THE REVIEWS ARE IN!

"Mai Donohue weaves together a wrenching tale of poverty, rebellion, enterprise and unwavering tenacity. Set against the backdrop of a rural hamlet in Central Vietnam and the urban swagger of a wartime, 1960's Saigon, this is an uplifting story of survival and, ultimately, the power of love."

– SanSan Kwan, PhD, Assoc. Prof/UC-Berkeley, and Author of "Kinesthetic City"

"It's not fashionable to say, but I happen to think there are too many unearned memoirs being churned out these days. Mai Donohue's breathless, riveting journey, from being a child bride in an impoverished Vietnamese village to a middle class mother of six in a wealthy American suburb, is astounding and inspiring, a true tale of survival against incredible odds. Her experiences are searing, but matter-of-factly told and I couldn't stop reading about them. This is a memoir from someone who's earned the right to have one, a hundred times over."

– Lauren Iannotti, Executive Editor of Brides Magazine; former Senior Editor of O Magazine

"Through Mai Donohue's riveting memoir we experience the French and American Vietnam Wars-- the barbarous tactics of the Communists and others, the family divisions, the degrading treatment of women and much more. Forced into a brutal marriage as a young teenager, Mai narrowly escapes to South Vietnam after several failed efforts. Through enormous courage and ingenuity, Mai manages to carve out a life for herself during the peak years of the American Vietnam War. It is a story of survival against insurmountable odds but it is also a story of love and hope."

– Gerry Tyler, Professor Emeritus of Political Science, University of Rhode Island

"Mai Donohue's amazing story of war, survival and love conquering all is an inspiration. We never tire of Mai's stories and life lessons, learned the hard way."

– Marty & Porter Halyburton (former POW in North Vietnam)

"I read this book in a single sitting and since then have used it as a personal day to day tool to take measure of what's really important."

– Molly Schiot, author of "Game Changers: The Unsung Heroines of Sports History"

CROSSING THE BAMBOO BRIDGE

Memoirs of a Bad Luck Girl

by
Mai Donohue

CROSSING THE BAMBOO BRIDGE
Memoirs of a Bad Luck Girl

by Mai Donohue

First Stillwater River Publications Edition

ISBN-10: 0-692-72876-7
ISBN-13: 978-0-692-72876-5

Library of Congress Control Number: 2016943447

1 2 3 4 5 6 7 8 9 10
Written by Mai Donohue
Cover Image Provided by Mai Donohue
Cover Design by Nami Studios
Published by Stillwater River Publications, Glocester, RI, USA.

Publisher's Cataloging-In-Publication Data
(Prepared by The Donohue Group, Inc.)
Names: Donohue, Mai.
Title: Crossing the bamboo bridge : memoirs of a bad luck girl / by Mai Donohue.
Description: First Stillwater River Publications edition. | Glocester, RI, USA : Stillwater River Publications, [2016]
Identifiers: LCCN 2016943447 | ISBN 978-0-692-72876-5 | ISBN 0-692-72876-7

Subjects: LCSH: Donohue, Mai. | Vietnam War, 1961-1975--Biography. | Teenage mothers--Vietnam--Biography. | Mothers and daughters--Vietnam--History--20th century. | Vietnam War, 1961-1975--Atrocities. | Civilians in war--Vietnam--1945-1975. | Vietnam--Social conditions--1945-1975. | LCGFT: Autobiographies.
Classification: LCC DS560.72.D66 A3 2016 | DDC 959.7043092--dc23

Some names and identifying details have been changed to protect the privacy of individuals.

The views and opinions expressed in this book are solely those of the author and do not necessarily reflect the views and opinions of the publisher.

Table of Contents

BOOK THREE: HOPELESS CITY

BOOK FOUR: A NEW LIFE

CROSSING THE

BAMBOO BRIDGE

Memoirs of a Bad Luck Girl

BOOK ONE:

Escape from Duc Pho

CHAPTER 1

Running Away

The first time I ran away from home, I was six years old.

I had made my mother angry and she sent me to get a stick for my switching.

I remember standing in front of a guava bush near our thatched roof house in the small hamlet, trying to choose. Even at that age I knew my mother well. The stick had to be just right – too big she would think that I was challenging her; too small she would think that I was trying to undermine her.

My thoughts were jumbled. One minute I feared to choose the wrong stick and the next minute I was angry.

I will not pick my own stick!

In my own mind I defied her. I decided to run away. I didn't know where I would go or who would take me in but anything was better than a whipping. I started running down the path.

Big mistake.

My mother must have been watching me from the house. As fast as my small feet touched the ground, just as fast in the same direction my mother chased after me.

When I reached the bamboo bridge I stopped. I could hear my mother getting closer but I was afraid to cross the bridge.

I will fall in the water and drown like my ancestor.

I had heard the story, over and over.

"None of you children must ever come near the water! One of your ancestors drowned in this river. His spirit has no rest. It cannot go home until it is replaced. He is waiting for one of you! He will drown you so that his own spirit can be free!"

The fear of drowning and becoming a cold ghost had stopped me in my tracks. I was afraid and I was angry. I stamped my feet. I screamed. I yelled for her to stop running toward me.

The lifelong battle between us began that day.

While I screamed and yelled at my mother, all the farmers watched us from their rice fields. As much as my mother didn't want to lose face she was also afraid that if she pressured me too hard I would jump into the river current.

I moved one step backward. Two more steps and I would be on the bridge. Suddenly my **mother** rushed me and grabbed me by the hair. She yanked me off my feet and behind her. As I landed safely on the other side of her, all the farmers cheered her on. Her fear turned into anger. Her eyes were red and her black teeth were shut tight. She grabbed whatever she could reach to whip me. *Swat, swat!* I half ran, half hopped and crawled on the ground.

That night my older sister, Chi Hai, or Sister Number Two, came to me with a bowl of salt water. She used her fingers to cleanse my cuts and bruises. The salt made my cuts sting. I cried. My sister begged me not to be so stupid.

"Little sister, please obey Mother! Oh, Cam," she said, using the name my family asked my ancestors' spirits to give me. "Don't make her mad. She could have killed you today!"

She was crying.

"You must learn to be a good girl. If you do what you are told I will give you anything I own! Little sister, I don't want to see you punished like this again. You hear me?" She sobbed. "You make me very sad."

I said nothing. I just cried. That night my sister cooked sweet potato soup for me. I couldn't lift my arms or open my mouth so she spooned the liquid into my mouth a little bit at a time.

After that, I tried my very best not to make my mother angry but the battle line had been drawn. I was always in hot water. My mother punished me for almost everything, to the point that when she yelled my name I would bring her a stick to save time.

According to my mother I was born in the year of the monkey—probably 1945—I will never know for sure. During the war my mother did not have the time to track the moon.

My mother always said I caused problems for her even before I entered this world. That I was born into the world under a cloud of bad curses, a bad luck girl.

Whenever she was angry with me, she would say, "You were a trouble child before you were even born. I carried you for thirteen months!"

She called me her elephant child because she believed that somehow she had walked under an elephant while she carried me, and that she had been cursed for this and had been punished. Whatever the truth, she carried me longer than any other woman in her village had carried.

She would go on.

"Then you almost killed me during childbirth. I was in labor for three days. I was dying! I sent your father out to get a coffin and what did he do? He came back with some high class broad! She walked in with her briefcase —she just looked like Madam [like a French woman]—and walked over to my bed and lifted up my shirt and looked at my big belly. She shook her head and walked away.

Then she ordered everybody in the house to do this, and do that! Boil the water, cut the clean cloth, move the curtain, send the children away! If I had enough strength I would have gotten out of my bed and come over and choked her! On top of all of that she smoked a cigarette! Can you imagine that? Here I am in pain with the elephant child inside of me kicking nonstop! I am dying, and there she was, this woman, having a cigarette, filing her fingernails!"

What really happened was that this 'high class broad' saved my life and my mother's life. She was a nurse and a good one. The Vietnamese didn't like the French but the French had helped educate many people in our nation. This nurse had been taught by the French, so she had some sort of education in medicine.

She wasn't like the ignorant midwife who lived in our hamlet and believed that childbirth was like a flower, that when the child was ready it would come out, that if things went wrong and the child or the mother died, well, it was the decision of our ancestors. She'd plant a banana tree at the foot of the grave and when it bloomed say it meant the child had been born on the other side. Luckily, my father had enough sense to go to the city and get this nurse.

It wasn't only my birth that caused her trouble. While she was carrying me, my father brought home a young second wife who was already pregnant. My mother desperately wanted me to be a boy, but no such luck. In the end it didn't matter because the second wife also bore a girl, my half-sister. However, to compete with the second wife, my mother decided to get pregnant again right away, and had my brother Ming this time.

Unfortunately, my father never saw his son born.

At that time my grandfather, the patriarch, was a major landowner in the valley and possessed hereditary power and wealth as the village chief. His father, and his father before him, and his father, had all been born and lived in the same house. Large tracts of the land surrounding our house and hamlet at one time had all been owned by my family, the Tran clan, which had belonged to Vietnam's nobility in centuries past. Even the hills behind us were named for our clan. Unfortunately, my grandfather had also chosen, in a valley of Buddhists, to worship the Cao Dai religion.

One night, when I was one year old, jealous local Viet Minh came to our home and killed my grandfather, my father and his two brothers. They threw my mother, seven months pregnant with her fourth child, into jail. Then they seized the family home and slaughtered all the animals for a banquet. As their excuse, the Viet Minh – who were also our neighbors – said my grandfather was supporting the Japanese. That was a cowardly lie. The truth was that he was Cao Dai. He had worshiped the wrong religion.

The sad thing was that many of my mother's brothers and brothers-in-law were Communist Viet Minh supporters. They all turned their backs on us after my father and grandfather were killed, either because they did not want to associate with us or because they were afraid of the Viet Minh government. Whatever their reasons, my sister, my brothers and I became orphans to them, the village underdogs.

We had no father now, and the family no longer had wealth. Our mother was in and out of jail so many times she soon stopped caring what happened to her. She became fearful and angry, hard and full of hatred. She beat us whenever her fear took over her heart, which was quite often. With no man in the house we became fair game for relatives and our neighbors.

And, through it all, the bamboo bridge waited patiently.

CHAPTER 2

War Child

Throughout my childhood there was always war—with the Japanese or the French or the Viet Minh. From 1945 until 1954 our village was occupied by Viet Minh soldiers. The reason I remember this so clearly is because the local Viet Minh government took over our big house and used it to store cotton. The rest of the house was occupied by Bo Doi, the Viet Minh army.

The effects of war on us were always local because we had no communications and knew little about the world beyond our village. In Vietnam, villagers did not travel very far. The average Vietnamese man traveled only within a fifty square mile area around his home, and the women and children even less. People were born and grew up in the same place as their father and father before them. They worshipped their ancestors, they worked on the land and raised their family, and they minded their own business.

Farmers usually did not wish to be involved in politics nor were they allowed. They seldom thought of themselves as individuals, nor were they allowed to make choices. When it came to politics, most decisions had already been made by the well-educated, the rich and well-to-do, and people such as my grandfather when he had been the village chief.

I was always getting into trouble because I wanted to learn, because I was curious, and because I was stubborn. My mind was always working and always hungry to learn about other people and other places. I knew there were Frenchmen in our country because often I heard the people in the village or the Bo Doi talk about them. We were afraid of the French because they had airplanes and could shoot us from the sky. Sometimes the local farmers would come to market and tell horror stories about the Chinese, Japanese and French. All the children would listen. Most country people have crude, earthy humor. And they loved to scare children.

The farmers would say that the Chinese kidnapped babies and killed them and stuffed the babies with opium so that they could transfer the opium to Hong Kong without getting caught, that the Japanese would kill you with their bare hands and tear you in half and eat you. As for the Frenchmen, they loved to have young Vietnamese girls. They would buy girls by the dozen and have their way with them. According to the farmers, all the Frenchmen had big noses. Their other bottom parts were very long too. When they had sex with the women the bottom parts were so long they went from one end of the women, through her stomach and up to her throat!

The stories did not stop me from being curious. I was always getting into trouble.

One day my oldest aunt, Auntie Hai, asked me to take care of her grandson. I did what my aunt asked me but when her older son had a meeting in secret I decided to eavesdrop. I overheard her son and other men talking about revolution. They said, "We must dig more trenches. We must recruit more young men in the village to fight! The French have the airplane and guns, but we have the will! We must be patient. We need more support from the local citizens. Here is the list of the young men—"

At that minute I heard my aunt's footsteps walk toward me. I worried she would catch me eavesdropping. I was in such a hurry I tripped over my own feet. I scared the baby who started hysterically crying. I tried to cover his mouth but it was too late. The next thing I know everybody in the house was standing there looking down at me. My cousin jerked the baby out of my arms and walked away. My aunt slapped me so hard that I saw stars. And when I stood up a book I had borrowed from an older girl that was hidden under my shirt fell on the ground. I could see the anger in her eyes. But with her good manners in front of her son's friends she just gave a faint smile. "I will tell your mother and see what she will think about this." She bent down and took the book and walked toward my house.

On the way home from Auntie Hai's house, I stopped at a bamboo grove. I peeled off the hard outer layer of bamboo shoots and went into the pigpen and wrapped them around my butt under my trousers. By the time I got into the house Auntie Hai was there. She made sure that I would be punished: she wanted my mother to know that her daughter was a bad girl. I did not wait for my mother's order: I knew the routine well enough. I went outside to the courtyard and broke off a big enough stick and brought it to my mother. I went over to the dirt floor and lay face down.

My mother announced my crimes before she began my punishment. Then the first blow landed hard on my protected butt. I thought I was outsmarting my mother, but I had forgotten something, I had forgotten to pretend to cry like I was hurting.

Looking back, I think it didn't make a bit of difference if I had cried or not. My aunt was there and she knew what I was up to. She stopped my mother's hand and went over to me. She pulled my pants down to my knees and showed my mother the bamboo wraps. I did not dare move a muscle. I thought about escaping but it was too late. My mother was so angry because she had lost face with my aunt. She shoved my aunt aside and began to whip me with all her strength.

By the time she was done with me I had lost count. My butt was raw and I had bitten into my lip until it bled. I prayed to my father's spirit to come to take me home with him. I could not remember what happened to me after that, either I fell asleep or I passed out. When I awoke there was the sound of an airplane flying over my hamlet and I heard a bomb explode.

There was no one inside of the house except for my little piglet and me. I was terrified. I wanted to call out for my mother, my brothers and sister, but I was afraid. There was a terrible pain all over my body. I crawled over to the door and thought I should run to the bunker but my legs and arms were sore.

My fear was a good thing. It was just open field between my house and the bunker. If I had run, the pilots may have seen me and they might have shot me down before I even reached the bunker. Then they might bomb the whole hamlet and we all would be dead. I thought about stamping my feet and screaming for help but then I thought if the French were somewhere nearby they might hear me. I didn't know what to do. Finally I crawled back into the house and went under the bed and cried myself to sleep.

That evening when all the bombing was over my mother found me. She cleaned me up good and changed me into clean clothes. She gave me some sweet potatoes and brown sugar to eat. She sent my sister to the neighbor's yard and brought back some special kind of leaves. She washed the leaves and ground them into a paste. She carefully tended to all my cuts. She told me next time not to be so stubborn and not to embarrass her like that in front of my aunt.

After that incident my mother was less angry with me than she used to be. Later on she told me how scared she was when she realized that the bomb had dropped and she found out I wasn't with her in the bunker. She even praised me for my bravery.

"You are a smart girl and you are brave. You didn't get scared and you didn't run out when the airplane flew over our house."

She was sweet to me that night and I was happy that my mother loved me. In some way I was glad that I had been beaten because my mother had paid so much attention to me that night.

My siblings and I were always hungry. In fact, we would have become beggars if the neighbors had let us.

We tried.

Often, when my mother was away looking for work, she would leave us in my older sister's care. Usually there was nothing in the house for us to eat. One time when our next-door neighbors, who were also our distant uncle and aunt, were celebrating the death anniversary of an ancestor they invited almost everybody in the hamlet except, of course, us.

The smell of the food cooking made our mouths water and our stomachs growl. My sister couldn't stand us whining. She told us to wash our hands and faces and change into our best clothes. Then she told us to go run back and forth in front of Uncle Hai's house. We all hoped they would invite us in, if only to eat leftovers or chew on the bones.

After an hour we gave up. We were so hungry and tired. We all walked home with empty stomachs like dogs with no tails.

When my mother found out she was angry and very upset with my older sister. She sat us all down and gave us a lecture that we never forgot. She told us that we came from a good family, that we didn't beg. We were upper class and must act like upper class! "A princess is always a princess even if she lost her throne! From now on, if I hear any of you are begging for even one sweet potato chip I will sell you all to the Frenchmen! Is that clear!?"

What my mother said didn't make much sense to me. After all, we were dirt poor. Yes, there was our big house but we could not live in it. They forced us to live in a small hut beside it. We slept on dirty bamboo mats. During the cold rainy seasons we had no blankets. Our lands were sold or lent to other people in the village because we didn't have a man in the house. More often than not even our small hut was shared with the Bo Doi. Later, when the South government took over, they did the same thing.

For some reason, unknown to me then, the girls in our hamlet liked the military men very much. I couldn't understand why my sister and her friends acted so stupid among those men.

Just before the Dien Bien Phu bombing there were Bo Doi camped at our house. My sister and her friends were all acting so silly. Some of the soldiers taught the girls how to play the *cai dung* - Vietnamese guitar. They told the girls wonderful things that happened in other parts of the country. Some of the men even promised that when the war was over they would return and marry some of the young women in our village.

I used to sneak around and listen to the older girls talk. They said if they had their way they would follow those men. Even my own sister dreamed of going away, but in our society marriages usually were arranged. And she was engaged to Vi.

More Viet Minh troops were moved into our village. There were more new trenches dug around our hamlet. The children used to play hide and seek inside of the trenches. We could go from one end of the hamlet to the other without coming out of the trench. The villagers also planted fruit trees, such as banana and pineapple and passion fruit, near the trenches to hide them. In some parts they even planted bamboo. Eventually the new trenches and the old trenches were connected and covered with trees.

After the collapse of the French at Dien Bien Phu the Viet Minh marched through the villages more freely. Hundreds of troops of the Viet Minh Army rolled into our tiny hamlet, bringing less food and less space and more taxes to support the army. They also brought a major shift in our village. The poor people who had supported the Viet Minh had more privilege as the communists became more in control. My mother's brothers had been longtime Viet Minh supporters. Now they had even more power. Their power had very little benefit for my mother, though. Her family ignored her, at best.

After the Dien Bien Phu bombing the country was somewhat at peace. Nothing can be more beautiful than the Vietnam countryside in peacetime. The morning sunrise and the evening sunset, the farmers coming home from their long day out in the fields. I remember most evening twilights, the sound of my mother's voice singing the folk songs on her way home. On the evenings when the moon was bright my mother and the women in the back of the hamlet would gather and spin the cotton threads. They would recite the national poem, The Song of Kieu, and chew *trau* – a betel nut and areca leaf mixture that was a mild stimulant. Sometimes in those evenings my cousin Thao and I would pretend we were detectives. We followed the footprints in the dirt to snoop around and see who was doing what. Sometimes we found the footprints of old men who were Peeping Toms. One night a chicken thief stole my mother's chickens. We followed his footsteps all the way to his home. We confronted him and he promised never to steal from us again.

Life was peaceful and beautiful.

Then came the Geneva Accords in July 1954. I heard people talking about North and South, about Vietnam divided in two halves – one for Uncle Ho and one for Emperor Bao Dai, and then later for Ngo Dinh Diem. As for Diem, no one in our village had ever heard his name before he became the president of South Vietnam. However, the Geneva Treaty not only divided the country, it also divided many Vietnamese families in half.

I remember those days well. Many of my aunts, uncles, cousins, my half-sister and other relatives were sent North by order of Uncle Ho. My family was excited and sad at the same time. I was envious. I thought the people going north were the luckiest people to have been chosen. Everyone said, "They are the best of the best, that's why Uncle Ho loves them and wants them." Their families had special privileges. "Two years," that was what they were told. "Two years and we'll all be back, one country."

My mother's youngest brother, Bin, who was in his twenties, had fallen in love with a girl in my hamlet. Xi was very beautiful, but my grandmother forbade Bin from seeing her. As did her family forbid Xi from seeing Bin. He was about ready to leave for the North, but because of the family problem he could not see her. He asked me to deliver a letter to her. He told me to tell her that if she loved him she must meet him at the ghost hill where no one would look for them. On the way to her house I wanted so much to open the letter but I was afraid if my uncle found out I would be dead, so I didn't. That night my uncle came to my house and took me with him. He told me that if I was a good girl and stood guard while he and Xi talked he promised me in two years when he returned I would be his favorite niece. Two years went by but my uncle did not return. Xi refused to marry anyone else. Later, she joined the Viet Cong and was shot and killed.

The first six months after the country divided there was one big confusion. Southerners went north and the Northerners came south. There were the new groups of Northerners migrating into our small district. They spoke with a different dialect. These North Vietnamese who came to our poor village were not upper class by any means. They could not afford airplane tickets to the cities, they traveled by bus as far as they could, and then walked. They came to our village and settled down alongside of Highway One, near where my grandmother, my mother's mother, lived.

They were exotic to us simple country folks. I was fascinated by them. I used any excuse to visit my grandmother who, like everybody else, treated me as if I was some kind of disease, a bad luck child. But I didn't care. I wanted to see these new people.

They looked almost like us but somehow were different. They wore clothes like the people in an old book I saw on the teacher's desk. They spoke a Vietnamese I had never heard. They worshiped a strange religion called Chua Troi (Jesus Christ). I remember sneaking to their church hut to watch them pray. Their God was hanging on a cross from the ceiling. They did not look anything like our Buddhists or Cao Dai. They didn't even burn incense. No incense, I wondered, then how did their God know when they worshipped him?

One night as I watched them praying their camps were suddenly caught on fire. I wasn't sure if it was an accident or someone had set them on fire. But the weird thing was that this group of strangers just kept on praying. I still don't understand why they didn't put out the fire. In the days after the fire they all slowly, one by one, moved farther South. Within weeks our village went back to our routine. Nobody cared if the strange people stayed or left.

In the first two years after the Geneva treaty the countryside was peaceful. In some small ways the new local government was helpful. We no longer looked over our shoulders and reported each other to authorities. If we wanted to kill the chicken for a special occasion we did so. We ate white rice without three parts of dried potato chips added to it. We wore new clothes that were dyed black and not gray.

Some people in our village traveled back and forth from Quang Ngai to Saigon. They brought back money to feed their family. Some in our hamlet even joined the church groups. That was something new. The churches provided food and clothing to those who joined them. My mother thought these farmers had degraded themselves to go to church and beg for foods and clothes. She said they traded their own culture, tradition and religion just to satisfy their bellies.

My mother, for ten years a single mother and survivor, under the new local government rules now was free. She already knew how to take care of herself and provide for her four children. When she needed a man to help with the work she paid him well. She became an entrepreneur.

She used to make her illegal rice wine and sell it to the local drunkards. Now under the new government she was free to make her rice wine as much as she wanted and to sell it to whomever, especially the rich. She was also a good dyer. She would dye cloth as black as can be because it was fashionable and people were willing to pay for her services. She raised her own silkworms and spun beautiful silk. She would pick out the silkworms that were too fat and too lazy to go through metamorphosis and chop them up very fine and add them to our rice soup. She didn't know how to read or write but she knew what protein did to the body. Sometimes I wanted to tell her I didn't care for the taste but I didn't dare.

After she spun the silk she wove it into beautiful clothes. She also sold the pupae to the local market to get more money. She raised pigs and piglets and sold them to people around the village. Also, there were many, many chickens and ducks to lay eggs. Unlike during the Viet Minh time, when she killed a chicken to worship our ancestors we ate it without fear.

I remember back in the Viet Minh time my mother would only kill the chicken and cook it in the dark and wake us up in middle of the night to eat our meals. Afterwards, she would bury the bones so the local government didn't catch her. She forbade us to tell a soul because the communists would not allow any of us to live "lavishly," meaning high on the hog. To kill a chicken for family fare was to commit a crime. Duck eggs were to be sold and the money sent to support the army, so they could buy weapons to fight the French. Under the Communists we had always been told what to do and what to eat.

The Communist government had also controlled all our crops. They gave only so many cups of rice for each family. They wanted the farmers to work hard and to support Ho Chi Minh. They would make us yell, "We are Vietnamese children. We are con Ron Chau Tien (children of the Dragon and nieces and nephews of the Goddess.) We will fight for our country until our last drop of blood!" Any one of us in the village who did not follow the rules would be harshly punished.

I was so glad that we were no longer living under the Communist control. Now my family life had improved. My brother Ming said it improved because my oldest sister was married to her husband, Vi; that now that we had a man in the house people began to respect us. I didn't agree. I said it was because the South Vietnam government let our mother be free and have the chance to be an individual and work for herself. In the end, it didn't really matter which of us was right as long as it was good for us.

CHAPTER 3

School Days

When I was small, girls in the village usually didn't go to school. It was too expensive. They thought girls didn't need it. Although my mother didn't know how to read or write she wanted all her children to have an education. My brothers and my sister went to a different school because my mother thought they were smarter than me.

My first school was not really a school. It was a ghost house. No one knew why but a whole family had died there with no friends or relatives to inherit the property or to care for the family altar or clean their graves.

There were rice paddies around the house. There was a small winding dusty path leading to the twig gate. There was an old pigpen at the back of the house. Overgrowth of bananas leaned against the bamboo fence. Spiders and other creatures had made their homes in it. The big boys used to go there to catch snakes to scare the girls. Near the water hole a tall betel nut tree stood against the bluest sky. On the far side of the house was the old cow pen with half a roof. It was used to store old rice straw.

The house had a dirt floor and the walls badly needed a new layer of mud to cover the old rotten straw. Most of the house was closed off, bolted with bamboo. You could tell no one had been in that part of the house in a long time because the bamboo was rotten, the mold was gray and furry, and small mushrooms grew between the cracks. On top of all of that, spider webs hung over the doorway. The house had a roof but the roof had so many holes that when it rained we had to wear cone hats. In the monsoon season sometimes no one came to class.

One room was used as a school for fifty students from kindergarten to grade five. Only six girls. There was a small blackboard and desks with benches linked to them. The walls were made from bamboo and clay mixed with water and rice straw. The straw was old and some of it stuck out. The boys would pick out the straw and blow it at the girls' hair when the teacher wasn't looking. If we didn't yell the boys kept on blowing. If we yelled we got in trouble. The teacher would send us to the back of the classroom and make us face the wall.

My teacher was Mr. Phuoc. His name meant kindness and caring, but he was the meanest teacher you could imagine. He used to scare us by telling ghost stories, especially about the owners of the house. He told about how they all died. He usually used the smallest girl to discipline as an example because she was a crybaby and a scaredy cat.

He didn't like girls very much, especially me.

For one reason or another I was the one most often sent to the back of the room. He would tie me to the chair and tell me the ghost hiding in the other room would come out and take me to his grave, or that it would stuff rags in my mouth so I would not ask so many questions!

I used to believe him. When I would hear noises behind the wall I would wet my pants and cry.

When I was in third grade we moved to a nicer school with more rooms and an open courtyard. It had a red roof and cement walls and was surrounded by pine trees. Mr. Phuoc was still the teacher but there were no more ghosts.

In the courtyard at recess, the girls were allowed to jump rope. I was the champ. I could even beat the boys at tree climbing. Only problem was I would rip my clothes. Then I would get punished by Mr. Phuoc and also by my mother. That didn't stop me.

In spite of Mr. Phuoc's strict rules I started to learn how to read and write. I would borrow books and hide them from my mother. I collected the paper leaflets that dropped down from the sky and hid them away and read them. Whenever I could, I read. It made my mother crazy. She punished me whenever she caught me reading. She said a girl who read too much would dream too much. She was right. One of the books I read told about another place, another time, about girls who wore flowers on their hair and sang and danced under moonlight, things that were forbidden for us Vietnamese country girls.

One beautiful sunny afternoon at recess I talked all the girls in class into going up the hill with me. We picked flowers and made flower bands and put them on our hair. We sang and we danced. We picked the tiny sour fruit and chewed them to make our teeth black like our mothers'. We went into rice paddies in our good clothes to catch fighting fish. By the time we got back to school it was too late. Someone had told Mr. Phuoc.

He was waiting for us at the door, the ruler in his hand.

"Kneel down," he ordered. The ruler was pointing to jackfruit skins on the floor. Jackfruit skin has sharp needles like nails that could punch into our knees. The other girls were crying but moving toward the skins.

Not me. I stood there and didn't move. Mr. Phuoc raised the ruler up and struck me twice on my back. I jumped back and cried out loud.

"Kneel down," he howled.

"No!" I yelled.

He struck me again, grabbed my neck and forced me down on the jackfruit skin. He whipped me hard. The pain on my back and my knees made me moan. I heard some boys in classroom whisper, "Good, serves her right."

"You will learn to obey me!" he yelled.

He turned and walked toward the back of the room.

"Run away with me!" I whispered to the girls.

"No, he will kill us," they said tearfully. They were so scared.

At that point I didn't care what he would do to me. I picked up my book and ran out the door. I could hear screaming and heavy footsteps behind me but I didn't look back. Later I found out that the girls did run but not fast enough. They got caught by the big boy Mr. Phuoc sent after them.

When I got home I was nervous and scared. Sooner or later my mother would find out. I snuck into the house and hid under my bed.

My little pig joined me.

Mr. Phuoc came to the house after class was over.

While he was talking to my mother my little pig left my side. It went over and peed on Mr. Phuoc's sandal. He got so angry he kicked my pig to the corner. I crawled out to rescue my pig but it was too late to stop him. I was crying and screaming.

My mother and Mr. Phuoc were arguing.

I didn't hear what he was saying. I only heard my mother's voice. She was yelling at him and pointing her finger in his face. Finally she chased him out of the courtyard with her broom.

To my surprise I didn't get punished. Nor did my mother ask me what had happened.

That was the end of Mr. Phuoc. We got a new teacher, Mr. Ban.

I promised myself that, with this teacher, I would try harder not to ask so many questions, not be disobedient, and especially not to cause trouble for myself or my mother. Mr. Ban was young and took pride in his job. He didn't crack my fingers with his ruler when I didn't write cursive very well. He didn't whip me when I asked him to help me with my math.

When Mr. Ban first came, my class standing was fifty out of fifty-three students. By the end of that year I was third in the class. Mr. Ban promised me that next year, when we returned from summer break, he would help me to fulfill my dream.

"You will be a good teacher some day," he told me.

On my way home my feet barely touched the ground. I was singing and skipping without a worry in the world. I thought of how happy my mother would be. I could not foresee what would happen to me.

My mother met me by the door.

"Your brother-in-law's cousin died this morning. They need me to prepare his body for burial. I will be home late. The animals need to be fed. Then make dinner and haul in water to fill the barrel."

"But Mother, I want to tell you about—"

"Cam, why are you always so difficult, and so selfish? People are dying left and right in the village and all you care about is yourself. For once do what you're told."

"Mother, but my teacher said—"

She didn't even let me finish the sentence. She walked out the door with a small bottle of rice whisky in her hand.

I followed her because I wanted to tell her about my school.

When I got there I hid behind the door. I saw the family crying while my mother cleaned the dead body with the whiskey. Watching her made me ill. I ran home and cried myself to sleep.

This death wasn't the end of it.

People in their thirties and forties in our hamlet were suddenly dying. Each time, my mother was called to a different family to prepare the body to bury it. Each time the drum pounded to notify the hamlet of the death. I started to count the beats.

I also counted how many deaths there had been. The next one was the fifth. His name was Thuong. His family lived two houses away from us. He was an only child, newly married, and his wife was three months pregnant. His death made everyone in the hamlet mourn.

I couldn't know, when I skipped home from school that day that the last, and youngest, victim of the mystery disease would be me.

I was also the only survivor.

However, it took me four long months to recover. I lost all my hair. My skin became so yellow and my face was puffy. It would be embarrassing for me, but I couldn't wait to go back to school.

In order to do that my mother had to sell her last piece of land. Or so I thought.

I stood there and watched her sign her name. With her shaky hand she held the ink pen inside of her palm. She made her 'X' on the paper. Her face was like stone and her lips so tight. I wondered, did she know all that was written on the paper? Did the new farmer who bought the land?

That piece of land was supposed to be my dowry. I was happy that she sold it for my education instead of to buy me a husband.

That night I lay on the bamboo mat and dreamed of my new school. I thought how wonderful it would be to once again join my little brother Ming and my cousin Thao for school. I would wear the piece of black cloth with tiny flowers over my bald head. I had been sick for a long time, my hair had all fallen out and only a little had grown back. It was very embarrassing for an eleven-year-old girl, but the thought of being in school again made me overcome my baldness.

The next day I was already awake before the rooster crowed. I carried the water and filled up all the barrows. I fed the pigs and chickens and ducks and watered the flowers and vegetables. I swept inside the house and outside in the courtyard where the black birds ate the five-star fruits and made a big mess. I washed my hands and face and changed into my second-best set of clothes that I had helped my mother to spin the cotton and weave the cloth for. I took the black crushed charcoal and used my finger to rub it on my teeth, because we didn't have any toothbrush or toothpaste back then. I sang my lullaby song with a happy tune.

When I finished everything I walked out to the courtyard where my mother was standing, with her hands on her hips, looking out to the rice fields. I knew she knew that I was coming toward her because I made a lot of noise, but she didn't turn her head. I stepped in front of her with my hands folded in front of my chest, and bowed. I was about to ask her permission to go to school. She stopped me short.

"Cam," she said quietly. "Cam, you can't go to school anymore."

I thought I was hearing it wrong. I was about to ask her why but she walked away. She left me standing there with no one to comfort me. I cried a lot, but it didn't help me any. My brother Ming would go back to school instead of me. He was younger, but he was a boy. My mother believed he could take care of her in her old age. I was just a girl. A bad luck girl. Useless.

It would be years before I went back to a classroom.

CHAPTER 4

Betrothal

Even though my mother didn't let me go to school any more, my dream to be a teacher had not yet died. In secret I would borrow a textbook from my cousin Thao or my brother and go to the back of my house. I had no pencil or paper so I used my fingers to write on the dirt.

My hope was that someday my mother would change her mind but that dream was crushed when I was thirteen. My mother announced that I would be married to a man named Binh whom I had never met, a man from a family who lived over the hill behind our hamlet.

"You can be someone else's problem," she had said.

At first I just thought she was angry with me, because I was sneaking around trying to learn how to ride a bicycle. She was afraid I would lose my virginity to the hard bicycle seat. I didn't understand, but she was serious.

"You better behave like a good girl when his family comes to visit because he will be your husband. You will show his family you are born with good grace. After you serve tea to your future husband, you will bow to him and back yourself out into the kitchen. Do you hear me?"

My mother had been training me since childhood to be a good Vietnamese wife. Besides serving tea properly I had also learned how to fold the *trau* perfectly corner to corner. Everything had to be beautiful to show how elegant and high class you were.

I couldn't help but wonder who this boy was and why my mother wanted me to marry him. He was not the first boy to come to my house to look at me. There had been others, but she chased them away.

Who is this boy?

Binh was a woodcutter. He also was a first son. That definitely attracted my mother. As for me, I wasn't prepared to like him even before I met him because my mother was forcing me to be married.

His family name was Thach, like the legend of Thach Sanh, the demi-god woodcutter. Binh himself thought, and acted, as if he, like the legend, was also an immortal.

The first time he came to my house to check me out I thought he was the ugliest boy. His hair was long down his neck. He used so much Vaseline to slick it back that if a fly happened to land on his head all it needed was a pair of chopsticks to ski down to his shoulders. His face was covered with zits, like burned rice stuck to the bottom of the pot. When he smiled at me there were two ugly gold teeth like the pirate's in the book I used to read. And he looked at me as if he already owned me.

I was thirteen. So much for my mother's instructions.

I did everything wrong, from the *trau* ceremony to serving tea.

Out of the corner of my eye I could see my mother's angry face, but I had no fear. I gave Binh a dirty look when I handed him his tea. I was supposed to back into the kitchen like my mother had taught me. Instead I turned my back to him and before I entered the kitchen I patted my butt.

Behind the bamboo curtain my cousin Thao and I laughed. But the laugh was on me. My mother had made up her mind.

"He is not rich, but he is strong. You will be the first wife of the first son. All his ancestral land will someday be yours. You will marry him whether you like it or not." I tried so many ways to plead with my mother to call off the engagement, but she refused.

One day I stopped Binh on his way home from the market where he sold his wood. I told him that I could never be a good Vietnamese wife.

He laughed at me and said, "A wild horse can be tamed. When she is tamed she will be a good horse."

I pleaded with my mother not to marry me off. She refused to listen, turning her back to me. Finally I stopped arguing. Then, a few days later, I told her I had to go to the Buddhist temple in the district center for a scout meeting to audition for a Buddhist festival play. Since I was at Buddhist scout meetings often, she let me go.

Across the bamboo bridge I went.

I was not going to the temple. I was going down to Highway One to flag down a bus and run away again. The problem was I hadn't thought beyond that. Actually, I hadn't thought at all.

Somehow, my mother's younger sister, Auntie Moi, knew what I was up to. There I was, standing beside Highway One waving frantically at the bus slowing down, and she was walking toward me furiously.

I knew I was in big trouble.

"Come with me, stupid girl!"

At first I tried to convince her that my mother had sent me on an errand.

"Mother sent me to the other hamlet to pick mulberry leaves to feed the new silkworms, Auntie! I was sidetracked watching the buses go by! I was bored, Auntie, I was just playing a game with the bus! Honest! I wasn't running away!"

She knew I was lying through my teeth. She gave me a sharp look and slapped my face.

"I was not born yesterday! Be quiet, stupid girl!"

I started to cry and beg her not to tell my mother. She ignored me. After a while I gave up, because it wasn't working. I pulled at the corner of my shirt and wiped my tears.

I will take my punishment, I told myself.

I stopped at the guava bush and picked out a stick. I dragged my feet in the courtyard behind my aunt, walking as slow as I could without getting slapped again.

Mother can beat me all she wants, I thought, *I am not scared.*

I would grind my teeth, I decided. I would not cry.

My mother sat in front of my sister's home. She could hear us coming nearer but she didn't bother to look up.

Auntie Moi came to a stop in front of my mother and announced the list of my crimes.

"Sister Number Six, what are we to do with this child!? She is a conniver, a liar, and a thief! Luckily I caught her before she had a chance to do bad things. I saw her flagging down the bus on Highway One! Then she had the nerve to lie to me! She abused your good name on the streets and on the highway, too!"

I wanted to rebuke her, but I didn't dare.

You are the liar, I thought. *I didn't steal anything. How did I become a thief?*

I stood in front of my mother and waited for my sentence, my head bowed low and my arms folded in front of my chest.

I glanced over at my sister and my older brother's wife. They were terrified. By now there were some neighbors there also, avid spectators. Once again I was to be the hamlet sideshow.

For whatever reason, I was no longer afraid of my mother, or my aunt, or least of all our gawking neighbors. I was not afraid, only ashamed.

Ashamed of myself for getting caught so easily.

Standing in the middle of the highway! Stupid girl! Where everyone could see you flagging down a bus! How could you be so stupid? Take your punishment, girl. You will not cry. Do you hear me? You will not ask for mercy!

My mother knew I was standing there, waiting for her. Silently she chewed her *trau*. She didn't answer my aunt or acknowledge me.

At first I was content to wait. However as the silence stretched on, I felt the air was heavy and my chest was tight. I had trouble breathing. I felt as if I was suffocating. I didn't know how long I had been waiting for my mother to speak. It seemed like hours.

I wished she would yell at me or get up and beat me. Why the silent treatment? What kind of punishment was this? I was confused. I didn't know what I was supposed to do.

I blurted out, "Mother, do what you want with me, but for the thousandth time, I don't want to marry!"

I don't know what made me say that. I had meant to lie to her, to tell her how sorry I was, but I didn't. It just came out.

She didn't look up but her voice was ice cold.

"Do you know what happens to disobedient girls here? I should have suffocated you when you were born! I should strip you naked and tie you to a pole at the edge of the village so everybody could see what kind of a girl you are! I should let the dogs lick your private parts to teach you a lesson about running away! I should tie you on top of a fighter ant nest! I should do so many things to show you what it means to disobey your mother! But I won't. I am too old and I am too tired. I went to all this trouble so you can have a *decent* husband! So you could be a *first wife* and someday be *important* in this society! And what do I get! Shame and embarrassment!"

She picked up her *trau* tray.

"As far as I am concerned I have no daughter. She died in childbirth." She got up, dusted off her pants, and walked into her house without looking back.

My body went limp and I fell.

I lay curled up like a child, weeping.

I knew my sister and my sister-in-law were whispering to me, but all I could hear were my mother's words ringing in my ears and in my head.

"I have no daughter. She died in childbirth."

My mother's new tactic threw me completely off my balance. She hadn't beaten me or done any of those other horrible things but her words had totally demoralized me, had taken away my will, my ability to fight.

Now all I wanted to do was to die.

I began to dream of ending my miserable life, of becoming a powerful ghost. *Yes! That would show them!*

I would make sure they never forgot who I was! I would make them build a little shrine to me in every corner of the village! People near and far would come to worship me! I would punish those who had hurt me, and do good things for those who loved me. I wanted to see my mother feel my pain. I wanted to see her weep over my dead body.

I would have my justice!

There was only one problem. I wanted to be pretty when I was dead.

Day after day, and night after night lying awake, in fact every waking hour, I was looking for the most beautiful way to kill myself. My first thought was to jump in front of the bus down on the highway. But there was that picture of the girl in Sa Huyen who had jumped in front of the fast-moving bus. Her body had splattered all over the road. That was too messy for me.

I thought about hanging myself. But there had been that young man from Saigon who had fallen in love with the girl down by the highway. He had followed her all the way to Duc Pho, but her parents forbid her to date him. Hopeless and desperate, he went out in front of the girl's house and hanged himself that night. The next morning they found his body hanging in the bamboo grove. He had no family and no one would claim his body so he hung there almost all day.

I had gone down to see him. His face was purple and his tongue was sticking out. I had nightmares for a long time.

Forget about that, I thought.

Maybe I could eat the forbidden poisonous fruit.

But then there was the wife of our neighbor. She had been sick and tired of being beaten by her husband and his family. Her own family was poor and wouldn't take her back. She felt she had no other way out. She chose to eat *trai thi* to end her life. She was violently ill all that day.

I went to her house to watch her while she was suffering and dying, her three young children weeping beside her bed. Near to the end she had a change of heart. She began to beg the neighbors for help, but by then it was too late. The poison had entered into her veins, her blood. We had no doctor, no nurse, and the wise man said she deserved to die. She died a horrible death. And nothing changed. Village life went on. Within a year her husband married the girl whose boyfriend had hanged himself. There was no remorse or guilt in either family.

And I never did see any of their ghosts.

Then I decided to kill myself by cutting my wrists.

The only problem was my mother's knives were too dull. I had to wait for a sharpening man to come by on his rounds and sharpen our knives. While I was waiting, one day my mother broke her silence to send me to see the butcher, Mr. Duc. She had sold him one of her pigs, but he had not yet paid her. She sent me to collect the money. When I got there the pig had already been slaughtered. Its throat had been cut. The sharp knife in Mr. Duc's hand was still covered with blood. I was scared. I wanted to throw up. I covered my mouth and ran out of his house as fast as I could without looking back. I could never stand the sight of blood.

I was definitely running out of options.

That night I questioned myself.

What if my time in this life had not yet ended? If I cut my life short, what would happen to me in my next life? What would happen to my spirit, to my ghost? What if I had done so many bad things in my past lives that my suffering in this life was not yet enough to redeem them?

What would happen to me?

Would I have another chance for reincarnation? If so, what would I become? A beggar? A dog? A turtle? A pig?

I definitely didn't want to waste all my energy and time just to come back as a beggar or some animal! A stinking stupid pig? No way!

I want to reincarnate as a beautiful princess who lives up in the sky! I will ride those beautiful cloud animals! I will fly out to the fairylands of the ancient stories!

I had to rethink this.

Day after day, in my head, I negotiated with Life, with Death.

I reexamined each situation carefully. As much as I didn't like the way my mother treated me, it was better than being sold to the French.

It was better than to die like those people who took their own lives, so messy, so ugly. I wanted to die beautiful so my ghost could be beautiful.

I also decided that I no longer wanted my ghost to scare people. I wanted my ghost to be kind. If I had to die I wanted to wear my best cotton shirt that my mother had made for me once, spinning the cotton into threads and weaving them into the cloth, which she carefully stitched together. It was so long ago but I still remembered that shirt. I wanted to be buried in that shirt. Yes. I wanted my ghost to wear the beautiful cotton shirt my mother had made for me.

No. I couldn't just kill myself the way those other people had done. The more I thought about it the more I was convinced I had done too many bad things in my past lives. I needed to repay them before I left this earth. I could not help but imagine myself as one of my mother's fat pigs lying on Mr. Duc's butcher's table! No, I had to repay with suffering in this life so I would be free in my next life.

I would obey my mother's orders.

Even though my mother hadn't beaten me, the silent treatment had been a hundred times worse than a beating. All my dreams and hopes had vanished. My mind was blurred. My will had been cut into a thousand pieces. My soul was empty now.

I became a living, silent ghost without a purpose. I did whatever I was told, whenever I was told. I became the obedient daughter my mother wanted me to be.

That was the last thing my mother expected.

I almost got what I wanted.

Whether my total collapse worried my mother or whether she had a change of heart I will never know. I do know that secretly she went back to Binh's family and tried to call off the marriage. I know this because after I was married to Binh he often taunted me with the knowledge.

My mother couldn't just withdraw her consent, though. By now everyone for miles around knew what I had done. If my mother just backed out she would be the laughingstock of the village for having given in to her spoiled, uncontrollable daughter.

What she did was to raise the bride price much higher than what had been set. Too high, she thought, in her simple mind. She was sure Binh's family would refuse to pay it.

She was wrong.

Within a year I would be married.

Binh wanted me for his wife at any price.

CHAPTER 5

Married Life

The night of the wedding Binh had left me alone.

The next night when he came to me I was terrified to let him touch me. I tried to put it off, saying it was late. His mother came to the curtain at the end of the bed and scolded us.

"You kids go to sleep or you'll keep us awake. We have work to do in the morning."

We quieted for a while and I was dozing off when I felt his hands on me. He had one hand over my mouth and with the other was pulling my pants to my knees. He put his mouth to my ear and whispered,

"If you don't let me get what I want, when I bring you back to your family tomorrow *the pig will have only one ear!*"

In our tradition, when the couple returned to the bride's family on the third day, the groom's family carried with them a pig's head. If the bride had been a virgin the pig's head had both ears. If she had not been a virgin one ear was cut off to let her family know. Her family then had to pay the groom's family money. More importantly, it brought great shame on the family name, especially on the bride's father.

I begged Binh not to do that, not so much for my mother but for my father's spirit. I stopped fighting and let him have his way.

Very soon I was pregnant I wasn't even 15 years old.

It changed nothing for me.

I had come to Binh's family as a daughter-in-law.

As such, I was treated as a servant. I had to obey the rules of the house and serve everyone in the family first. My new in-laws also had the right to mistreat me any way they liked. It was allowed in our culture.

With the war raging, there weren't many males left in the village. Binh and his father were among the few men in the district that had not publicly joined either side—they always tried to be on the side of the winner. As woodcutters, both sides needed them working.

In my seventh month of pregnancy my mother came to my in-laws and asked permission to take me back to her house. This was traditional. The first-time mother would be returned to her own family to have her baby.

I was so happy to return to my mother's home.

My younger brother Ming had gone north. My older brother An was in the South army. I still had my mother, my sister, and An's wife for company, as well as my nieces and nephews, whom I loved to be with. But I knew my time was fast coming when the child would be born. As my belly got bigger and bigger I was getting more and more depressed.

Many nights I lay on the straw mat in my mother's house and prayed to my ancestors to take my baby and me during my childbirth. I couldn't bear going back to the cruelty of Binh and his family. I wanted my life to end in such a way that did not dishonor my family. That way my spirit would be free and my mother would not lose face with relatives and neighbors. When I would dream of this precious death, the only thing that made me sad was that my body would be brought back to my in-laws' land to be buried in their field, not in my own.

Although I couldn't understand why at the time, my prayers were not answered. My son Han was born and I was still alive.

After the birth I was left alone in my grass hut. I lay on bamboo strips in the corner at the back of my mother's house. The blood was dripping from my vagina into the clay pot of sizzling charcoal underneath. The flies were buzzing, landing on my face, but I had no energy to move. I was relieved the baby was out. I knew it was a boy, but I hadn't held him yet. The midwife had used a sharp piece of bamboo strip to cut the baby's umbilical cord. She had given the baby to my mother-in-law to hold. She had pressed the afterbirth out and given it to my aunt to make some kind of medicine.

It must have been a hundred degrees outside. In my hut, the pot of hot coals under my bed made it unbearable for the others to stay but I felt so cold I was shaking. The blood still dripped. I listened to everybody outside congratulating each other for the job well done. They poured tea and chit-chatted. I could hear my mother-in-law and my husband brag about how fortunate the Thach family was to have a son to carry the family name. I felt nothing. I was neither happy nor sad at that minute. Eventually I drifted to sleep.

I was awakened by my mother's footsteps. I opened my eyes and there she was. In one hand she carried a heavy bunch of freshly steamed leaves. She bent over and unbuttoned my shirt. She laid the hot leaves over my breasts and began to squeeze. I grunted in my teeth and tried not to scream, but the pain was so great.

I started to cry. "Mother, Mother, please stop," I whimpered. She gave me a slap and told me to stop.

"This is not for you. It is for your baby. Do you want him to have stomachaches? You think I have nothing else to do? I have to squeeze all the young bad milk out so the new milk won't hurt your baby."

Both families were happy. Everyone told me I should be happy, too.

"You have a son, the first son in the family with all the privileges. He will carry on the family tradition. He will take care of the Thach ancestors and he will look after his grandfather's lands. One day *you* will be the mother-in-law and then you will understand how our traditions have passed down from one generation to the next!"

Six weeks later, it was time to go back to my in-laws.

Binh's mother came to my house with the traditional offering. My mother told me I must cross that hill one last time and return to the Thach family, that from now on that was where I belonged.

The gift basket of fruit, sweets and tea that the mother-in-law had brought was displayed on my own ancestors' altar. My mother had lit the incense sticks to ask the ancestors' spirits to protect her daughter and her grandson on their journey. A few words were exchanged between the two women. My mother-in-law picked Han up and ordered me to follow her.

I said goodbye to my mother, my sister, my sister-in-law and all my nieces and nephews. We were all crying. I saw water in my mother's eyes but I wasn't sure if she were crying or if her sweat had got into her eyes. If she did cry, I didn't believe at the time that it was for me. She loved her grandson and hated to see him go.

I remember that morning so clearly, the winding path that took me out of my small hamlet and up the hill. I remember each step I took. Each step was a nail pounding deeply into my heart. I felt once again that I was being sent into slavery. This was the same route they had taken me on my wedding day earlier in the year. I wanted to lie down on the railroad tracks and hope for the train to go by and take me away. Except now I had my son who I loved more than my own life. I couldn't bear the thought of leaving him on this earth alone without me.

When we arrived there was the same house and the same bed. The same mother-in-law, father-in-law, and husband. My fear kept rising. I could not control it. The only time I had ever felt at ease was with Binh's younger sisters. Whatever the reason, I was not afraid of them. Now I prayed my baby Han would be my savior, my protector.

The night had slowly crept in. It was dark but not too dark. Moonlight shone through the window. I wished I were back at my mother's house. I could hear my mother-in-law warning her five-year-old daughter Ut.

"Don't suck so hard. You are hurting me!"

A slap followed the warning and the girl cried.

What a family! Five years old and she is still breast-feeding?

I heard footsteps and then more men's voices outside in the courtyard where Binh and his father were sitting. I couldn't see the newcomers' faces but I knew who they were. They were the relatives who had become Viet Cong. They would go up deep into the mountains for some time. In the past year they had been very active in the district. Like Binh himself, these relatives believed they were descended from the legendary Thach Sanh and the goddess. They believed they were invincible, that no one could hurt them.

There was a lot of whispering and Binh followed them out of the courtyard gate. I was relieved but not off guard. I didn't dare lie down. I sat behind the curtain, hiding in the corner of the tiny bed with Han sucking on my breast. I was praying to Buddha to keep Binh away from me tonight and every night.

It was late and I must have been very tired, because when I awoke I heard heavy footsteps moving closer and closer to where I was hidden. I was in a panic and my heart was pounding.

It's not working, I thought, *my prayer is not working. I didn't pray hard enough! The Buddha didn't hear me!*

I could smell Binh's sweat and it made me sick to my stomach. *I must sit still and try not to move, try not to breathe.* There was a shadow over me and then there was the whole body. The hands, the hands came closer and closer to me.

"Where are you?" Binh snarled.

I tried to curl up tight. The hands touched my feet and I kicked him hard. I struggled to get up and escape but there was no room. The tiny bed was stuck in the corner between the close walls.

Binh stood at the foot of the bed, blocking me.

He was yelling, "Fuck your mother! What kind of bitch are you? Did you know where I went? I went to fuck my old girl friend and come back here and now I will fuck you!" He grabbed onto my feet and pulled me down onto the bed.

I screamed for help.

His mother came to the curtain but not to help me. With a chilly voice she said, "Your husband is entitled to whatever he wants from his wife. If you don't let my son get what he wants I will come into that bed and hold down your hands and your legs so he gets what he wants!"

My fear turned into anger, I told her to go to Hell, that if she dared to even think of doing what she said that I would swallow my tongue and kill myself, that my spirit would come back and haunt them all – *and believe me it will!*

She mumbled something but I didn't hear what she was saying because by that time Binh was out of control. He slapped me and punched me. I was screaming and the baby was crying. He stamped out the door, and cursed my mother's name. At that moment I promised myself, *They may have my body but I will never let them take my soul!* The punches still hurt but I preferred them to letting him rape me.

I thought I had won this one.

My victory didn't last very long. Binh soon returned, not with a stick for whipping but with a handful of the hottest peppers he had picked from yard. He was wild. He used all his force and ripped off my clothes. He threw me down and spread my legs open. I tried my best to fight him, to escape from his powerful arms but it was useless. He cursed my mother again, "Fuck your mother! If I can't fuck you. I will make sure no other men ever fuck you!"

His hand with the hot peppers went between my legs and up inside my private parts. I could feel it like fire burning all through me, all over my body. "Oh my God, help me!" I screamed. I kicked him hard and dropped my baby and ran outside without any clothes. The pain was unbearable. I was rolling on the ground, howling like an animal. I always knew he was vindictive, but never did I think he would be this low. What Binh did to me was more than an outrage. It was unspeakable.

"God will punish you for this," I cried. I said it over and over while trembling on the ground with pain.

The next morning, no one seemed to care what had happened to me the night before. Binh and his father had gone back up the mountainside to cut wood. The rest of the family had gone out into the fields.

My chores were to take care of the two younger sisters and feed the animals, haul in the water for the cows, and do whatever else needed to be done. My black pajamas were half torn, and my cone hat covered only a part of my face. Han was in my arms as I worked. The burning between my legs made me groan with pain. My tears rolling down my cheeks mixed with my sweat and dripped down to my mouth. Revenge was all I could think of.

You will all pay for this, I promised myself.

As much anger as I had toward Binh, I was angrier with my whole society, especially with my own mother. She had sold me to this vicious man. She knew she was wrong, especially after my many attempts to run away from him. She knew I had even wanted to commit suicide, but in her stubbornness and pride she wouldn't admit her error. She wouldn't give in. Now more than ever she wanted to prove to all the people in the village that *she* had control.

As for me, the angrier I became the more determined I got.

I will climb over that hill again. I will go home! I will crawl or creep, either way I will escape from this place once and for all!

That next morning, before dawn, I bundled Han and crept out of the house. I started up the hill trail in the dark. As the night went on I became more disoriented, but I wasn't afraid. Nothing out there in the darkness could be as bad as what I was leaving. But I hadn't slept the night before, and I was in much pain. Very soon I was tired.

One more step, and one more step, I told myself. *Soon you will reach the top before the sunrise.*

My mother was surprised to see me back and not happy. She said I was more trouble than I was worth. A girl who refused her husband was asking for trouble. None of her brothers' daughters had ever made such fools of themselves and brought shame to the family, that if I knew what was good for me I would return to the Thach family at once, that I belonged to them, not to her.

At first I had not wanted her to know what happened that made me run away, but when she rejected me I became angry. I dropped my pants down to my ankles.

"Take a good look at this! Is this what you think I deserve, Mother? Look at this so you know if you send me back that this is what *you* do to me, not them! You think I am so much trouble? You haven't seen anything yet! I will never go back. If you try to send me back I will kill myself and

41

my baby! You, Mother, you will be responsible for my death for the rest of your life! Do you hear me, Mother?"

My older sister had been there all the while, listening to us. She knew my mother's rages and now she was terrified for my life. But my mother didn't beat me for being disrespectful.

Silently, she walked away.

During the time that I stayed with my mother I thought about running away with my son to Saigon. But I didn't have the nerve or the money to do so. Also, I had a fifth-grade education and no skills. I could not even support myself, how could I support my son? There were no welfare or government programs to help women in need, especially one who had run away from her husband. What could I do? What I was supposed to do? Leaving my son behind was out of the question. I loved him too much.

Binh had come down to my mother's house during the daylight a few times demanding that I return but each time I had refused. Meanwhile the villagers who came to visit would talk about me, even in my presence, as if I weren't there. They laughed at my mother now for having lost control over me. They said it was a good thing that I wasn't *their* daughter. They said that if I were *their* daughter they would take me down to the sea and use me as bait for sharks and whales. Some of them said they would take me up to the mountains and feed me to the tigers or wolves. "No daughter of mine, no wife of mine, would act up like this and still be alive."

I didn't care what they said but unfortunately for me, Binh and his father had also become laughingstocks of the district. And I had become so sure that Binh and his father would not risk their lives to come to my village after dark that I became careless.

One night, as I swung back and forth in the hammock singing a lullaby to Han while he sucked on my breast, I wasn't paying any attention to what was around me. I didn't see Binh as he snuck around the back of the house. Later we found out he had poured rat poison into the barrel of my family's drinking water. But suddenly he was there in front of me.

He told me to get out of the hammock to go with him.

I didn't move, thinking I was safe.

I told him if he wanted me to go with him he must carry me or kill me otherwise I was not leaving. I had not even finished speaking when in the moonlight I saw his father step out from the corn stalks. Before I could move they had unhooked the hammock and rolled the baby and me inside it. They dragged me out of my mother's house. It happened so fast the only thing I could do was yell for help.

About that time my mother was coming home from the market and was near the house. Later, she told me that her instinct had told her something terrible had happened to me. Instinct or a guilty conscience? Whatever, she was right. When she heard me scream she dropped her packets and ran toward our house. My sister had just had her third child and was not allowed to come out, but she yelled to my mother and told her what had happened. My mother grabbed the frying pans and banged them together as she ran. She called the neighbors for help and most of the people did come out to help.

Binh and his father were on the back path out of the hamlet, one hand holding on to their bikes with the other dragging me between them. They heard the noise behind them of my mother and the neighbors coming after them. When they knew my mother was near they stopped.

Binh's father gave the order, "Kill her."

They had poles lashed to their bikes that they used to secure and carry wood to the market. Now those poles landed on my defenseless body, over and over. I heard a popping sound and a thousand lights sparked before my eyes, then darkness.

Six hours later, when I regained consciousness, I was in my mother's kitchen. My baby was crying and I was trying to find him, but I couldn't lift my arms.

I had a pounding headache. Salty water was dripping into my mouth. There was wetness around my neck and ears and a sticky feeling. I thought it was water, but it wasn't. It was the blood dripping down from a big hole in my head. I must have been hit very hard, I thought.

My face was so swollen that I couldn't open my eyes. I used all my strength to lift up my hand and went over my cheeks. I pressed my finger to my skin and it felt like it had blown up like a balloon. I used my thumb and my first finger to hold open my eyes, and I finally got them half opened. Through the dim light from the coconut oil lamp I saw my mother curled up on the dirt floor in front of the kitchen god's altar. The incense stick was burned low. My mother was sound asleep.

For the next six weeks I had to take care of my own wounds. Our village had no doctor and no modern medicine. Binh and his father had hit me so hard it left the deep hole in my head. I tried to measure the wound by using my fingers. It was wider than my two fingers put together and down inside of my skull.

To care for the wound my mother would go around the house and the pigsty to gather spider webs to use for a bandage. To wash my own wound I had to collect the pee-pee from my nephews. At one point my wound was infected. There were white maggots crawling out of my head.

Luckily my cousin Kham, who was a student nurse, lived next door. Even though Kham's mother didn't like my mother or me, Kham still cared about me. She gave me a small pack of *thuoc tim*, which was some kind of medicine with purple color. I used a tiny bit of the powder medicine and mixed it with boiling water and cleaned the wound every day until the infection was gone.

My bruises on my face and my body slowly disappeared. Soon there was no apparent trace of any sort of injury. I also started combing my hair in the opposite direction to cover the big hole in my head. The hole would be there for the rest of my life but I was alive.

I also no longer had any wish to die.

No more precious death for me as a way out. I told myself that if they wanted to kill me they had to find me first, but I would never voluntarily surrender, either to my husband or to my mother. I told myself that, from this moment on, I was on my own, that I must stop feeling sorry for myself. I must think only of ways to escape this miserable place.

My next chance was not long in coming.

CHAPTER 6

My First Escape

Being small and sickly had always given me advantages. For one, I didn't have to work in the rice fields, which had given me time as a child to learn other trades.

I was famous around the village for my *nong la,* my cone hats. Now I started in earnest making cone hats and within a month I had woven over a hundred hats. I sold them to the merchants and saved up my money. I befriended the merchants and drivers in the village market to find out where they resold the hats. I knew they didn't sell many in our village because we were too poor.

One of the buyers, Mrs. Thi, was my primary source. I had known her from the time I was a small child. Her youngest daughter, Be, was the same age as my older brother An. When Vietnam was divided, Mrs. Thi's husband chose to go north. He left her without money or property and with three almost-grown children.

After 1954, Ngo Dinh Diem's regime was always looking for reasons to break the bond between family members that were related to the communists. They focused mainly on the poor people because the poor were more likely to join the Communists. When Mrs. Thi's three children became of legal age they were ordered to relocate to different parts of the country. Mrs. Thi, however, chose to remain in our hamlet.

Without family, and with no land, Mrs. Thi was as poor as it gets. Like my mother, however, she was a crafty woman. She found different ways to make a living. Soon, buying and selling cone hats became Mrs. Thi's business.

One day, I saw that the truck to take her to the city market was parked next to the village market. I looked around but Mrs. Thi and the driver were nowhere to be seen. Without hesitation I lay Han inside of the truck and carefully climbed up myself. I used all my strength to move the heavy stacks of cone hats to give me enough room for me to hide. My heart was pumping so fast I had trouble controlling it. To keep Han quiet I pulled out my breast and fed him.

There was noise outside.

More hats were being piled into the truck.

"Check and make sure the hats are secure," Mrs. Thi ordered the driver. "We will stop in Tam Quan for candies but I want to reach Quy Nhon before dark."

The truck gate slammed shut, with me and Han inside. It was pitch dark, hot and not much air. Han was crying and the stacks of hats were sliding back and forth. I tried to protect Han and myself from being crushed to death by the cone hats. I didn't know how far we had gone but by the time the truck stopped and the back gate was opened I was ready to give up the fight.

The driver and a South Vietnam police officer stood by the open gate staring at me. The driver's face turned white as a ghost or something. He howled out to Mrs. Thi to hurry up and come out from the truck.

When she saw me with Han she stopped chewing her *trau*.

The police officer looked at her. "What is this all about?"

Mrs. Thi gulped down the *trau* and caught her breath before she could answer him.

"I didn't know she was there, officer! She is a foolish child!"

She was thinking fast.

"Her husband joined the South army, like you. But he was not lucky as you. He was wounded at Ban Me Thuot. Her family didn't want her to go to him because it was too far. She asked me many times to take her with me, officer, but always I said no! I didn't think she was this stupid! She almost got herself killed, and her baby, too, you see?"

Before the officer could ask my name she said,

"Get out of the truck and tell the nice officer your name and show him your identification card!"

She hit me on the head hard and pulled me out of the truck. "Or don't you have your papers either, you stupid girl?" she said furiously.

Standing there with Han in my arms, I thought it was all over. With all my plans and my trouble now I would have to go back again. But this time I had got Mrs. Thi in trouble too!

The officer didn't speak to me. He just motioned Mrs. Thi to step away from the truck and follow him. A few minutes later she was back. She gave me a fierce look of disapproval. Then she turned and told the driver to climb in the truck and help me up.

She opened the front door and said to me, "Get in!"

The driver handed Han to me and helped Mrs. Thi get in and then walked around the truck and got himself in. He looked at me and shook his head. As we drove off the policeman was out of sight.

"Young lady, you have a lot of explaining to do! And you just cost me a lot of money!"

Mrs. Thi was angry with me but she was angrier at the police officer. She turned to the driver. "I swear to God, these policemen are just highway robbers! They don't even try to catch the Viet Cong. They are just out here to rob the hard-working citizen! Sometimes I wonder which side are the bad guys!"

I could see why Mrs. Thi was so bitter. Ten years earlier the North had taken her husband, leaving her with three small children. Then the reforms of Ngo Dinh Diem had sent her three children away because she didn't own any land. Now the police were taking her money, too. I was sorry, but not that sorry.

I was still in the truck. I was getting away!

It was the flood season. The roads were covered with water, sometimes too deep to pass, and we would have to wait. The trip from Duc Pho to Ban Me Thuot normally took two to three days, but in the rainy season, it took us ten days.

We stopped alongside of the road and asked for shelter in people's houses. We slept on damp, dirt floors without blankets. We ate whatever the farmer who lived alongside the road had to give to us, which usually meant nearly nothing. From the little money I had saved, I repaid Mrs. Thi what she paid the policeman. I also gave a little to the driver for my transportation.

The last time we had lunch together, away from the driver, Mrs. Thi told me, "I will stop at my daughter Be's house and ask her husband to let you stay there with them. Be's husband was dismissed from the army. Now he has trouble working, and he stays with the children. You better be nice to him, you understand? They are poor, but you are the poorest! You had better remember that. You will be safe here. Your husband doesn't know where you are. Nobody does. This driver doesn't know who you are, and I won't tell anyone. In the future, I will stop by from time to time to see Be and the children. I will let you know what is happening back home. Be a good girl now. Do you understand?"

Then we were there.

A tiny little shack sat alongside of the road. Be ran out to greet her mother with tears running down her face. She looked ten years older than when I last saw her. I remembered Be as a friendly teenager who liked boys, especially my brother An. My mother said she was a tramp. I didn't know what that meant. Even so, many families wanted their sons to marry her but she left the hamlet and married some guy no one knew.

Now she had two children and a sickly husband. Their living condition was so poor. *Land Reform*, I thought. I wondered what would happen to Han and me while we were here. It didn't look promising.

In 1959 when Ngo Dinh Diem forced many poor peasants to relocate, she and her husband were caught in it. Land Reform was actually a resettlement program where many peasants from small distant villages were ordered to move to densely populated areas controlled by the South. Instead of a few families who knew each other, the peasants were lost among thousands of strangers, far away from their ancestral tombs and their temples.

Every day Be and I woke up very early in the morning. We took the rickshaw to the market to catch the farmers who brought goods to sell. We hurried to buy rice, fruits and vegetables and everything else we could from the Montagnards, the hill tribes. When we had spent our 'market' money we carried everything we had bought in our bags. On the way home we sold our goods to the plantation workers or to poor soldiers. For each cup of rice we sold we earned about half a tablespoon of rice. For every ten eggs we sold we may get one for our profit.

If we were lucky, by the end of the day we may have earned a cup or two of rice and a few eggs. With these, and the leftover damaged fruits and vegetables, and whatever else we couldn't sell, we went home to feed our family of six. Sometimes if we made a little more money we bought some cheap bony fish. We never had enough money for chicken or pork. We also had to buy Be's husband cigarettes and cheap rice wine so he watched our children.

One night the Viet Cong came to our shack to talk. They said they had heard that Be and I associated with the South Vietnamese Soldiers at the market. They said they had not come to punish us for that. They only wanted us to find out what was going on in town. They pointed at me and told me, "You are a pretty girl. You should be friends with the soldiers and bring them out here. They love good food and good loving. They will tell you what we want to know." Happily I didn't have the chance to do what the Viet Cong had planned for me.

War, politics and power usually go together. The overseer of the local plantation was also the village chief. He was in his forties – an old man to me. Worse, this old man already had two wives. One day he went to the market place and saw me. He thought I was pretty and he decided he would like to marry me: he wanted me to be his third wife. When I refused him he ordered his plantation workers and the poor soldiers guarding the plantation not to buy anything from me or from Be.

In one week Be and I lost all our business. We could not even feed our children. Soon Han was so weak he had no strength to suck on my empty breast. Be's children couldn't get out of bed. They constantly asked for food. They were starving. Some of the villagers tried to help. One night some hunters skinned a deer carcass outside our hut. They took the skin, meat and bones but left the intestines on the ground. The next morning Be and I fought the army of flies and ants away. We washed the slimy intestines and boiled them with some herbs from the roadside. First we spooned the broth into the children's mouths. Then we let them chew slowly on the meat. It was soon gone.

We went up the mountains and dug up roots and wild berries, but very soon the berries also were gone and Han got sick. Be's husband wanted me to leave. He said I was bad luck.

I went back to see the old man and begged him to give me money to buy medicine for Han. He told me he didn't know that I had a child. He wanted me to give Han up to an orphanage. I remember I was crying when I left his office. I didn't want to give up my son. All the way back to the shack I cried, "No, no, I will die first before I give up my child."

But when I returned home, Han was violently ill.

I had to go back to see this man again. He knew he had me where he wanted me. I promised that I will marry him, but before I gave up my child I must get him healthy first. The old man listened to my reasons and finally he gave me money.

I went to the store and got the medicine. That night the old man came to our shack. He brought a chicken, rice and some sweets. He brought Be's husband beer and cigarettes.

"We are celebrating my engagement," he said.

He told Be's husband to keep an eye on me, that he would return the following night to collect me.

That night I took Han and snuck out while everyone slept. I was sorry for Be but I went anyway. The road from Ban Me Thuot to Saigon would be bumpy and hilly with South Vietnam police at every checkpoint. Even though I had almost nothing to take with me, I vowed I would make it. Once again I was running away with Han, this time not from Binh, but from an old goat.

Days later, I finally arrived in Saigon as the sun was going down. In the late afternoon the streets of Saigon were jam packed with cars, motorbikes and with cyclos, or motorized rickshaws. With Han in one arm I was standing on the roadside waiting for the traffic to stop. I didn't know which way I should start or where to go.

I knew there were people in my village who had come to Saigon to avoid the war. Many of them worked here as housekeepers, cyclo drivers or as food sellers on the streets. Some of them who had the money had opened up small businesses. Most of them lived outside of the city. I didn't want to go near them. I didn't want Binh to know where Han and I were hiding.

I remembered my older brother An had once mentioned that my great-aunt Ving's sons lived somewhere in Cho Lon, the Chinatown of Saigon. I had never met them or their family before and I didn't know what they looked like. Besides, they were my third cousins, not my first. And they were rich, my brother had said. Should I just show up at their door and beg for food and a place to stay? What would they say when they found out I had run away from my husband?

By now Han was cranky from the long trip. We were both hot, thirsty, and hungry, with no way to go. I felt I had failed him. I ached for what I had done to my child. I headed for Cho Lon. When I found the address, the housekeeper let me in after I told her who I was.

She also told me what the situation was in the house.

Since the death of his first wife the older son, my cousin Tuan, had lost his mind. He was always gambling and spent most of his time at nightclubs. He had left his three young sons in the care of the housekeeper or in private school. Tuan's younger brother Hong had three different wives and ten or more children. The big house was always full of freeloading relatives from the countryside (like me, she implied) who needed the place to stay. So many people, so many problems, the whole house was in chaos. Even so, Han and I could sleep on the floor in the corner of one of the rooms.

It didn't last long. The second week there, the housekeeper told me to leave. She said my cousin Tuan had not been home for many days and there was not enough money to buy food for everyone. Since I was not a close family member, I had to leave. The only thing I could think of then was to try to find Mrs. Thi's second son, Sau Trung.

Sau Trung had left the land reform place he had been sent to, and had moved his family to Saigon. Mrs. Thi had told me one time that he was a cyclo driver and his wife sold food on the street. Now they were renting a tiny place just big enough for one bed somewhere in the Phu Nhuan section. They had three children. Later I found out the real reason Sau Trung had moved his family to Saigon. He was Viet Cong and he had been assigned to Saigon. At the time we didn't know it but there were Viet Cong in every block and on every street. They were blending with people in different classes. This was how Ho Chi Minh worked.

Sau Trung and his wife were not happy to see me show up on their door, but they didn't tell me to go away. They were kind enough to share their bed with us. But on the second night Han had a stomach problem. Needless to say it happened in the middle of the night. Nobody could get any sleep. The next morning we had to leave.

For the next three days I wandered the Saigon streets looking for a job. I was willing to do just about anything for room and board, but no one would accept Han. Soon what little money I had was gone.

At night the pavement was our bed. Han was getting sicker and I didn't know what to do. In my desperation I took Han to an orphanage. My hope was that the orphanage might help by keeping him while I looked for work, and that when I found a job I could help support him at the orphanage. But when I got there and took one look at the place, I was terrified. I ran out of the orphanage as fast as I could.

On a downtown street under a shade tree I lay Han's tiny, motionless body inside an old cone hat. I was weeping.

Oh, Heaven, I beg you, my son is dying!

What was I thinking to give him up to the orphanage? It was the most horrible sight I had ever seen. What had I done to this child? I had denied him his father's land. Now he was dying of starvation, all because I wanted to be free. My selfishness could cost him his life. What kind of a mother could do this to her own son?

Oh God! Oh Buddha, please help me. I will do anything you ask of me but please let my son live. Please help me to take him home. My hands covered my face. I was sobbing, "My son, my baby son!"

There were strange voices speaking above me. I looked up. Two giants stood before me, Westerners. They dropped some money into my cone hat and keep on walking. I picked up the money and ran after them. I wanted to return their money and tell them it was a mistake, that I was not a beggar! But my legs were short and I was tired. I couldn't run as fast as the giants walked. I yelled after them, "Money, too much money!"

As soon as I said this, I stopped talking. My first instinct was fear. There were many real beggars on the street. If they knew that these men had given me this money they would hurt me and take the money.

I scooped Han out of the cone hat and quickly walked to a food stall and bought two hot embryo duck eggs. I squatted on a stool close to the ground. Han was lying on my lap, his eyes closed.

Oh please, God, please, Buddha, don't let him die.

I put a warm teaspoon of embryo water into Han's mouth. He slowly started to swallow. Little by little he finished the water. I took the tiny cooked ducks and chewed them very fine. I fed Han like a bird, from my mouth into his. Then, like a miracle his eyes opened and he gave me a weak smile. I cried, "Oh, my God Buddha, he is alive!"

I used the rest of the money to buy two small loaves of French bread, and a can of condensed milk.

And a bus ticket back to my home village.

CHAPTER 7

Family Secrets

Most of the people from my village who had gone to Saigon and returned came home with new wealth and honor. They were celebrities.

When I came home I brought nothing but shame.

I *had* been the disobedient child. I had brought so much shame and heartache to my mother. Still, when I came home she would never say so, but I knew she was happy to have me there.

Me and my baby son, Han.

One evening I found out she had been in jail while I was gone.

We had finished our meager meal of rice and boiled sweet potato leaves dipped in the cheapest fish sauce. I had cleaned our few dishes and come out to the courtyard to sit with her, my little nieces playing around us in the courtyard.

She told me the story her own way.

After telling me to prepare her *trau* for her, my mother picked up Han and lay down with him in the hammock. She swung back and forth, talking to my baby.

"Your father is a monster and your mother is stupid! You are lucky to be alive! But you are a good boy."

She spoke as if I weren't there. She snuggled Han. She rubbed his hair and kissed his forehead. She blew on his stomach and tickled him to make him laugh out loud. As much as I didn't like my mother ignoring my presence, I didn't dare to speak up. After all, Han and I were sheltering under her roof.

Finally she looked over at me.

"Why don't you say something? What are you thinking?"

"I was just—

She had always had a habit of asking me questions but never waiting for an answer. Nothing had changed. Without waiting, she went on.

"Did you know your older brother An had to come home to save me? Do you know what those monsters down to the city did to me? They caught me coming home from market one day. My basket was almost empty. It had only a few shiners that I bought to feed my grandchildren. They threw me in jail for that! Then they made up a fake charge against me and said that my younger son had joined the Viet Cong!"

I interrupted her.

"He did? You... you know where Ming is, don't you! You lied to me! You told me he ran away"

I remembered the morning Ming left, wondering where he was. He went to school and never returned.

All day long I wondered about him. By nightfall I was very angry with my little brother for not returning home. I was angry with him because he made our mother cry. I was angry with him because he had sold the bicycle that I had bought from my hard work and sweat to help our mother. I was angry with him because he was a spoiled child who did what he wanted most of the time.

I was especially angry with him because he was the one Mother had chosen to send to school, not me; that he always made me cry; that he was a boy and I was a girl; that he was Mother's favorite. I was angry with him because he had not cared enough about me to stay home to defend me when I was beaten nearly to death.

Yet, for all that, I loved him and worried about what had happened to him. He was only a boy! I remember thinking that. I went out that night to look for him, asking everyone I knew where he could be.

When I returned that night Mother sat in the darkness and chewed on her *trau* one after another, without saying a word. I tried to comfort her by telling her I would find him, but it was no use. She knew Ming had made up his own mind and didn't want to be found. She knew he had gone to join the Viet Cong.

Now she was shushing me.

"What a stupid girl you are! What makes you think that I know where he is?"

"Well, you have an idea, don't you?" I asked.

She spit out some red juice, ignoring my words completely.

"Where was I? Oh, yes, my arrest. At first they kept me in the local jail. They wanted me to sign a paper that said my younger son was a Viet Cong. I refused! I told them I didn't know where my son was. And it was the truth! I told them that he just left home, that he was missing, but they didn't believe me. They beat me up very badly."

She spat again.

"They whipped me until my clothes were torn and my skin was cut. They poured soapy water into my mouth and made me swallow it. I fought with them, I twisted, I turned, but those monsters held me down and forced my mouth open. I couldn't stop them. They kept pouring and pouring. My stomach was this big- She arched her hands over her belly. -so they stepped on it! I opened my mouth, and let it out."

As she spoke, I could taste my salt tears. I used my shirtsleeves to wipe my eyes.

Even as I felt sorry for my mother, I kept asking myself, *What did she do in her past life that was so evil that she must suffer this much? How much more must she repay in this life for her past wrongdoing?*

My mother was still speaking.

"They didn't get a thing out of me! I'd rather die than tell them where my son is!"

I said impatiently, "Mother, how did An save you?"

She didn't bother to answer.

"Do you know they beat me up so badly that I couldn't walk? Then they threw me into a shack behind the jailhouse. I lay there on the dirt floor in my own blood. The roof of the shack was tin. Do you know how hot it was at noontime?"

I shook my head.

"The sun had heated the tin roof so hot the shack was like an oven. I thought I would cook to death. My clothes stuck to my skin because the blood had dried and glued them together. I lay in my own urine. Do you know how painful it was, and how stinky I was?"

I remembered as a child when the local government took over my sister's kitchen for a jail, how they used to bring in people they suspected were VC and beat them with sugar cane sticks. Years later, I can still hear the screams.

My mother continued.

"When they didn't hear me complaining or begging, they took me outside and dunked me into the water. They ripped off my bloody clothes. The pain was so bad, I felt like every hair on my head was standing up like a porcupine. All I could do was scream. I yelled and cried and cursed them, but they didn't care. They keep sticking the paper in front my face and telling me to sign their phony document that I was a VC supporter!"

"Did you sign it?"I asked.

"No! I never did."

Her face was hard, her eyes filled with hatred, victory in her voice.

I had sat there motionless, with goose bumps on my skin, while I listened to my mother tell me her stories. Now I was outraged.

"Those animals, those scum! I want to be Viet Cong! I want to go to their houses and shoot them dead!" I yelled.

My mother looked at me and said, "Nonsense."

She turned her head and looked out beyond the gate to the rice field.

I used to hate my mother's stubbornness, her hard head, but at that moment all I could do was admire her courage.

She stopped swinging and moved Han from her lap onto the hammock. She bent over the side and spit out the areca leaves she had been chewing.

Without her asking, I got up and went to the back of the house. I came back with a coconut bowl filled with water and handed it to her. She took the bowl and rinsed her mouth. Then she drank the rest of the water and threw the coconut into the corner.

I neatly folded slices of nut and paste into another areca leaf and handed it to her. She accepted it but before she put it in her mouth she said, without bothering to even look at me, "You didn't use too much paste, did you?"

I was annoyed.

"No, Mother, you know I've done it a thousand times before."

Although I calmly answered her, I said to myself, *They should have kept you in jail! See how much paste they would put in your trau!*

As usual, I felt ashamed for my evil thoughts.

"You know the worst part? They didn't let me chew my *trau!* Yes, I almost had a nervous breakdown. I was *this close* to signing that phony confession!" She pressed her index finger and thumb together.

"When they didn't get it, they were so mad. Then they sent me to the province jail, thinking I would get a harder time, but they were wrong!"

She laughed.

"Hah! The Quang Ngai province jail guards gave me *trau* to chew! In exchange, I cooked and cleaned for them and mended their clothes. But even though they had no confession, no evidence, they still were going to keep me in jail for three months. Three months! For nothing wrong!"

She looked at me then and smirked.

"Your brother must have sensed something was wrong. He took a leave of absence and came home."

With a proud voice she said, "An walked into that prison in his full uniform. He looked so handsome. He marched into that jail and demanded to see me. He asked the warden where was the evidence that his mother was a Viet Cong supporter? He asked them how could a woman send her first son to fight for the South and turn around to support the enemy! He scorned them.

"Do you think I went to fight in the war so you can just sit at your desk? So you can jail my mother without proof? I want an answer and I want it now!"

She lifted her chin up.

"Well, they let me go right there and then. They told me to go back to my shelf to get my belongings but I would have none of that. I just turned my bum to them and walked straight out the door with my first son!"

I thought my mother was laying it on a bit thick. I had never seen An act like that. But if that is what she believes, fine with me.

I asked her, "Did you tell my brother An how proud of him you were? Did you thank him, Mother?"

She gave me a dirty look.

"I carried him nine months. I brought him into this world. The least he could do was to take care of me when I needed it. It is his duty to take care for his ancestors and for *me*, his *mother*. He is the first son!"

As for me, my escape had all been for nothing.

Nothing had changed in my situation. I still belonged to Binh's family and now I also had to deal with the local Viet Cong.

More and more of the young men and women in the village had become their cadets. Even my best friend Chun, who had let me borrow her birth certificate for my escape, informed me that very soon she would be going up into the mountains for training.

As my neighbors saw it, I had only two options. I could become a Viet Cong or I could return to Binh's family. Either way, it was an intolerable decision. I definitely didn't want to return to live with Binh.

No way, I told myself, *you were not born to be an obedient wife. If you return to Binh, you will have more babies and, you being you, either you will kill yourself or he will kill you. Either way your children will not have a mother.*

It seemed that I would have to join the Vietcong, that I had no choice. But I quickly decided that wasn't right. After all, a choice is what *you* make. A choice is not what people make for you.

I asked my mother to care for Han. I told her I wanted to leave Han with her and return to Saigon to work. Mother wasn't angry with me for putting her on the spot. She just said no and then she walked away. I went to my sister and asked her for help.

She was furious with me.

"What kind of mother are you?" she yelled. "You are not even an animal! Animals take care of their young ones. They don't abandon their kittens or their puppies. You are selfish and inconsiderate! You, you – all you think about is you!"

I remember I was so angry with my sister. I was crying. I don't remember what else I said. I only remember thinking, *I am not a mother who doesn't care, who goes away to be free of my responsibility. I go away to make something better for myself and my son!*

I was so upset with my mother and my sister that again, the only thing I wanted was revenge. Not only on my family but on my whole society as well. The idea of becoming a Viet Cong was looking better and better all the time.

I will go north and find Mr. Hung, our neighbor, the man who killed my father. I will make Han's father's life miserable like my own. I will make the villagers terrified of me!

The Viet Cong had guns! The Viet Cong had power!

The day after our big family blowout my mother went to the district chief and got my birth certificate. She carried it with her wherever she went, and at night she would hide my birth certificate and what little money she had. She also took Han away from me and brought him in her bed and let him suck on her empty breasts. I thought she was doing this to keep me there.

At the time I thought she was mean and malicious. Only now, when I look back, do I realize she was preparing for me to go. Although I didn't know it then, each night when she hid my birth certificate and her money, she did it in such a way I could see where she put them. If I left, well, then, I left. She'd have no direct responsibility of my action. In this way she wouldn't have to answer to the Thach family or to the Viet Cong.

But should I go? Did I dare to go?

63

CHAPTER 8

Crossing the Bamboo Bridge

The rainy season in Duc Pho was miserable.

One night, after we ate a meager supper, my mother took Han up to the main part of the house, leaving me with the pots and bowls to clean, the small cooking area to tidy up, and the pigs to tend.

I hate the rain.

I had to go outside again, out into the rain. I had to bring in a banana bunch to chop up and add to the pig's slop pot. I looked down at my bare ruined feet. Earlier in the day I had asked my nephew, Bang, to pee on them to hopefully kill the infection. But the rain and the dirty wet ground just made them worse. The sores had cracked open and the toes were bleeding. I felt sorry for my feet.

I had no money to buy even a pair of rubber sandals. *Don't talk about shoes. What do you expect, foolish girl?* Day after day, my poor feet pounded the muddy ground. *And just look at your hands, your dirty*

clothes! My hands were wrinkled and my clothes were always damp—
I didn't have any other dry clothes.

*How much more can you take? Cam, you've got to get out of here.
You have delayed long enough!*

Every day I made my plans to escape. But every time I looked at
my baby, I didn't have the heart to leave him. He had gotten better since
we were home, but he was not yet completely healthy. His ears still
discharged white pus, and every morning they crawled with maggots.
No matter how many times during the day I cleaned his ears, the bad
smell attracted the flies. His nose was constantly running. His small body
was all bone and skin, his head too heavy for his tiny body.

At night I would light incense sticks and kneel down and ask the
Buddha for help.

"Buddha, please help me! If I take him with me he will die. But I
don't want to leave him here. What should I do? Please give me a sign.
I will obey. If you want me to stay here to take care of him I will do it."

The rain was pouring down hard.

I decided not to do the dishes so I took them outside to let the rain
rinse them for me. "I'll get up early in the morning and do them," I
muttered. I still had to cook food for the pigs, though, and let it cool
before morning came. *Stupid pigs!* If the pigs didn't get fed when they
woke up they would squeal, loudly. Mother would kill me.

Damn fat, stupid pigs!

I reached up to take down the raincoat. It was no ordinary
raincoat. It was made from palm leaves woven with bamboo strips.
When I had to wear it I looked like a big moth. With a cone hat on my
head I looked like a turtle wearing a moth's body. The coat was so old
that leaves had worn off. My mother had used bamboo tiles to patch it.

The coat was heavy. When it was wet, it smelled awful.

I hated the coat.

As I put it on I mumbled, "Why doesn't she throw this stupid thing away?" The cone hat on my head was no better. *Here comes the turtle moth!* Out of habit I bent down and rolled my wet black pajama pants above my knees. I held onto my cone hat with one hand and my palm leaf raincoat with the other. I pulled my chin into my chest, like a turtle.

I dashed outside into the darkness, the wind, and the rain.

I couldn't see anything in front of me.

Too late I sensed someone. Startled, I opened my mouth to scream but my voice didn't escape my mouth. Strong hands pulled me forward against a grown man. His hand covered my mouth. My heart pounded, punching me under my wet pajama shirt.

"Don't scream, we are friends. I won't harm you if you do as I say."

I thought about kneeing him between his legs, but my strength was gone, my body limp.

"Who is in the house with you?"

I shook my head and tried to make a noise. His hand covered my mouth so tight I could not talk. He must have realized that, too.

"You will not scream. Understand? I will remove my hand."

I raised my hand to my mouth and peeled off his fingers. I used my wet sleeves to wipe the salty, cigarette taste off my lips. The thought of those dirty hands, of where they had been, gave me goose bumps. I turned my head so he and the men he was with wouldn't see me and I spit on the ground.

I was still shaking.

"You scared me half to death," I told them weakly. They seemed not to care. Maybe they hadn't heard me.

Once again the older man asked me, "Who is in the house with you?"

"M-my mother and my baby."

"You're not lying to me, are you?"

He didn't wait for an answer or to be invited in.

"Dong chi Ming, vao nha coi thu!" he ordered.

Cadre Lac, go in the house and check!

The young cadre cautiously entered the back door. When he emerged he waved to the others. "No one in the house." Softly they walked into the kitchen. I followed them, quietly.

A coconut-oil lamp was burning.

In the dim light I recognized the young Viet Cong cadre, an older boy named Lac.

He was only a few years older than me. He used to live down near Highway One. We used to go to the Buddhist temple as boy scouts and girl scouts of the Buddha. We knew each other but we weren't close friends. I hadn't seen him for a long time.

He ignored me. In front of his commander he pretended he didn't know me at all.

It didn't surprise me. When you joined the Communist Party, you gave up your personal life. No more parents, no more family, no friends. In 1945, when my father's family was killed, most of my mother's family were Communists. Their father was killed, too. Later, they said it was a mistake, but who knows? I mean, they couldn't save their own father?

Or they wouldn't.

No, I wasn't surprised this boy would not acknowledge me.

In a low voice I called for my mother.

"Mother, we have... company."

My mother appeared in the room with Han in her arms before I could finish my sentence. She must have heard the noise. I saw her eyes blink. She nodded slightly, with a faint smile.

"Xin chao, cac dong chi."

It is an honor to welcome Viet Cong cadres.

"Please take off your coats and warm yourselves by the fire."

She didn't wait for them to answer or take off their coats.

"Cam, go outside and get some more rice straw to build up the fire. Hurry, the men are cold!" The orders flowed. "Get more water to boil for tea! Bring out the dry sweet-potato chips. There is some brown sugar in the barrow, up at the main house. Hurry up, child!"

I could hear the nervousness in her voice. I started to speak. She gave me a sharp look. I knew what that look meant and kept silent. Like a wet dog I bent my head low and scurried out to the back of the house to dig out some dry straw.

When I returned, I saw the men sitting around the fire on the dirt floor, warming their hands over the fire and smoking Mother's homemade tobacco. I dropped the straw beside them, took out the sweet-potato chips and began to cook them.

While they were cooking, I told my mother I had to go up to the main house to get the molasses to add to the chips.

Lac got to his feet. "I will help you," he said.

The two older men looked up and winked at him. Before I could refuse, Lac picked up a coconut lamp and walked toward the main house. I had no choice but to follow him.

He said softly, "Do you know I used to like you a lot? I did. Don't be afraid of me. I am still your friend."

I nodded my head but said nothing.

He looked back at the kitchen. Then he whispered while we scooped out the molasses.

"Tonight they have come to check you out. They want you to join us. You better do what they say. They won't take you to the mountains yet. You have to stay here and work for them. If you do good work then they will take you up to the mountains. Then you will belong."

I lifted my hand out of the large barrow. I glanced over at his worried face. I wanted to ask him why he was worried but I saw his index finger pressed to his lips. The concern in his eyes told me he was afraid. We said nothing more. At that moment I thought I heard footsteps nearby and my heart jumped. When we returned to the kitchen the two men and my mother still sat where we had left them.

Finally, it was agreed. I would meet them on the hill at midmorning. I would go with them. After the men left, my mother, without asking, took Han with her to bed.

Alone, I stacked the pots and pans with the coconut bowls I had used to serve the Viet Cong. Then I threw everything out the door with the rest of the dishes. I didn't bother cooking the pig food either.

I just went to bed.

As I lay on my wooden plank, I watched the lamp burning on my ancestors' altar. *I have brought so much shame to this family.* I couldn't bring myself to pray to their spirits that night.

How can I dare ask them for help?

I looked up at the ceiling and listened to the wind blowing, the rain dropping, the bullfrogs roaring in the far distant rice fields. Under my bed mice were scurrying. In my head my thoughts were scurrying just like those mice.

What should I do? What?

Should I do what those men want? Should I go with them?

I thought about having revenge, about having power. If I joined the Viet Cong, people would be afraid of me like those men made me afraid of them. Yes, people would fear me! Then I thought of the communists killing my father, my grandfather and uncles. How could I ever forget that, forgive that?

Then should I return to Binh and his ugly family to be the wife I was supposed to be? Oh yes, my mother would love that. The thought of Binh's hands on me made me shudder.

No, Mother, you won't have your wish.

My head was beginning to hurt.

Or should I escape to Saigon to make something of myself. But what? I didn't know how to do anything in the City. I was just a country girl.

A country girl. Oh yes, I could just hear my sister's voice.

"Cam, why can't you be *normal* like the rest of us? You are only a girl! Why are you always so much trouble? You bring so much hardship on yourself! You saw what happened to Miss Giang who lives in the house behind us. She fought like you, she cried, she fussed, and what did she get? Her father beat her up so badly her head broke and now she is half crazy. Everyone laughs at her. And she still ended up marrying that guy! How many girls in this village didn't want their husband? Too many, and so what! They still ended up doing what they been told. Sister, if you keep swimming against the current you will drown for sure! Please, Sister, stop. If you go too far, someday you will be sorry. But it will be too late. Accept your life. You are just a girl... a country girl."

Finally I slept. My dreams were terrible and confused.

When I awoke at the rooster's first crow, my decision was made.

Carefully, very quietly, I rolled up my straw mat. I tiptoed to the ancestral altar and nervously lifted the cover off the bronze jug. I reached inside and pulled out a small pouch that my mother carried with her during the day wherever she went. At night she hid it in the jug. She knew I would know this. The pouch contained some money and, wrapped in brown paper, my birth certificate. I took my certificate and put the money back in the jug.

CROSSING THE BAMBOO BRIDGE

From the clothesline in the corner of the kitchen I took my two pair of damp black pajamas. I neatly folded them and put them on a bamboo tray. Then I moved the rice jug where I hid my own money and put my money with the clothes. I tiptoed out the back door to the banana tree and cut off a big leaf, making sure I did not wake up the pigs. I brought the leaf inside and wrapped it around the tray to protect my clothes and money from the rain.

Barefoot, I walked softly to my mother's bed and bent down to kiss my son. I froze. My mother's body had begun to shift.

Oh God, she will get up! I am dead!

My heart was racing. I stood utterly still, waiting for her.

She didn't open her eyes. Her hand reached over to Han and pulled him closer to her and away from me. I stood there waiting for a few more minutes. It wasn't to be. I would not be allowed to kiss my baby goodbye.

Sadly, I went back to the kitchen.

There were two raincoats hanging on the wall, side by side. I picked the better one and put it on. Then, for whatever reason, I decided not to wear the new one and put it back, taking the old one and an old cone hat. I covered most of my face. Then I picked up the bamboo tray, moved the thatch door to the side, and let myself out like a thief.

I hurried out to the gate and down the muddy lane. At the edge of the hamlet I paused. The path forked left, right, and straight ahead. I went straight ahead. Before me was the old bamboo bridge.

Memories flooded me of the time I tried to run away when I was six and my mother caught me at this bridge.

I hate this bridge.

Now here I was again, facing it. Except, this time I wasn't just running away. I was leaving my sick child behind.

The only hope for me was that someday my son would understand. In my heart and head I tried to explain to him. "Han, my baby son, you are a first son. You are a boy. You will have all the privileges. For me, I am nothing. I am the property of your father's family. They will break me now if I stay. I will die if I stay! But you will die if I take you with me!"

I had planned to escape since the day we had returned from Saigon. But Han was so sick for so long that I could not bear to leave him. Now I felt I had no choice. The Viet Cong were forcing my hand. If I stayed they would eventually take me from my baby anyway. In a few hours they would be looking for me.

I could not stay.

Standing there, I wasn't prepared for the pain.

I can't do this.

"Oh, Buddha, oh, Heaven and Earth," I prayed, "Please let me do the right thing!"

Unexpectedly, an old song popped inside my head.

Chieu, Chieu, cau gang dong dinh.
Cau tre luc lac gap gen kho di.
Kho di me dat con di.
Con di truong hoc me di truong do.
Evening comes, we cross the bamboo bridge.
The nails are strong but the bridge is shaking.
The child goes out to school to learn.
Mother goes out to learn the way of life.

I moved toward the bridge.

One foot in front of the other, one hand holding my tray and clothes, the other grasping the rail, I stepped onto the shaky bamboo bridge. The bamboo planks were wet and the river current beneath me was strong. I thought about nothing except my next careful step.

As I stepped onto the muddy road again I turned and looked back.

A heavy mist hung over my little hamlet. I could hardly see my mother's house. I tried not to cry but my tears wouldn't stop. My heart ached for my baby. I wanted to run back to him. The voices inside my head were screaming at each other.

Your child will never see you again! Running away like this will cause more harm to your family. You are an unfit mother. You are worse than an animal. You didn't even say goodbye to your baby son. You left your baby to save your own skin. Bad mother, bad mother! Your child is better off without you!

I begged the voices to stop but they would not be stopped.

I ripped off my heavy raincoat and threw it into the rice field. I turned my back to my hamlet, and started to run toward the highway.

I ran and ran down the muddy rutted road through the rain.

I passed my grandmother's house, then my Aunt Number Di Moi's house. I passed the Duc Pho market. Soon I had crossed the railroad tracks. I was on the other side of the village now, walking alongside Highway One in the dark.

Bus after bus went roaring by me. I waved at them desperately, trying to flag them down, but they didn't stop. Their wheels splashed mud on me as they passed. I was soaked to my skin, filthy and cold.

I was far from my home and my family. I was far from my hamlet, from all the people I had known all my life.

I was far from my child.

Bad mother, bad mother!

Far, far away.

CHAPTER 9

Bus Ride to Hell

I t was getting light out.

My bare feet no longer wanted to move.

My legs were heavy. My stomach was making an awful noise. My eyes were stinging and sore from crying. The road was wet and muddy. If I sat down to rest my bones I would get a bad chill and sicken.

I thought about lying down anyway and letting nature take its course.

"Stupid girl, stupid girl," I yelled at myself. "How stupid to run away again! Now you can't go home! What were you thinking?"

An old yellow bus was approaching. I raised my hand.

One more try.

As the bus went by me, I thought there was no hope for me. I turned to walk on and saw the bus stopping. The driver was trying to back up while one of his helpers jumped out the bus and ran toward me.

"*Di dau, di dau?*" the helper yelled.

Where are you going?

"Saigon," I yelled back. "How much?"

He didn't bother to answer. He grabbed my hand and pulled me toward the bus.

At the bus door he picked me up under my armpits and shoved me inside, squeezing in behind me. The door was not yet closed when the driver took off, roaring down the road.

Eight hundred kilometers to Saigon and the road was bad.

I pushed my way into the crowd and stopped. There was no room for me to sit down.

I can't travel all the way standing up.

The motion of the moving bus was dizzying. The smell of live, unwashed chickens and pigs, of fish and fruits and rotting vegetables, was sickening. People were vomiting. I felt ill.

"I want to get out!" I screamed.

"Go sit down!" the helper yelled as he pointed to the back.

"I can't move!" I shouted. People were watching us.

He stepped from the bus stair up into the aisle. He shoved through passengers and ordered the ones in seats to squeeze in further. He ordered me to follow him to the back.

Lurching after him, clutching my belongings, I tried not to fall into people's laps but it was too late. The driver had run over a bump at high speed, faster than was safe. The bus tilted first to one side and then to the other. The driver almost lost control of the bus.

I fell backwards into an old woman's lap.

She slapped me on my back and yelled at me for being careless. The helper turned and looked at the old woman. A young boy was sitting next to her by the window.

"You only paid half price. Get up," the helper told the boy.

The boy complained but finally got out of his seat. I felt bad for him, but not bad enough to refuse the seat. Besides, I knew the helper would do the same to me if someone older came aboard. That was life at the bottom of the barrel. It was also the way Vietnam buses operated.

I was too tired to be a hero. I was happy that I would have a seat by the window, but no such luck. That old woman was faster than me. She shoved her butt over to the window. She also took extra room. She put her live piglet next to her, behind me. She left me seated on the front edge of the seat with no room for me to lean back.

Almost sobbing, words jumped unbidden out of my mouth.

"I wish my mother were here."

We traveled most of the day.

As we approached Qui Nhon the driver announced we would be stopping for the day. The road from Qui Nhon to Nha Trang, over the mountains, was too dangerous to cross at night. Narrow hairpin turns and steep ledges. In the old times bandits would stop the buses, robbing and killing the passengers.

Now the road belonged to the Viet Cong.

The helper took us to the lodge, a small shack in town.

There were two rooms, one with a dozen wooden sleeping platforms with mosquito nets and the other with only a hard cement floor. The lodge owner said if we wanted to stay we had to pay for straw mats and mosquito nets. Space on the platforms would cost the most.

I thought about asking someone to share a space but I didn't trust them. I thought about renting a mosquito net and sleeping on the cement floor but it was damp and cold.

Mosquito net or straw mat?

I chose a mat.

I will sacrifice my blood to save for a loaf of bread.

I lay my straw mat in the corner and rolled myself inside it like a cocoon to keep myself warm and protect myself from pickpockets. I dropped instantly asleep.

As exhausted as I was, I felt my body being moved.

I smelled someone next to me. I opened my eyes.

A woman laid beside me, very close, her hands under my belly where my pocket was. I was a bit scared but I didn't let it show. I slapped her hand hard and kicked her away.

"You try that again, I will bite your hand off," I hissed.

Quickly she moved to the other side.

I lay awake all night for fear she might come back.

All next day we were in the mountains.

The passengers were fearful and talkative. The road was most dangerous during rainy season, they said. So many accidents, so many deaths. I knew it had to be true. On this particular stretch of road, small shrines had been built alongside every curve and at the top of every crest.

Someone's spirit was there.

It was so dangerous and yet so beautiful. The scenery was spectacular, breathtaking, the lush green mountains above and the beautiful seacoast far below. I was too depressed, tired, and scared to enjoy any of it.

The bus slowly crawled higher and higher. Sometimes the bus shook when the driver went over bumps or potholes. A few brave souls were oohing and aahing over the scenery. Many of the passengers were too sick to care, groaning and moaning. Some were vomiting their guts out.

If I thought I was scared on the way up, nothing prepared me for the way down. It was pure terror, the same narrow roads, hairpin turns, and bumps and ditches but now at high speed, the bus swaying dangerously, brakes burning.

Oh God, I thought. *One wrong move and we're all dead!*

Clutching the seat in front of me, I wondered what would happen if I died up here.

Would anybody in my family miss me? Would they come here to light incense to invite my spirit home? Or would I become just another unknown ghost, a hungry ghost, doomed to wander forever without hope or purpose?

There was a bone-crushing bounce and someone screamed.

Would I be a good ghost or a bad ghost? I wondered.

The bus reached Nha Trang in the early evening.

Nha Trang, the second biggest city in the South, was a beautiful seaport with flawless white beaches and quaint fishing villages around it. The Emperor Bao Dai's summer home was here. All the elegant villas of the French were here, their summer retreats, their flower gardens.

The bus driver yelled out as we pulled into the bus stop.

"Get out and find something to eat. We will check the engine and the tires and refill the gas tank. We will leave here soon. Don't be late. We won't wait for you!"

The passengers moved out the door like a flock of smelly sheep, leaning their sweaty bodies against each other. They pushed and shoved and argued with each other like children.

I sat on my seat, knees curled up to my chin.

I didn't move.

I didn't need to go anywhere except to pee. I didn't have enough money to eat in the shops. A loaf of old bread would suit me. Besides, the bus was surrounded by peddlers selling all kind of food, some of them reaching up to the windows.

I was the last one off the bus.

I went out back of the bus stop, trying to find a place to relieve myself. Some people from the bus were there before me. The urine smell was so strong I had to cover my nose. I hurried up and did my business. Finished, I went over the water well, dropped the bucket deep, and pulled it up full of water. I didn't know if the water was good water or bad. I didn't care. I was so very thirsty.

There was no cup, no bowl. I drank out of the bucket.

I could feel the water dropping to the bottom of my empty stomach. I took a breath, then drank until I was no longer thirsty. I rolled up my sleeves and dipped my hands into the bucket, rubbing them together to wash them. I poured water over my head, my face, letting it drip dry. I rolled my dirty gray pajama pants above my knees and poured water over my legs and feet, rubbing them together. I cleaned all the mud of Duc Pho from my body.

I felt clean and refreshed.

I walked up the alley toward the bus. With each step I took, my stomach, so full of water, made a funny sloshing sound.

Blub, bloop, blub.

As I neared the road, the smell of the food cooking in the shops was irresistible. I could no longer control my appetite. My mouth was watering. I stopped walking and stood in the middle of the alley. I closed my eyes and let my nose take in all the heavenly smells. I shut down all my other senses.

When I opened my eyes an old woman was standing in front of me.

She was so old that her back bent over halfway to her knees. Her skin was weather beaten, and the wrinkles in her face were deep as gullies. Her cheekbones stuck out and her toothless mouth was shrunken. Her hands shook as she held out her tray.

Small boiled yucca roots. Corn that looked no better than she did.

"Miss, please buy my food. I will sell cheap. I am so tired. I want to go home."

I didn't respond. I looked around to see if anyone were nearby, watching us. I thought about stealing one of her small ears of corn and running away.

My conscience wouldn't let me.

Cam, you can't do that. It will add to your lifetime debt. You will never be free. You will return in the next life as this old woman!

I looked at her wrinkled face, her frail body.

I struck a bargain and the old woman agreed to sell all her food to me. She carefully wrapped it in banana leaves. She gave me the rest of the banana leaves for free.

I took my seat on the bus, my food and belongings held tightly. I unwrapped an ear of corn. Eat slowly, I told myself. Make it last. As hungry as you are, do not eat all the food! After all, we were still a long way from Saigon. Besides, there was nothing to brag about my dinner. The corn was nearly expired, and tasteless, but it filled my belly.

The yucca roots would be worse.

Chewing on the old ear of corn, I thought about my mother.

As often as she would beat us to release her anger or her fear, she seldom let her children go without a meal. Sometimes she could only feed us poor sweet potatoes, bad rice, cheap fish, and the dregs of fermented fish sauce, but she fed us.

The old tasteless corn reminded me of a meal I had shared with my brothers and sister.

It all started because Mother was out late.

We were hungry. There wasn't much of anything in the house to eat, not even dried sweet-potato chips. My sister scraped down to the bottom of the tin and came up with only a half cup of rice. She sent me out to pick water spinach, even though there was no water to grow it, it being the dry season. She started the fire and cooked the rice. I found some vegetables, brought them home and washed and cleaned them.

They were old and stringy. I was having a hard time slicing them so I chopped them up.

My sister took one look at my vegetables and shook her head. "You can't even cut up vegetables to put in the soup. How will you find a decent husband?"

I was eight years old.

That night under the full moon the four of us sat in a circle around a bamboo tray, our bowls half filled with watery soup. "Eat slow now," my sister reminded us, "That's all you will get. We have to save some for Mother." We were so hungry we slurped the tasteless soup.

Our mother walked into the courtyard.

My sister hurriedly got a bowl, scooped into it what was left of the soup and with two hands offered it to her. Mother squatted down beside us. As she took her first mouthful of soup I watched her reaction. She tossed the bowl on the ground and turned around and spit out the soup.

I was suddenly afraid for my sister. She was the oldest, the responsible one. If anything went wrong, she was the one to take the blow. All of us waited fearfully. Instead of hitting my sister, my mother reached out to grab us, pulling us to her. She was crying, her eyes full of tears. In a choking voice she said,

"I promise you. You will never have to eat this crap again! I will steal, I will cheat, I will kill, but you will all have food!"

I chew my tasteless corn alone.
How I yearn for that tasteless bowl of soup,
For my sister, my brothers, my mother's arms.
Life was so hard, we always thought
We children, we four against the world.
Now I sit on a bus alone, looking back.
Hard times were not so hard as this seat.
My childhood memories burn my eyes.

I miss you, my family. I miss you, my home.
Where are you, my brothers, my sister?
Where are you, Mother?
Oh to be together again, eating our tasteless soup.
Will we see each other again, I hope?

Now the bus engine was roaring and the horn was beeping loudly. The helpers were hanging out the bus doors, waving their hands and yelling to signal the people on the street that the bus was ready to depart. Slowly the bus pulled out onto the highway. Near me, the young helper was waving his hand at the city.

"Goodbye, beautiful Nha Trang!" he yelled. "I'll see you on my way back!"

He thinks he is so cool, I thought, but he's not. He is ugly as a dog. He is obnoxious. I can't stand boys like that!

On this run we had an extra driver on board. He was there to help the senior driver bring the bus back to Nha Trang. It made it more crowded because he took one of the best seats.

A few hours out of Nha Trang the bus gave out a dreadful noise and slowly stopped.

The bus helpers opened the doors and jumped to the ground, cursing. The bus drivers rolled down their windows and poked their heads out.

The senior driver ordered the helpers. "Du, go underneath and check the axles and the brakes! Tien, open the hood and check the oil and water!"

The drivers looked at each other, and whispered something, nodding.

When both the helpers returned, their faces did not look happy. They signaled to the drivers to get off the bus. While the four of them were outside talking, some passengers started shouting. Others stood up and looked through the windows, to see what going on. Some others acted like they knew it all. They were the loudest.

"Bandits have done it! They came down from their hideout and sabotaged the road! They made the bus break down! Now they're out there hiding, watching the bus! Waiting for darkness! They will return to rob us! They will take the young women to their hideout!"

The senior bus driver must have heard the commotion. He was angry when he stepped up through the door. He yelled down the bus at the loudmouth passengers.

"Hey, we have a problem here. We don't need loudmouths scaring the women and children. There are no bandits! If there are, they must be you guys! Now shut up or I will stuff dirty underwear in your loud stupid mouths! You understand? You got that? Now, everybody off the bus! We've got work to do."

One by one, like mindless ducks, we got off the bus.

Standing in the aisle, waiting to get out the bus, I looked out through the windows. *What a joke,* I thought. *All that rush to leave beautiful Nha Trang and now look at us, the bus broken down in the middle of nowhere!*

Behind us were mountains and barren hills. In front of us were large salt farms and dikes, and beyond them the sea. No houses, no one to help us. *What we will do if there are bandits? Worse, what would I do if the Viet Cong came?*

The drivers and helpers, four grown men, all lay in the dirt road underneath the bus trying to repair the damage. I took my banana leaves and went by myself out to the salt dykes. I went far enough from the bus for privacy but not too far. I wanted to be away from the crowd. Also, if bandits or the Viet Cong did show up, I would have a chance to hide.

I spread the leaves on a salt dyke and sat down, dangling my bare, bleeding feet into the water. I thought the water might help heal them.

My mistake. The salted water really stung. Well, at least my feet will get cleaned, I thought.

I looked up to the clear sky and searched for my lucky star. I couldn't decide which one was mine because they were all brightly blinking and full of life. One by one I started counting them to calm my nerves. I had counted up to one hundred and five when some slimy thing crawled up onto my foot.

I shrieked and scrambled to my feet. I ran to the bus in horror.

One of the helpers, the obnoxious one, crawled out from under the bus. He yelled at me for being a silly girl and then grabbed my hand, laughing.

"You want attention? I will give you attention!"

He pulled me to his filthy body.

I fought back, kicking at him as hard as I could in bare feet. I screamed for help. The passengers turned their heads and watched but no one moved to help. By now I was using all of my strength to pull free, but his strong grip gave me a sharp pain up my arms.

The older bus driver must have heard me. He rolled from under the bus and yelled.

"Du, stop it! Let go of her and get back here now! I need you!"

The helper let go of my hands, his grease stains all over me. He grabbed my chin, smearing my face, and glared at me. In a low voice he cursed me and said,

"You just wait, stupid girl. I will get you later."

As I pulled myself away, he kicked dirt on me, mumbled something nasty, and crawled back under the bus. My heart still raced. I was more afraid of him than of that slimy thing, or bandits, or even the Viet Cong!

Everyone squatted by the side of the road, waiting for the bus to be fixed. After a while the drivers came from under the bus, anger on their greasy, tough faces.

The bus needed new parts. We couldn't get the parts until morning. We'd have to wait in the bus tonight.

Many of the passengers were angry. They yelled and cursed the bus drivers and the helpers. They wanted their money back. I did, too. I wanted to look for another bus. I wanted to get away from that awful young helper. But I didn't say anything.

My fear was what could happen if no other bus went by. The drivers and helpers were already feeling threatened and angry. And I was alone. The young helper might take his fear, his anger, out on me. So I said nothing, keeping back out of sight. A good thing, too. As it turned out, no bus went by that night.

The senior driver took command, speaking strongly.

"You people like it or not, we have to wait until morning. All of you, return to your seats and try to get some sleep! I'm not responsible for anybody who decides to stay out here!"

He turned around and pointed his finger at me. My stomach twisted. "You, girl! You, troublemaker! Go in first and pick up your belongings!"

My fear rose up. *He's throwing me off the bus!*

I was scared and my tears were about to burst. I didn't move. He lit his cigarette, took a deep drag, and slowly let out the smoke. All eyes were upon me.

"Girl, did you hear me? Go in the bus and get your belongings. You will sit right behind me, in the second row seat by the window, where I can see you!"

I didn't know why he had singled me out. When I glanced at the helper, I saw new anger in his eyes as he stared at me. I wasn't sure whether the older driver just didn't want any more problems on his bus, or if he had some plans of his own. Whatever, I grabbed my stuff quickly and scrunched down in my new seat, trying to be invisible.

I sat in the dark in the filthy bus crammed with live chickens and pigs, with children and men and women, old and young. I sat in the noise and the putrid air. Babies were crying. Mothers were trying to calm their children. A young woman in the back was complaining that someone had grabbed her breast. The helpers were taking turns telling dirty jokes, the younger passengers laughing.

The bus driver shouted with authority. "Everybody shut up! Enough of this! Get some sleep."

I curled up in my seat, my back against the window. I closed my eyes and tried not to think about anything. Not even the danger I would have to face. The harder I fought them, the stronger the fear and sadness took over me.

Someone in the bus opened a bottle of cheap fish sauce.

Its pungent smell reminded me of my home life. My mother used to ferment tiny anchovies in a lot of salt to make this sauce. The smell was truly awful but I had grown up with it.

Fish sauce, fish sauce, why can't I be like other girls in the village? Why do I dream so much? Why do I always swim upstream? In the dark, I could hear my mother's voice.

"You read too many silly books!"

Maybe she was right. Maybe the books had poisoned my mind. I had dreamed too much. I had done things that country girls were not ever supposed to do.

I should not have climbed trees when the boys dared me. I should not have beaten them with my wooden shoes when they grabbed my breasts. Or gone with them and caught better fighting fish than they could. I should not have played detective and made the neighbors nervous. I should never have questioned the authority of the elderly. They had earned it and I had not. Definitely I should not have talked so much, so often. Most of all, I should never have climbed the barnyard tree and peed on Dau's head, the nasty bully, when he walked unawares beneath it. Later I blackmailed him into leaving me alone. I never told anyone, except my cousin Thao who promised never to tell.

I wondered, now that I was gone, if Thao would break her promise and tell on me. Did the neighbors finally know?

I could hear the voices of the neighbors talking about me.

"If she was my daughter, I would take her up into the mountain and feed her to the tigers!"

"I would use her as bait to catch sharks!"

"I would sell her to the Frenchmen; let the long-noses rape her all night!"

"I would suffocate her at birth!"

If she was my daughter.

"She was a bad luck child before she came out of her mother's womb!" they said.

"Her father took in another wife because her mother was pregnant with her! Now what can you expect? I mean, after all, a girl without a father? Like a house without a roof! Yes, she is too stupid to know any better!"

Stop. Please stop. I know you all hate me.

I could see my mother's tired face.

Oh, Mother, please forgive me!

My tears were wetting my filthy shirt. I was filled with shame and grief, remembering how my mother had fought to keep me and my brothers and sister together through those very difficult years. How she had cared for us, defending us against vicious, mindless cruelty.

Oh, Mother, you could have run away and left us at the mercy of our relatives, those horrible people who would have made slaves of us!

But you didn't. You stayed and you fought and fought for us! You always made sure we had clothes to wear and food to eat. You even sent us to school! I am so sorry! Truly, I am an ungrateful child! I will come back home to beg your forgiveness. I will not run away again. I will take care of my baby! I will obey you! Mother, I will make you proud—

"Stupid girl! Stop kicking me or I will break your legs!"

Someone was slapping my legs. I was awake. I was startled.

At first, I thought I had returned home, that the angry voice, the slaps, were from my mother. Then my eyes adjusted to the semi-darkness. An old woman with hostility on her face was close to me, glaring at me. I was puzzled. I didn't know her, or where I was. Where...?

I was on a bus with strangers.

Why was this strange woman angry? What had I done?

I must have fallen asleep while thinking about my mother. I must have dreamed. Then I remembered my dream. My Aunt Number Nine was being beaten nearly to death. I had to get help for her but my hands and my legs were tied. I had tried to free myself, kicking my legs and swinging my arms. I must have kicked this cranky old lady by accident.

"I am sorry," I told the old lady.

She turned her butt and pressed me hard against the window. "Sure you are!"

I don't know whether it was the old lady or my bad dream but I couldn't go back to sleep. My mind was racing with so many things that had happened in my life.

You get in trouble wherever you go.

I had to agree with my neighbors about one thing. I must not be very smart. A smart girl would have accepted her life with Binh. A smart girl would have worked it out. Yes, she would have been his good wife. She would have done the right things.

What right things? asked the imp on my shoulder. *Letting him beat you to death? Hah!*

My mother had said, "He wouldn't have beat you that badly if you hadn't defied him." Maybe not. Then again, if I'd been as smart as my brother Ming, I'd still be in school and Binh would still be raping sheep! Yes, if I had been smart I would have become a teacher!

But I'm not, and I won't. I am stupid.

"Just like your Aunt Number Nine," everyone said.

I felt the sadness deep in my heart.

Face it, Cam. Your mother didn't love you as much as your brothers and sister. You can't go back home, Cam. You acted so dumb back home. You did so many bad things. No one loves you now. Not even your son. Yes, he is just a baby but when he grows up, he will hate you, too.

No, you can't go back, Cam. You are just a stupid girl.

I was lonely, hungry and depressed.

The smelly old woman had me shoved up against the window. My body was aching.

Nothing I did was ever right! If I'd been a boy, I could have done anything! Why hadn't I been born with a penis? Why couldn't I pee over the grass standing up? No, I had to sit down!

It wasn't fair!

I couldn't get the story of my Aunt Number Nine, my father's younger sister, out of my mind. I was trying hard to avoid it, to no avail. She had been a simple woman, with the kindest heart.

No, don't think about it. It is forbidden. You promised!

CHAPTER 10

Auntie Thua

I had promised my mother I would never tell a soul. I never did. After awhile, I couldn't. I had pushed it down to the black pool of forgetfulness.

Now it was rising, dark and ugly.

Leave me alone! I don't want to remember!

The sweetest woman, my Auntie Thua. What happened to her was more intolerable than anything I could imagine.

No! It never happened. It's just a bad dream!

Sitting there in the dark, in the low hour of life, my mind was nagging my soul. I was no longer able to control my outrage.

I closed my eyes tight but the images kept flashing in my mind. The newborn baby girl, her little hands, her tiny face. My aunt's bloody bottom, and her sorrowful eyes looking at me.

Her eyes forever haunting me.

And the others. The first wife with her thin lips gawking at me. The old man staring at me. His bushy eyebrows.

Suddenly I could hear my mother's stern voice.

"Cam, what did I tell you? Never tell anything about this! Didn't I forbid you? Didn't I tell you that if you ever say *one word* I will cut your tongue out! *Didn't you hear me?*"

Her finger pointing at me in the dark.

"I forbid you!"

I covered my ears, screaming silently.

Why are you all mad at me? I'm only a child. I didn't know anything. I did what I was told. You are all evil! You're all liars, not me!

I had buried the memories so deep.

The truth was I really didn't know what was going on at that time. I only knew what my mother told me, that my Auntie Thua had a growth inside her stomach and that I had to go with her to the big city Saigon, eight hundred miles away, and take care of her there. I didn't understand why everything was kept a secret. Even afterwards, no one ever told me. I figured it out myself.

Young children in the country were not supposed to know about sex. We were not supposed to talk about sex. All I knew was that women got married before they had babies. Some babies were found on the sweet growth of potatoes. Others were found in the pumpkin patch, or up on the hill.

As far as I knew I was the only baby in the village ever born from its mother's womb. I knew this because my mother had told me that I had been a 'trouble child' before I was even born, that I had nearly killed her. She told me often.

My older sister had married and had babies. Her first son died right after birth, from lack of oxygen I now know. The wise man said an evil spirit had swallowed him whole. The older girls were always talking about sex but what they said was over my head. I didn't understand it. Besides, they were girls. Only women had babies. Sometimes even without a husband, which I also didn't understand. Very seldom did those babies live, though. Sometimes they were left in the bamboo grove where the wild animals got them. Sometimes their tiny bodies were found floating in the river.

People whispered, but no one ever said who did what.

Truly, during my childhood in the village I didn't know one illegitimate child.

Actually, the only one I ever heard about was the child of my step-grandmother, a girl. My step-grandmother had been very young. No one knew who the father was. My step-grandmother decided to keep her child. However, the girl was badly treated by the family and by society. The ridicule and cruelty were unending. The girl chose to take her own life in her teenage years. After she died, I heard people in the village whispering about how lucky it was for my step-grandmother that her shame was ended. Even so, they said, my grandfather had been a fool to take her as a wife. He had lost face to take in such a woman but since she had been only a second wife, it didn't count as much.

That was how much I knew about having babies.

In fifth grade, when my mother told me I was no longer allowed to go to school, she immediately assigned me more of her duties. One of them was to carry sweets and teas to distant relatives, as altar gifts, and to represent the Tran family in ancestor worship on death anniversaries. I got the job because no one else ever wanted it.

It turned out to be a highlight of my young age. I got to meet people, especially young people, outside of my village. I also had a chance to borrow books from my older cousins who had more advantages than I.

At first, though, I was resentful. My mother piled so many duties on me. As young as I was, I also had to care for my little nieces. Then my mother started lending me to relatives for free. I had so many relatives sometimes I couldn't remember their names. I even ended up taking care of my older cousins' children. More often than not, these relatives treated me like I was their servant. When I would complain about it to my mother, she would scold me for being selfish.

Sending me with Auntie Thua was scary, though.

Auntie Thua.

My grandfather had six daughters. Two of them, Auntie Thua and Auntie Lon, became second wives to wealthy men. These aunts were kinder to me than the rest of my relatives. In fact, of all my relatives, Auntie Thua was the only one who never beat me. I loved their children, especially the girls.

Auntie Lon was the more advantaged. She had the looks and she was more outgoing. Auntie Thua was quiet and simple.

My grandmother died giving birth to her last child. Soon after, my grandfather remarried an attractive but difficult woman who hated his children, especially my Auntie Thua, who was slow in her head and not as pretty as her sister. Step-grandmother would often make up lies about her that made my grandfather mad. Sometimes he beat Auntie Thua badly to please his new wife. Everyone in the family also felt they had the right to decide Auntie Thua's future. They wanted her to get married, of course, but they worried she would never find a suitable husband.

One day a distant cousin, a woman, came to ask Grandfather to give Auntie Thua permission to join the woman's household staff as a second wife to her husband. Grandfather was more than happy to do this. Everyone said that it was a blessing for the Tran family.

It was true at first. Auntie Thua's new husband was the only child of a very prominent family, the Nguyens. His own mother had died when he was young but his father had never remarried. By not remarrying, his father had acquired, in the eyes of his village, the power of a saint.

Auntie Thua's new husband was married to Cousin Five at the time. The first wife, we called her. She had borne her husband two daughters, but no son. Like Abraham of the Bible, the family had decided he must take another wife to try to have a son. The first wife would choose.

There were several reasons why the first wife chose my aunt. My aunt was from a wealthy old family of the nobility, our family, the Trans. So, even with her low intelligence, she had good bloodlines. Secondly, she was a relative. Both of them being married to the same man would keep the wealth in the family. Lastly, the first wife chose her precisely because of her low intelligence and lack of beauty. Auntie Thua would never have the brains or the looks to gain control over the husband. The first wife would always have the power, even if Auntie Thua bore a son.

Regardless, Auntie Thua never had any say. Grandfather Tran and the Nguyen family agreed how it would be. Her duty was to obey and to produce an heir for the Nguyen family.

At first they were all disappointed. Auntie Thua gave birth to a beautiful girl, Yen.

Everyone was unhappy except Auntie Thua. She loved her daughter more than her own life. However, without a son she was still no better than a servant in the Nguyen household. The next year she was pregnant again and this time she bore a strong son, Lam.

Unfortunately for Auntie Thua, that same year the first wife also gave birth to a son. Auntie Thua and her children, especially her son, were suddenly unwelcome. Not long after the boys were born, the first wife had Auntie Thua and her babies moved out to a small house in the corner of the compound.

Soon after, the young husband came down with a mysterious illness and died, leaving his wives and children in the care, and control, of his saintly widowed father.

CROSSING THE BAMBOO BRIDGE

Since all land and property passed down from first son to first son, the old man now owned everything that had been in his son's name. If the widowed first wife remained unmarried, at her father-in-law's death all the wealth would belong to her son, and by inference to her. However, if she remarried she not only lost this fortune, she also lost her children, who belonged not to her but to her husband's family.

Auntie Thua, however, could only own property bought for her either by her father-in-law or by her husband. When her husband died, Auntie Thua owned next to nothing. Mr. Hien, the elegant old man, the saint, owned everything.

The jolting bus brought me back to the present. The nasty old woman beside me was snoring. I looked past her out the window, trying to make more poems. Perhaps they would ward off the bad memories of that old man.

> *My legs are numb and my back is bruised*
> *Carefully I turn my body*
> *I lean my forehead on the glass window*
> *The deepness of the sky and the high moon*
> *Always the beauty of the land*
> *Majesty of mountains high*
> *Green hillside shadows of mountain light*
> *Low salt fires glistening under the sea moon*
> *From high mountain pass to low salt dike*
> *High to low, linking*
> *How could I find fault on this beautiful land?*

It didn't work.
Many years had passed but I still remembered that old man.

Long after the Viet Minh revolution, not only had he kept his life, he had kept all his lands. His home was a palace compared to his neighbors. His gardens had many unusual trees. All neatly carved into animal shapes. His courtyard held many different fruit trees, lush and green and blooming throughout the year.

People far and near came to him to ask his advice. When they arrived, they would bow and address him by his inherited title of nobility, Huong Bo Huyen, or Lord Huyen.

His appearance, his manner, matched his title.

Huong Bo Huyen was tall, taller than the average Vietnamese male. His snow-white hair grew down to his shoulders. His long, thick eyebrows were also white. His neatly combed white beard grew down below his chest. His skin was tanned in season, not from labor under a hot sun but from sitting out in the trellis-filtered sun of his courtyard, drinking his tea and writing his poetry. His daily wear was silken white pajamas, worn with grace. When he drank his tea, he held up his teacup in such a way that I can never forget. His thumb and forefinger grasped the handle of the delicate teacup, his middle fingers supporting, and his little finger loose, its long nail curving like a talon.

He would stroke his long beard before he would to speak. His voice was resonant. He spoke always with deep authority.

Most people in the valley looked up to him. They thought of him as a saint. They thought in his past life he had been some kind of god who had done something that displeased the father god. That he had been sent back to live as a wise man to atone before returning to Heaven.

People never questioned his authority.

He had raised his son alone after his wife's death. In Vietnam that was as rare as a rooster raising its own chick. Now his beloved son had also died, leaving him with two young wives and five young children to care for. This was his punishment and suffering to regain Heaven.

In all, he was one with the high mountains, the hills, the salt dikes under the sea moon.

All of that. Yes, he was all of that to the eye, to the simple country mind. But underneath his elegant white pajamas he was just a man with his dark secrets, with his foul appetites that made him less than a man, much less a noble one.

As my mother had said when I expressed my awe of him, "Don't let the looks fool you, stupid girl!"

I remember that afternoon.

I knelt down on the dirt floor beside my mother, parting her greasy hair from side to side, my eyes fixed on her scalp. I was searching for lice. There were times I hated this duty but in a way I also enjoyed it too. I was good at it and I loved the physical contact, the peaceful opportunity to be close to my mother.

Like a child my mother went right to sleep, my hands roaming her scalp.

I was bone tired. I wanted to stop but feared to disrupt her peaceful time. As my hands moved gently over her scalp, I let my mind go elsewhere, frustrated. I wanted to go and catch a few fighting fish. I wanted to sneak out back and read my silly new book I had just borrowed. My hands moved by themselves as I looked out on the empty rice fields.

To my surprise I saw Auntie Thua approaching. She came into our courtyard. I wondered why she was out in the brutal noonday sun when everyone had taken refuge inside. She looked tired and distressed. I stayed kneeling but withdrew my hands from my mother's head, folded them in front of my chest and bent my head to greet my aunt.

"Chao, Co Thua" "Hello, Auntie Thua."

Children always addressed adults by their family rank number, never by their name. Thua meant eleven.

My mother, still half asleep, opened her eyes. She took one look at my aunt's face and immediately ordered me out. "Cam, take your spinning wheel and go outside and do some work! I don't want you running around to the neighbors getting in trouble. You stay where I can find you! You hear me?"

Obediently I picked up a spinning wheel and walked out to the big mango tree. I put the spinning wheel in the shade of the tree. I knew my mother couldn't see me there, that I could sneak back and eavesdrop.

So I did.

My aunt was crying. At one point my mother slapped her and said how stupid she was.

"How stupid of you to let it happen. There's no way you can back up your story! Who would be dumb enough to listen to you? People will say you made it up. They will not listen even if they believed you, even if they knew it was true!"

My mother was as mad as a wet hen in our chicken coop.

"He has money! He has power! It will be his word against yours. Who will they believe, you or him? They will stone you, or hang you! I can't believe you waited this long to come and tell me. You are stupid, *stupid* to let this happen!"

She spat her *trau* juice on the dirt floor, not in her spitting pot. She never did that.

"Now I have to clean up the mess," I mumbled.

Who is this man they talk about, and why is my aunt still crying?

"Stop the boohoo, it won't do you any good. You should have crossed your legs when he came near you."

Between sobs, my aunts said, "Sister Six, please believe me, I did! But it didn't work. Now if I don't keep quiet about it, he will kill me and take my children."

My mother didn't let her finish her sentence.

"Stupid girl, how long has this been going on? Who else knows about this? Tell me to tell now or I will strangle you!"

My aunt was stumbling over her words.

"It happened – first time – my husband had just died. A few years ago. I told Chi Hai but she said I was a bad girl! Don't bother her! That I had done something wrong to attract him. That it was my fault! Oh sister, please help me! I didn't! I never—he had power—he was so strong! He forced me! Sister, I was so afraid!"

I heard my mother getting off the floor.

"My God, I know you are stupid, but I didn't know this stupid! This happened that long ago? And you didn't tell me? *I will kill that old goat!*"

I ran back to my spinning wheel, the cotton ball in my hand.

She stormed toward me. I pretended I was spinning. My mother was too angry to notice how much thread was on the spool. Lucky for me, I thought.

"Cam, get me my hat, and come with me!"

I stopped the wheel, got up from the dirt and ran to get her hat. She rushed out the gate in a rage, my aunt wobbling after her, pleading.

"Sister, please don't tell him I told you! Please! He – he will take my children from me! He will *hurt* them. *Please....*"

My mother mumbled something to herself but didn't acknowledge my aunt. Behind them, on my short little legs, I half walked and half ran, trying to keep up with them.

I thought the long walk under the blazing sun would make my mother more angry, but no. She was calm when she arrived at my aunt's house. Like a general she took command, ordering us to clean the house.

"Chin! Clear off the table! Bring out the best straw mat you have and lay it on the wooden divan. Clean your husband's altar and light the incense! I want this house in top shape before I invite him over. And clean yourself up! Make yourself presentable!"

I glanced at my aunt, but was afraid to speak. My aunt stumbled around, trying to obey my mother, the tears on her face blended in with her sweat. She was so nervous, so tired and sad. I went over and said softly, "Auntie, go clean yourself up. Have a rest. Don't worry, I will help you. I will clean up."

My mother inspected everything over and over.

"Cam, go boil some water and make some tea."

She walked around my aunt's house, straightening things, wiping off dirt. She closed the windows. After she was satisfied nothing more could be done, she sent me over to the main house to invite the head of the family, Huong Bo Huyen, to attend.

I was about to ask her, "Why invite *him*?"

She gave me a sharp look. I didn't ask my question. She went on, telling me what I was to say to him.

She turned around and looked at my aunt.

"Thua, where are your children?"

"At the main house," my aunt replied nervously. "Please, can Cam take my children to your house?"

My mother nodded abruptly. "Cam, you heard your aunt. After you've delivered my message, take the children!"

"Yes, Mother."

I walked slowly across the compound.

Nervously I entered the beautiful paved courtyard, my bare feet burning on the hot surface. Each step I took seemed heavier and heavier.

Huong Bo Huyen sat in his ornate hand-carved wooden bench in front of me. He was having his afternoon tea. I was always afraid in his presence. I bowed my head, my arms crossed. I was so nervous I couldn't speak.

The old man put his teacup down and looked at me. In a cultured voice he asked me, "What do you want, my child? Did your mother send you here to ask for a favor? Or did you come here to play with your young cousins?"

I shook my head. I looked to the left and to the right. No one was near. I could back out of the courtyard if I dared. But I didn't. I didn't dare disobey my mother.

My eyes were on his elegant sandals.

"Huong Bo Huyen, my mother invites you to have tea with her at Auntie Thua's house. She needs to talk to you."

I didn't look up. My knees were shaking.

"Child, what does she want to talk to me about? Why didn't she come herself if she needs something from me."

"I don't know, Huong Bo. She said she wanted to see you in private."

I rattled off my mother's instructions as fast as I could.

"She said you would know why she wants to see you at Auntie Thua's house. She also said it was entirely up to you whether you came. She said it would save you public embarrassment."

I didn't understand the words. I didn't make them up.

I did leave something out.

"He'll come if he knows what's good for him! If he doesn't, I will make sure his good name is added to the crow's menu!"

She had been so angry then that I didn't dare repeat them.

That evening when my mother returned home with a hard face she chewed her *trau* to no end. I knew she was in a bad mood so I stayed away. I saw this hard face too often, so why stick around?

I stayed out of reach but close enough in case she wanted me. I was out in back feeding the ugly noisy pigs when she walked up to me.

My heart started to pound. *What did I do?*

"Cam, you will take Auntie Thua to Saigon."

What?

"Why?" I asked. "Don't ask," she answered, her voice soft and low. She thought for a moment.

"Cam, I know you are getting to be a big girl now. Something has happened that we can never talk about with anyone, ever. You are a big girl. We will keep what happened today to ourselves. Right now you are still too young to understand. Someday I will explain, but for now you must *never* talk about this to the neighbors! Especially not to the first wife's relatives. Especially not to them! Do you understand?"

"Yes, Mother, but what happened? Why does Auntie Thua have to go to Saigon?"

"Don't ask questions. Auntie Thua has a growth in her tummy. The doctor will take it out."

"Oh."

That's all? Then fearful thoughts went through my mind.

"Is she going to die? Is it contagious? Will I get it? When are we going? How long we will be there?"

Question after question I asked my mother.

"What did I just tell you? Don't ask questions, especially silly questions!" she said with exasperation. Then, looking at me, she shook her head.

"No, your aunt is not dying. What she has is nothing to be afraid of. It's not contagious. I don't know how long it will take. Now you listen carefully."

Her voice got higher and stronger.

"I want you to promise me you will not talk about what happened today to anyone! *No one!* Not even your big sister! You must *promise me!* Do you promise me?"

I nodded my head, "Yes, Mother."

"Yes, Mother *what?*"

"Yes, Mother, I promise."

As I said, being her helper, going on all kinds of errands, was nothing new. My mother made money any way she could. She dyed cloth for people to make clothes. Sometimes she secretly cut and sewed for women in the village whose husbands or mothers-in-law forbid them to own even a decent outfit to be buried in. Most often my mother was paid in small installments. She would send me to collect for her. She also raised silkworms and sold silk. She would send me to pick mulberry leaves to feed the silkworms, sometimes in villages far away. And, of course, she often sent me to represent the family at death anniversaries. Sometimes those trips took half a day of walking. Sometimes I would have to stay overnight.

This time, the thought of going to Saigon with my sick aunt scared me. *What if I got lost? How would I find my way home?* Worst of all, I couldn't tell a soul about this trip. *If I disappeared who would find me?* I was scared, confused, and afraid to talk.

I don't remember much about that first bus ride.

Everything was strange to me. I never knew where I was, or where I was going. I don't remember what part of Saigon we lived in either. All I remember was the alleyway, and a tiny flat only big enough for one small bed that we shared.

Most days, I helped my aunt go to the market or to the hospital. Every day I went to the water well to carry water home. I did the laundry for us. It wasn't much. We each had two sets of clothes, one to wear and one to wash.

There was nothing else for me to do. I didn't have money to rent books and I couldn't borrow them because everybody was a stranger. I was also afraid that if I made friends I might forget and tell them about my aunt and the growth in her tummy. I didn't want to betray my mother's trust. She had gone to a lot of trouble to set up this hideout. I didn't want to spoil it.

I was lonely and very homesick. I was a little girl. When I looked at my aunt's face and saw her sadness, though, I didn't have the heart to complain.

My fear was that she might die soon. Every time we went to the doctor they just sent her home! Her growth was getting bigger and bigger until she had a hard time walking. If she died, how would I explain it to my mother? She would blame me for not taking good care of my aunt. I thought about going to see the doctor myself and asking him for some special medicine for her. But I didn't have money of my own. And how could I buy medicine? There was no one I could ask for help. I wished my mother was here. She would know what to do. She always did.

I also thought my aunt was very cheap. It breaks my heart now to think how poor they kept her at home. But living in that alleyway as a young child, I thought she was the cheapest person I had ever known. She washed banana leaves and hung them to dry to reuse. She bought only a handful of tiny anchovies to last us a week. She made me salt them before cooking. She bought leftover water spinach that nobody wanted and boiled it with salt. We'd eat the vegetables and drink the water. She only allowed us to use chopsticks to scrape the salt anchovies from the rim of the pot, and we had only one anchovy for each meal. When I asked her to buy me a mosquito net and a straw mat, that I would sleep on the dirt floor, she said it was too much money. We wouldn't be there that long.

We were there four months. Four long months sharing one small bed. Most often I sat up at night. She had bad dreams most nights. She kicked and screamed and put me out of bed. When she awoke, she would cry. She missed her children terribly.

One night I was awoken by my aunt crying out.

I thought she was having the bad dream again. I pulled my shirt over my head and tried to go back to sleep. But she was awake this time.

She told me it was time to go to the hospital. She had a stomach pain. The growth in her stomach was too big. It needed to come out.

We went to the hospital. She was in such pain she couldn't walk. The nun took her inside to a room while I waited. There was no room for me to sit so I squatted down outside in the hall. My aunt was not alone. I saw other women who had also come to the hospital with big tummies. They were all in pain too. I could hear women in other rooms screaming. I tried to cover my ears so I didn't hear the screams. It didn't work. When I could no longer stand the screams, I wandered to other parts of the hospital.

It was late, very nearly dawn.

I didn't know where I was or how far I had roamed. Somehow I managed to return to the hall near my aunt's room. I fell asleep on the floor. A nun came and woke me out of my heavy sleep. She held a tiny baby in her arms, a girl, she said. She showed it to me and asked if I wanted to hold it. I shook my head and said no. I just touched the baby's tiny fingers. I thought she was a beautiful baby. I didn't know how the nun knew that I liked babies, or why she showed her to me.

The nun gave me a kindly look. I felt I could trust her. I asked her about my aunt.

"Did you see a woman with black teeth in there? She had a growth in her stomach! It gave her so much pain. She came here this morning to remove the growth. We came from very far away. Could you please tell me, is she all right now?"

The nun used her free hand to rub my uncombed hair.

"Poor child," she said. "You are such a good girl."

It had been a long time since anyone told me I was a good girl.

I blinked my eyes and said, "Thank you."

I asked her, "Could you please find my aunt for me. I don't know where to look. I don't want her to die! If she dies, what will I do?"

I was crying.

The nun smiled at me. "Your aunt is fine. She just had some bleeding, that's all. Wait here. I will be back after I place the baby. I will return soon. We will go see your aunt."

She lowered her arm.

"Would you like to see the baby again?"

I looked at the baby's face. I used my finger to stroke her on her soft skin. She moved a little, and that was it.

My aunt cried when she saw me. There was so much sorrow in her eyes. She turned her face to the wall. Her body was uncovered from the waist down. Her bottom was all bloody, the blood dripping down to a bucket under the bed.

I was terrified. I thought I knew why she was crying. The doctors must have told her the growth was bad. She was bleeding badly, I thought. She will die soon.

Oh God, Oh Buddha, please don't let her die now. I can't take her body home.

My prayers had worked. My aunt got better each day.

For nearly a week, every day I walked to the hospital to see her. Every night I went home with her dirty clothes. I had to wait until everyone in the alley went to bed. In darkness I washed my aunt's bloody clothes by hand. The smell of the blood made me ill. Every morning I took the little money she gave me to the market and bought a little food. I cooked it the way she had taught me and carried it to the hospital to feed her.

Each day my aunt got stronger and stronger. I no longer feared that she might die. I couldn't help but wonder why didn't she have her growth removed earlier. We could have returned to Duc Pho a lot sooner.

At the end of the week she decided to return to our flat. She was still very weak, and sad, and very grumpy. One day I told her about the baby girl I saw the same night she had her growth removed. I thought it would cheer her up.

"Auntie, you should see the baby girl the nun showed to me. She was so beautiful. She was tiny. She was so sweet. You should see her!"

My aunt was angry at me. "Stop it, or I will slap you!" She said. But she didn't. Shortly after, she announced we were going back to Duc Pho.

I was excited and relieved. I wanted to sing and dance.

"Oh, how wonderful it will be," I chattered to myself. "I will not have to wash her bloody pants!" I was so sick of the dirty work, and I was so lonely. I missed my nieces and my home. I missed my mother. I missed my everyday life.

I was a happy girl when I walked into my mother's home. My mother praised me for being such a brave girl. She treated me as if I was grown up. She offered to let me chew her *trau*. I had wanted to chew it for long time but didn't for fear of my mother. Now she was giving it to me! I thought I had gone to heaven. So I chewed it. After a few minutes I felt sick and everything was spinning. I felt as though I was flying. Then there was darkness.

I had passed out. I didn't understand that *trau*, though a mild drug, was too strong for my young body.

For three wonderful days all I did was sleep.

A few days later, early in the morning, there was violence.

I still had not yet resumed my duties. Mother was preparing to dye the bolts of cloth she had collected from her customers. I was still on my sleeping mat.

Auntie Thua's neighbors came running to our house. She said there had been an accident, that Auntie Thua had been badly injured. The neighbor was worried. We must go see her!

My mother dumped boiling water on the fire. She told me to get up and come with her.

My aunt was on the floor of the hut, half conscious. There was blood everywhere. Her children were crying. Of course my tough mother always wanted to know things first. She was shaking my aunt, demanding my aunt to tell her who had done this to her, but my aunt couldn't talk. My mother sent me outside to get help. I came back with two farmers from a nearby field.

The farmers went out and cut down a big bamboo stick and brought it back. My mother had taken down the hammock. The men lifted my aunt onto the hammock and hooked the hammock to the bamboo pole. That was how they carried her through the hamlets and the rice fields to the local hospital.

I followed them. My heart was pounding. I was in a rage.

Once again I was assigned to a hospital to take care of my aunt. Once again I had to wash bloody clothes! I remember how resentful I was. I remember thinking how unfair it was. My aunt had many older and younger sisters and many nieces! Even my own sister! Why did they all hang their heavy burdens on me?

I decided it must be because I was stupid.

Three weeks in the hospital did me in. I was exhausted. I was angry that my aunt was suffering. Most of all I was angry with my mother for making me wash those bloody clothes!

Eventually it all came out, at least to me.

The first wife must have found out the old man had given Auntie Thua a new piece of land. That had been my mother's price for not destroying his saintly reputation. The first wife probably had suspected all along there was something going on between my aunt and the old man. When she found out about the land, she assumed the worst. She was so angry with my aunt that she beat her, nearly killing her.

I remember how angry my mother was.

She went to the first wife and the old man. She demanded a written note signed by both of them that they both promised never to touch my aunt again. If they ever harmed her again, my mother would spill the beans, she said. She would drag the Nguyen family name in the dirt. She would make Huong Bo Huyen a *real* saint, she told him.

She would cut off his dick!

All of them knew there was no law in the countryside, that there was no proof. But in that village my mother was a force unto herself, indomitable. They signed that paper because they feared her. She demanded compensation for my aunt for her injuries. They paid it because my mother was known to be incorruptible. They knew everyone would believe her.

Their family would be dishonored for generations.

My mother made that old man pay dearly for repeatedly raping my aunt. My mother made the first wife fear to touch my aunt's body again. She had struck them both where it hurt the most. In their pride, in their vanity, in their pocketbook and in their land.

My aunt returned to her home and lived with her two children.

I had never told her secret.

"Everybody out of the bus," the driver yelled.

It was early morning now. The new parts had arrived. The men crawled under the bus. Cursing and spitting, by midmorning they had repaired the damage.

Once again the old yellow bus lumbered and screeched toward Saigon. Sitting behind the driver, bouncing and swaying, I thought about what had happened back then to Auntie Thua.

Looking out the window, I wondered what happened to that baby. *Was she still alive? What would have happened if my aunt had kept her? What was the relationship? What would my aunt tell her other children?*

"This is your little sister."

But she was not just their little sister. She was their aunt, their father's half sister. I felt sorry, not only for my aunt and that tiny girl child, but for the thousands of women in my country who had to endure a society run by men, for men.

I will never marry of my own free will, I thought.

I hate men!

BOOK TWO:

Saigon Streets

CHAPTER 11

Hau's Castle

The bus window was dirty.

I was as dirty as the window. I had been on this crowded, filthy bus for three days. I was tired, hungry, lonely and depressed. We were in Saigon now. I looked out on the crowded streets.

I wondered where I would spend the night. I had no home, no family and no relatives. The little money I had taken with me was nearly gone.

I shook my head in despair.

The bus was pulling into the Saigon bus terminal. Outside, running alongside us, grubby looking men were waving their hands, their hats, calling out to passengers. Women were carrying food packets on their heads and in their hands, pushing and shoving, trying to get nearer to the bus doors. The driver kept blowing the horn and roaring the bus engine, trying to move through the crowds. Black smoke was blowing from the exhaust and in through the windows. The driver's helpers were at the open doors, blocking them, kicking their feet out at the peddlers pressing forward, yelling at them to move out of the way.

"Hold tight to your belongings!" a passenger yelled, trying to warn us. "There are thieves out there! Not just the taxi and cyclo drivers! Watch out! They're out there waiting for you newcomers, you country folks!"

It was noisy in the bus, people grabbing their belongings, yelling and screaming. Some passengers had more possessions than they could carry. Some were careless, dropping things, yelling. Some passengers were fighting with each other to be the first to get out the door.

A man near me laughed. "Long trips make people's patience run thin," he said.

Outside the bus, it was chaos. The noise, the crowds, the peddlers shoving things at the passengers. I sat in my seat, not speaking to anyone. I clutched my belongings fearfully. I was too scared to get off the bus. The driver turned and saw me. He yelled at me angrily.

"Girl, what are you waiting for? Does my helper have to carry you out?"

Reluctantly, I got out of my seat and came to the door.

The obnoxious helper was standing on the ground, blocking my way.

He raised his two hands to me. I had no other way to get out. *Don't let him know you're scared*, I told myself. *Take his hands and step down. He won't do anything stupid. There are a lot of people here*, I assured myself.

I put my hand out to take his hand and step down. As I moved forward, he shifted his hands. Both of his hands ended up on my breasts. The other people standing around laughed out loud. I was so embarrassed I didn't know what to do.

The next thing I knew people were grabbing my arms. Others pulled on my shirt.

"Come with me, young lady, come with me!" they yelled. "I will take you where you want to go! Lowest price! I will take you!"

I tried to get free of those hands but there were ten of them to one of me. Suddenly, I felt my legs buckling. My throat was dry. I began to choke and hyperventilate. Everything was spinning. I fought to stay on my feet, to get out. Even today, I do not know how I got to the curb.

Dreamily, I stood there on the corner of the street, wondering where I was. Then everything came back to me. I checked inside my pocket. My money was gone. My clothes were scattered on the ground around me, tossed away. I closed my hands into fists and screamed my anger.

"You animals! You'll pay for this. You will pay!"

I was sobbing desperately but people just walked on by. Some of them glanced at me, but no one offered their help. With tears in my eyes I gathered my belongings.

I was in Saigon without my baby.

Sadness filled me.

I was totally alone. I had no money, no friends. I wondered again if I had done the right thing by coming here. *What if I can't find work? What if I fail?*

A man was calling my name.

"Cam, Cam, here you are! I've been looking everywhere! Where's your baby?"

I was shocked, and very scared. Too scared to look up at him.

Oh God, what bad luck! I just got off the bus and they've caught me already!

I thought it was one of Binh's relatives or friends. Frantically I looked left and right for a way to bolt. It was too late. A young cyclo

115

driver pulled in front of me, blocking my path. The instant I looked up at him I panicked. His lower face was covered by an old bandana. I couldn't see his face but I didn't think I knew him!

What? Who? Then he spoke again.

"You don't remember me, do you? Not so strange. It seems so long ago that we were young. I used to live in the other hamlet, across the monkey bridge, near your mother's home. I am Hau. I am so glad I have found you!"

My first reaction was fear.

Does he know Binh? Will he tell?

Suddenly I knew him. He used to live in the hamlet across the bridge from mine. He was a little older than I was. Yes, I remembered him.

He was the boy with the harelip.

I had never actually talked to him back then, or knew him personally. As a young child I had been afraid of him, of his deformity. Then, as teenagers, all of us kids in the village used to make fun of him. We used to mimic his lisp. We would laugh ourselves silly until we dropped.

Hau's deformity was relatively minor. Three others in our village were more serious. Two men had been deaf mutes. I couldn't remember their names, or if they had names. They were a lot older than my sister. The man who lived near my house was very nice and funny. As children we teased him, and sometimes he would get angry, but he never hurt us. The other man was big and strong like a buffalo. He was ugly. He was the scariest creature I ever knew in my childhood. No one in the village dared to mess with him, especially girls and women. He acted like an animal when he saw a woman. He made all kinds of ugly gestures without shame. He was terrifying.

The last person, a woman, was mentally retarded. The villagers called her Nam Ran, because she was poor. Her clothes had a hundred different color patches. Whenever her pants or shirt had a hole, she would find some rag and patch it. It didn't matter to her what color, size or shape the patch was. She also would mumble to herself for hours without stopping. I never saw her eat anything but salt, although she must have, to live.

Nam Ran had a very hard time in the Communist years. The government only gave each family a certain amount to live on. Her family was too poor to barter in the black market. I remember that my mother would take her in from time to time. Nam Ran was not a very good worker but my mother had a weak spot for underdogs. The thing I remember most about Nam Ran was her dignity. She wanted the villagers to address her as Miss Nam Ran. If anybody forgot, she would remind them. My mother looked after her like our distant relatives.

Hau....

We had two boys in the village named Hau. One had been short, ugly and always bothering me. I couldn't stand him. This was the other one, the tall Hau. Although I never had anything to do with him, I didn't have a very good opinion of him either. Not that he had ever done anything to me. It was just that I was my mother's daughter. Even though I never had coins of my own I still thought I was better than this poor soul.

Standing in front of him, my first reaction was disdain.

Oh great! Just what I need, another Hau to bother me.

Short, ugly Hau had pestered me until the day I peed on his head from a tree. After that he left me alone. Now, here was tall Hau Hare Lip! There was no way on Earth I would associate with this man. As I looked at him, I could hear my mother's voice.

"Cam, our family is suffering from bad luck now, but we are still the nobility! It is in your blood! A princess is always a princess, even if she loses her crown! This boy is not worthy to carry your shoes!"

That's what my mother usually said to me when she thought a boy was unsuitable for me. Me and my smart mouth, one time I had replied, "I don't have any shoes." She had swatted me. "Stupid girl, it is just an expression."

Now an unsuitable boy was standing in front of me, looking at me.

He's been searching for me? Why?

How did he know I was here, that I was coming? So many questions entered into my tired mind but I couldn't answer any of them. My mouth was wide open. "I can't believe this," I said. "You were looking for *me*? Hau, who else is looking for me? Did Binh set you up for this?"

He didn't answer me.

The bandanna covered the lower half of his face but his black eyes were gawking at me in wonder. My eyes shifted uncomfortably from his face to his cyclo.

He must have read my mind.

In a low voice he asked, "You never liked me, did you?"

I shook my head but said nothing, keeping my eyes on his cyclo.

"You're not alone, Cam," he said softly. "I'm used to people not liking me." He touched his bandanna but didn't take it off. "I know I'm not the most handsome guy in the hamlet, and I was poor. People looked at me like I was some kind of beast. I hope you are not one of them."

His voice seemed so sad. I felt sorry for him and ashamed of myself.

I was also embarrassed because he thought I was different from the rest of the villagers, but I was not. I could feel my blood rushing to my face. I wanted to ask why he thought I was different but I didn't have the nerve. I fidgeted instead, my bare toes digging in the dirt, my hands crinkling my dry banana leaves.

"Where are you going?" he asked, in his strange voice. "I will drive you there."

I didn't want to tell him that I had no place to go, so I lied.

"I am going to Phu Nhuan to stay with relatives."

He asked me where in Phu Nhuan my relatives lived. When I couldn't come up with the name of a street, I started getting nervous.

He must know I am lying.

He persisted, "Okay, so you don't know the street. Which part of Phu Nhuan do they live? I live in Phu Nhuan, too, and I'm done for the day. Let me take you there."

I tried to be polite. I didn't want to hurt his feelings.

"Oh, thank you, Hau, but I don't know what part. All I know is the bus route. Thank you, but I will take the bus." Nervously I turned and tried to walk back into the terminal. Hau was quicker than I was. He grabbed my shoulder, stopping me.

"Cam, don't be afraid! We grew up almost in the same hamlet! I've lived in the city a long time! I know what It's like to be new here! I want to do this, from one countryman to another! If you have some place to stay, I will take you there. If not, you're welcome to stay with me."

I didn't know what to say. My eyes were filled with tears.

Hau continued. "I will bring you to see your relatives! I know a lot of people from Duc Pho. You tell me their names and I will find them for you, I promise!"

Without thinking I blurted out, crying.

"I don't know anybody! I don't want you looking for my relatives. I don't want to be found!"

He gave out a happy laugh.

"Then it's settled! You can stay with me until you decide what you want to do."

He sounded so sincere, but I felt uncomfortable. Every bad story went through my head of young country girls disappearing in the big city jungle, of hunters waiting for young girls to fall into their traps. *Hau may be one of those hunters, Cam! Don't fall into his trap!*

I looked into the terminal. The thought of those animals in there made my heart sink. At that moment Hau tugged on my dirty shirtsleeve, pointing to the seat of his cyclo.

"Please, get in. It'll be all right."

I hesitated, then stepped up and sat on the front edge of the cyclo seat.

Hau pulled his cyclo out from the curb and mounted his bicycle seat behind me.

He stood on the pedals, pushing hard. Soon we were going faster. Too fast for me. As he proudly maneuvered his cyclo through the Saigon traffic, down the overcrowded streets, I began to regret my decision.

I gripped the cyclo rails, bracing my body. Exhaust fumes from the traffic blew in my dirty face, drying my tears and sweat. I tried to lick the dirt and salt from my chapped lips. Wiggling my toes, I tried to shake the dirt and clay from them.

An hour later, Hau finally steered his cyclo into a side street.

We stopped at the mouth of a big alley. He got down from his seat and tilted the cyclo forward to let me out. I was dizzy from the long ride.

"Here we are," he said. "I'll be right back. I have to return the cyclo and pay for the rental."

I nodded my head that I understood.

As I stood up and tried to step out of the seat, I lost my balance. Hau put out his hand, but I didn't want to fall into his arms, so I leapt. I landed on my hands and knees in the dirt, looking up at him. He laughed as I scrambled to my feet.

He pulled down his bandana and took out a cigarette. He lit it, took a deep drag and blew the smoke in the air, away from me. His eyes were on me, watching me. I couldn't help it. I gasped in horror. Part of his upper lip was missing. Two front teeth grew out of his nostrils. His tongue, or pink flesh, hung loose from his mouth. I tried to hide my fear but it was too late.

He flushed with anger.

He took another deep drag and this time blew the smoke at me.

The air was already hot and my throat was dry. I inhaled part of the cigarette smoke. I coughed harshly. My chest was tight. My throat was closing. Coughing, I tried to catch my breath. He gave out a laugh that went through my veins.

He looked at me coldly. "I love my cigarettes. You'll have to learn to get used to it. I'm not quitting them anytime soon, either you like it or not." His tone of voice had changed. Not looking at me, he guided his empty cyclo into the rental shop, leaving me there on the sidewalk.

I felt powerless.

Evening had fallen and darkness covered the alleyways. Silently I followed Hau through wide alleys and narrow alleys. Some parts of the alleys were lit and others were not. From time to time lights shone through windows or from vendors' carts against the walls. I was quickly lost. Hau took so many turns that I couldn't keep track. I couldn't remember where I had been.

Broken shells and rocks were poking into my bare feet. As if they weren't sore enough. I told myself that I should turn back. But which way? And where would I go? *This is Saigon, Cam, not your village.*

I told myself to wait until morning.

Immediately, the argument in my head began.

Wait until morning? What will you do if he's bad? You've already made him angry. At least tell the neighbors you're not his girlfriend! Laughter in my head.

Right, and who will believe you? What kind of girl goes to a man's house at night? They'd think you were just making trouble, crying wolf!

Another voice cautioned, *Whatever you do, don't let the neighbors know you ran away from your husband! With your luck, one of them will know Binh! Don't reveal yourself!*

My head was aching. *What should I do? Where could I hide?*

I couldn't wander the streets at night. If a policeman caught me I'd go to jail. Vietnamese police are monsters and I was a young girl. How could I protect myself? No, I decided, at least here I have only Hau to deal with. Besides, I assured myself, if there's a way out, I will find it!

"You wait here. I will get us dinner."

He vanished inside a small shop.

As I stood there waiting, a young girl approached me. She was about five or six, no older. Her clothes were torn and her face was covered with dirt. On her hip she carried a sickly looking baby. Her dark eyes stared at me. She held out her palm.

"Please, miss, do you have some change? My brother is hungry. He needs food."

I felt sorry for her and her brother. I wanted to help her but I had nothing. "I don't have any money. If you wait, when the man with me comes out, he may have some change to give you."

As I spoke, Hau came out of the shop carrying a six-pack of 33 beer, a pack of cigarettes and two packets of dry egg noodle soup.

When the little girl saw Hau she fled down the dark alley.

"Damn beggar!" Hau barked. "Did you give her your money?"

I shook my head. "No."

"Good! You're smart, and you learn fast," he said, satisfied.

Not so smart, I thought stubbornly. I would have given her some.
Well, Cam, if he thinks you're smart, pretend to be smart!

We had walked a long way from the main road. Ahead of us, between the shacks and shanties, I caught glimpses of bobbing lights on water. It must be the river! We'd reached a part of Saigon I never knew existed.

The Under City.

Row after row of huts hung out over the river, connected to each other by planks, held up by bamboo poles. The huts were of cardboard, warped plywood, uneven planks and rusty tin sheets, with roofs of thatch or palm leaves to shelter from the sun and rain. Across the narrow river were more huts, the river hemmed in. Between the huts were rickety walkways of old rotting wood.

The walkway creaked as I stepped out on it, following Hau.

We ducked under the ragged clothes hung across the walkway. Inside the huts, families with young children squatted on bare floors, in the oil lamp light, having their evening meal. Mothers were yelling at their children. Babies were crying. The elderly squatted beside the doorways, watching us pass, fanning themselves or swatting at clouds of bloodsucking mosquitoes.

The walkways were poorly nailed, with wide gaps. I looked down, stepping carefully, afraid of falling through. I could see dirty dark water underneath me. The stench of sewage in the river was unbearable, nauseating. I wanted to throw up. I wondered is this how country people live who come here to find the dream of wealth?

This is no life, no dream.
This trap of poverty.
I dream of a freedom I am yet to see.
      Hardship is my life, and dark miseries.

Myself, only me, to blame.
My mother is right, her judgment true.
I am the dreamer with my foolishness dream.
I leave my high mountain for the dream of another.
I climb the new mountain to discover, to rue.
I am lower than before!
My child, my home, my dream! My shame.
My ancestors have turned their faces from me.

In a proud voice, Hau announced, "This is it, Cam. This is my castle, and I am the master. Welcome to my home!"

An old plastic curtain covered the entrance. He pulled it aside.

I stood very still, afraid to move. His hut was the last one on the slum. It was built at the very edge of the water. If I made one wrong move I would end up in the dirty river.

In the dim light, I quickly scanned the inside of his hut, looking for a place where I could sleep.

The hut was tiny. In one corner, a small bed was shoved against the tin sheet that divided him from the family next door. In another corner was an old square table with a tiny, rusty kerosene stove on it, and an old chair.

This is where he cooks, eats and entertains, I thought.

Two short-legged red plastic stools were stacked under his bed. His old clothes and hats hung from the rope that ran across the room. Dirty towels were tossed on his bed. Beer cans, soda bottles, and cigarette butts were discarded on the floor.

He saw me looking.

"It isn't much, I know, Cam, but it is mine. I pay for it with hard earned money."

He held the curtain all the way open.

"Come in. Come in and make yourself at home."

He sounded more cheerful than he had since I got out of his cyclo.

He lit his lamp and his stove, boiling water for the soup. After three days of eating old bread and corn, the bowl of noodle soup tasted like one of my mother's special meals at Tet! Sitting on the low red stool, I was still uncomfortable looking up at his face, but with his food in my belly, I was not as scared. And I was grateful for the food and a place to stay.

I said softly, "Hau, thank you for your kindness. When I find work, I will repay you."

He gulped down his beer, taking a few more drags on his cigarette, blowing the smoke away from me, fidgeting. He was nervous.

He spoke in a rush, the lisp in his voice very heavy now.

"Cam, do you know I love you? I always loved you. I always look for you here, hoping to find you. I knew you would come to Saigon one day. I want to marry you. You will be my queen. I will take care of you. You won't have to work. I will give you anything you want out of life!"

I was in shock. Without thinking, I said, "Hau! Are you joking? You are just kidding me, right? You must know that I don't want to be married to anyone, especially to you! You poor soul!" The words jumped out of my big mouth. I couldn't take them back. Suddenly, my heart was in my throat with fear.

I was angry with myself at the same time.

You stupid girl! Can't you ever think first?

He glowered at me, his eyes burning with shame.

"You are in my house—and you—you say—!"

He stubbed his cigarette on the table and flung the empty beer can out the door. I heard it drop in the river. He moved to rise, reaching for me.

"Hau, wait," I beseeched. "Please, can we talk?"

His voice was thick and full of rage.

"Nothing to talk about! You don't like me! You don't want to marry me! You think I am ugly. I will show you how ugly I can be! After I finish with you— "

Oh God, I should never have gotten into his cyclo!

I raised my arms to protect myself, waiting for the first blow.

Nothing happened.

I peered through my arms. His eyes glared at me, but he hadn't moved yet. My first reaction was to tell him what I thought, that he was a pig like all men!

Not now, stupid girl, not now!

I looked outside. *Should I run?*

It was dark. The walkway was dangerous. I didn't know where I was. I'd never find my way to the road. I had no place to go.

Talk to him before he gets out of his chair.

"Hau, how did you know I was in Saigon?" I asked calmly, forcing myself to relax. "And I don't think you're ugly. But of all the girls in the hamlet, why do you want to marry *me*? I'm nothing but trouble. You must know that I ran away from my husband. Now I've abandoned my baby! Hau, I'm no good! I'm a terrible human being. I have shamed my family. You never did that!"

Blah, blah, blah, from one sentence to the next. I didn't even stop to breathe.

"Hau, there are many good women out there! A hundred times better than me! They would love to be your wife! I am always making trouble! I am too wild. I am too unpredictable. Hau, I can't even trust myself!"

To my surprise he didn't hit me or do anything else.

He settled back in his chair, reaching for the last warm beer. Using his forefinger, he popped the lid on the top of the can. He took a big gulp and lit another cigarette. He rocked his chair back and forth, finally stopping, his chair leaning against the wall, the front legs off the floor.

126

His put his hands behind his head, looked at me and said, "I have something to tell you. Do you know why men want to own a wild horse? I know why. Because if a man can tame that wild horse, she will be a champion some day. The man who can tame her will own her, will own a champion, for the rest of her life! Why do I want to marry you? Because you are my wild horse and I want you! I watched you from the time you were a young girl, but I knew my place in the hamlet. I said nothing. When you married I left the hamlet. I came to Saigon. I thought I would never see you again. When I heard you had run away from your husband, I knew you would come to Saigon sooner or later. I looked for you everywhere!"

He crowed, "Now, you are here in my stable!"

It was hot and there was no wind.

The palms of my hands were wet with sweat, but I felt a cold chill run up my spine. There were goose bumps all over my body. I was not flattered, I was terrified.

This creature has been following me since I was a little girl.

He took a big gulp of beer. Some of the beer dribbled from his ripped mouth and down his chin. He pulled his faded t-shirt up and wiped his mouth. He leaned forward, the front legs of the chair striking the floor. He looked down at me on the stool and he smirked.

He looked like he thought he was the smartest man on earth.

I wanted to reach over and pull the legs of the chair from under him. I wanted to take his own frying pan and hit him over the head. I wanted to rip off his rabbit face and throw it down into the river and watch the water carry it away. I wanted—

He just sat there, swigging his beer, puffing on his cigarette.

Suddenly I felt all my energy draining out of me. My eyes were swollen. I fought to hold back my tears.

"Hau, I am so tired right now that if I don't sleep I will collapse. Leaving my baby is breaking my heart. And the long trip was exhausting.

And the craziness in this huge city is not helping. Hau, I am already broken. I am emotionally and physically overwhelmed. Please, please let me rest for one night. I want you to know the truth. I have no money, no family, and no place to stay. You are the only person I know here, the only friend I have. Please be patient with me, I will answer your request another time, but not tonight. Please."

I could no longer control myself. I sobbed and sobbed.

"How about tomorrow night?" he said.

I was still crying. I was grateful for one more night, one more hour.

"Thank you so much for your kindness," I said tearily. "You are a true gentleman."

He was thinking about something.

"Yes, you are right," he said, nodding his head. "I should not make a hasty decision when you are emotionally unstable. Especially about a long-term relationship. I will be home earlier tomorrow. We will go to the Buddhist temple and make it legal. Then I will take you out and we can have a feast to celebrate."

Then he thought of something else.

"Remember, Cam, this is my turf, and I am a cyclo driver. I know every street and alley. I hope you don't have second thoughts and do something stupid. I told you, I've been living here a long time. I know a lot of people. I will find you."

I was relieved, and at the same time a little scared.

I lowered my head docilely, "No, I won't, Hau."

The little voice in my head whispered,

He thinks he's got you where he wants you. He's so sure of himself. He doesn't know you very well, Cam, he—

The last thing I needed was my little voice.

"Shush, shut up," I said, loud enough for Hau to hear.

"What?" he said.

I shook my head. "No, nothing. Just so tired."

He got up and tossed the beer can into a corner. Wearily, he walked outside to relieve himself in the river. When he returned he reached for my hands. I quickly lifted them to cover my mouth and gave a big loud yawn, moving to the floor.

"I am so tired." I said gratefully, "Good night, Hau. Thank you for everything." He threw his blanket to me and blew out his oil lamp. Then he crawled into bed and let his mosquito net down.

"Good night, my queen. I will see you in the morning."

As tired as I was, I didn't dare fall asleep. Hau might wake up in the middle of the night and change his mind.

Not that I could sleep anyway.

The heat and the humidity were suffocating. The low tide gave off a terrible smell. And the Saigon River mosquitoes were huge. I had rolled myself in the blanket against their bites but hungry swarms kept reaching me through the cloth, injecting long needles into my skin. They buzzed around my ears, landing on my bare face, stinging my back. I rolled over and covered my face.

It didn't help. And now I couldn't breathe under the filthy blanket. Between the mosquitoes and the heat rash I was going insane. I had thought I could tough it out but I could no longer tolerate the stinging, the itching and the sweat.

I knew in a minute I would be screaming.

Shamefully, slowly, I crawled under the mosquito net and into Hau's bed. I squeezed my tiny body against the tin wall at the bottom of his feet, carefully avoiding them.

Either he had drunk too much beer or it had been a hard day but he didn't budge, he kept on snoring.

I don't know if I slept. I tried not to.

The night lasted forever.

CHAPTER 12

Out of the Frying Pan

In the false dawn, I sat at the foot of the bed, listening.

I could hear footsteps in the next hut. Peering through cracks in the tin sheeting, I could see a woman moving. She was rambling back and forth in her slippers. I could hear dishes and spoons clacking as the woman arranged them in her basket. I could smell chicken soup.

I could hear her soft voice. "Wake up, my big son. Wake up. Keep an eye on your sister until I get back. Can you do that for me?"

A young boy whined, "Ma, I am so tired. Let me sleep. Take her with you."

"Oh, get up, my big boy. I will buy you some sweets if I have luck selling soup today."

Carefully I crawled out of the bed.

Should I wait for daybreak, for Hau to go to work?

The woman spoke again. "I left you and your sister some soup. Don't follow me to market. I will return after I sell my soup. It won't be long."

Follow her, said my voice.

Carefully, not making a sound, I picked up my belongings and hid by the door, waiting for her to come out. I prayed desperately, silently.

Please, Heaven and Earth, don't let Hau wake up! Come out, lady. Come out!

And there she was.

Her cone hat almost covered her face. Her bamboo pole sank deep into her shoulder, a heavy load on each end. At one end hung a lidded pot of chicken rice porridge, or *chao ga.* Atop the lid was a small clay stove filled with burning charcoal. At the other end of the pole was a pail of water, a basket of bowls, spoons, chopsticks and vegetables, and stacked short-leg stools.

She stepped out in her rhythm, gliding to keep the load from swinging or bouncing. With each step she took, the walkway creaked.

I followed her down the walkway and out of the river slum. My heart beat faster the further we went. In the alleys I stayed safely back from her, keeping her in view, frequently ducking into corners to see if Hau was after me. So far, so good. Maybe luck was with me.

When we reached the corner of the big alley the woman stopped walking.

She put down her heavy load and took off her cone hat, fanning herself with it a few times. She raised one arm and used her sleeve to wipe the sweat from her forehead. I stood in the dark, not moving, waiting for her to continue, but she didn't. Taking a short-handled broom from her waist, she started sweeping an area of sidewalk. She put her burning stove on the ground and set the soup pot on top. She lined up the stools in a row. Lastly, she lifted the pot lid and with a long spoon stirred the *chao ga.*

The aroma of the *chao ga* made my mouth water.

My feet moved of their own accord. Closer and closer I came to the woman's stand, my eyes fixed on a chicken leg sticking out. The woman looked up and saw me.

"Go away, you heavy soul!" she said angrily. "I need someone with light feet and a happy soul to buy my first bowl. To bring me good luck! Not a foot dragger like you! Go away! Go away or I will throw hot water on you!"

I knew why she was so angry with me. Superstition and tradition ruled our culture. If her first buyer had plenty of money or was bouncy and happy, she would have good luck. I had neither to give her. Hungry, sad, and ashamed, I slowly walked away.

I heard footsteps. My heart pounding, I ducked behind a booth.

I breathed a sigh of relief—it wasn't Hau.

A young woman walked up the alley. On her shoulder she carried a bamboo pole with two large empty tins hanging. She stopped in front of the soup stand.

"Greetings, Mrs. Heo. How is your morning?"

"Oh, what bad luck I had this morning!" moaned Mrs. Heo. "I had just uncovered the pot when here comes the rat! She stood right there and stared at my soup pot! She put a curse on my cooked chicken! I'll tell you, I shooed her away fast!"

While she was complaining, she lit an old rolled up newspaper and began to wave the burning paper in the air. She walked all around the soup pot and stools, waving the paper, smoking me out.

I watched her burn my bad luck spirit away. My pride hurt a little.

I don't need your stinky, greasy soup anyway!

But standing there in the dark, how I wished I could buy a small bowl of it or just one piece of that chicken to chew!

Enough of that, I scolded myself. *You better learn to control your appetite before you sell your own soul for food!*

Another young woman went past my hiding spot, carrying a water pail and humming a song. Like a shadow, I followed her to the local water well. What a noisy bunch at the well! They were all women, young and old. They talked, they laughed, and they teased each other. Some were washing clothes. Others had just come to carry the water home.

In the half-light I looked around the well plaza.

A middle-aged woman sat beside a huge basket heaped with clothes, a large empty wash bucket beside it. The clothes were in two piles, one already soaped and one not. In her hand she held a large bar of soap. She took a pair of pants from the dirty pile and began to soap them, her hands moving steadily, scouring the white long pants.

I stepped out into view and approached her.

"Ma'am, do you need some help?"

She raised her head and looked me up and down. She didn't answer, but asked gently,

"Where are you from and what do you want?"

At first I wanted to lie to her, but for some reason I didn't.

"Ma'am, I just came here from the country. I don't know anybody. Please, ma'am, I need a job."

She looked at her tall piles of clothes. "I can't give you a job. I work for people. I am just a maid, not a boss."

"Yes, ma'am," I said. "Can I just help you pull up some water? I don't mind, ma'am. It will give me something to do."

She gave me a kindly smile.

"Clever girl. Smart, too. You'll survive. Yes, you may borrow my bucket and pull up some water. Give yourself a good wash first."

Shyly, I picked up a small tin bucket, walked over to the well and waited my turn. As I dropped my bucket deep into the well, the other girls looked at me.

I couldn't see down the deep well. When my bucket hit the water I wanted to make sure it was full. I pulled it up a few feet and dunked it down again before pulling it all the way up. I walked back to the woman and poured the water into her big wash bucket. I repeated this many times until her wash bucket was full. I pulled the last bucket up for me.

The woman handed me her bar of soap.

I poured the bucket over my head and body without taking off my clothes. I washed my hair, my face and body, and my clothes. I scrubbed the dirt off my feet and toes. It was heaven. I couldn't remember the last time I had taken a shower.

I felt clean, fresh and alive.

I squatted down beside the woman and helped her with her work. When we were done I thanked her for her kindness.

She said, "I might be able to help you." She told me an address. "They are friends of my boss. I am Mrs. Ba. You can use my name as a reference. They are not nice people to work for, but if they are willing to hire you, at least you will have temporary shelter."

She handed me a comb.

"Here, comb your hair. Then go behind that wall. No one will see you. Take off your clothes and wring them out so they will dry quicker. Shake them out so they don't wrinkle!"

I combed my tangled hair and handed the comb back to her. Before I went behind the wall, I bowed my head low and thanked her again.

She put her baskets on her pole and wished me luck. "But remember, don't knock on their door until noon!"

I bowed and stepped away. In my heart I wished she had taken me home with her.

The sun rose and kept rising.

I wandered streets and alleys, hiding whenever I saw a cyclo.

I kept repeating the address Mrs. Ba had given me so I wouldn't forget it. I also begged the gods for help. *Please, Heaven and Earth, help me! Please make them hire me!* The sun was high now and the air was hot. I didn't have a hat so I used an old pajama shirt to wrap my head.

By force of hunger I kept coming back to the food alley. Fried shrimp, every kind of fish, soups, beef and chicken on skewers, stir fried noodles, aromatic sauces. In display cases hung succulent chickens and ducks.

Along the alley, in stall after stall, table after table, people sat and ate. All kinds of people. Young student girls in long white *ao dai's*, maids and office workers, taxi drivers, farmers in from the country with their produce. The ones who had money sat on chairs. The others squatted down on the ground. Everyone eating and eating, one hand holding chopsticks, the other holding a spoon. Slurping the broth noisily, shoving the noodles into their big wide mouths.

I would stand there and stare at their food, my mouth open, hoping someone would offer me a leftover, anything, but no one did.

"Get out of here, rat! Go away, bad luck girl!" They yelled, they threatened, they burned paper. I had to keep moving to protect myself. I was disgusted with myself for being so hungry all the time.

I was back in front of the house.

I had lost count of the number of times I had walked to this house, not daring to ring the bell because Mrs. Ba had said to wait until noon.

My clothes were long since dry. My feet were sore from walking on hot roads. My mouth was dry from thirst and my stomach was so empty it hurt. I looked up at the blazing sky. The sun was directly overhead.

"It must be time," I said.

Nervously, I reached for the doorbell and pressed it lightly.

I heard the rings, *bling, bling.*

I waited, my heart pumping fast. I heard flip-flops shuffling toward the gate. One eye peered through the peephole and a voice with a Northern accent said, "Who are you? Go away! You have disturbed our meal. Go beg somewhere else!"

Quickly I said, "No, Madame, I am not a beggar! Mrs. Ba, the maid of your good friend, sent me here. She said you may have need of servants."

I heard a light thump.

The lock rumbled and the gate slid open. I didn't wait for her to ask me in. Quick as a rabbit, I squeezed my body through. "Madame, I am a friend of Mrs. Ba. She gave me your name and address."

The woman closed the gate and shoved the bolt. She turned and looked me up and down as if I were meat in the market.

"Mother! Who is that?" Another female Northern voice from inside the house.

"Nobody important!" said the mother over her shoulder.

The mother asked me, "What did you say your name was? Are you related to maid Ba?"

My head was bowed low, my hands playing with my shirt. I knew she was looking at me, waiting for me to answer. I gulped down my saliva.

"My name is Cam. I am come from the country looking for work. Maid Ba is a friend of mine. We are not related."

She didn't seem to be listening, or to care. She looked at me sourly.

"You are not what I had in mind for a maid. You are too young, too small and you look sickly. I need someone older, with more experience. I don't have time to train you."

She was complaining now. "I have two grown daughters. They both work. I need someone strong to carry water, to clean the house and do the laundry. You are too small."

"Madame, please give me a chance! I am a quick learner. I am small but I am a very good worker. I will work hard for you."

She looked me up and down again.

"All right. I will give you one week. I will see how you handle the work. If I see you cannot do it, you will have to go. Understand?"

"Oh, yes, Madame! Thank you."

"Well, then, come in and meet my daughters."

We walked into the house. Two young women were there, eating.

"These are my daughters, Miss Nga and Miss Lan."

I bowed low, keeping my eyes on the floor.

One of them said, "Mother! Why did you even let this *thing* in the house?" The other one added, "Eww! She looks like a beggar. Get her out of my sight! I'm trying to eat my lunch!"

I flicked a glance at the table. It was covered with food.

I was angry with the girls. I was also starting to starve. I wanted to cry but the little pride I had left would not let me.

Ignore these ugly witch sisters. You need the job. You need food.

"Please, Misses, give me a chance, I will prove to you. I will—"

They didn't let me finish. They both laughed until they were choking.

"Mother, where did you get her? In the jungle? At a hick farm in the mountains? Mother, just listen to her accent! You should send her back to tend her pigs!"

"Now, daughters, be kind. There's work in this house that needs to be done. Would either one of you like to do it? Like to clean up after yourselves? I say we should try her out."

"Do what you want with her, Mother," the older daughter, Nga, said, waving her hand in dismissal. "Just keep her away from us!"

I sat on the beautiful dirty tile floor eating their leftovers.

A fish head and fish bones with some meat left on them, all soaked in fish sauce. A few stalks of water spinach in a bowl of water. A spoonful of sauce from stir-fry tofu with tomatoes. A full bowl of white rice.

I shoved the rice into my mouth with chopsticks. I licked the stir-fry sauce. I sucked and chewed all the bones from the fish until there was nothing left. I dipped the water spinach in the fish sauce, ate it, and drank the water. I didn't stop until all the food was gone. It was the first time in days I had even this little bit to eat.

While the family took their noon naps in their comfortable beds, I was in the kitchen on my hands and knees scrubbing the floor. The dirty dishes were waiting, the floor to mop and dry, and dirty clothes to be washed. The mother had taken me into the kitchen before I could eat.

"There are two floors in this house. The last maid left a month ago and we haven't found one yet that we like. There is a lot of work to be done. But first go give yourself a good scrubbing. I will give you some of my old clothes. Throw those rags of yours out! And try to stay away from my daughters."

"Yes, Madame," I had responded.

Alone now, clean and fed, I looked at my new clothes. They were three sizes bigger than my body. I told myself I would cut and sew them to fit when I had time.

When I had time.

The old woman had not been kidding. Her daughters did not like to clean. Their rooms were a mess, their dirty clothes piled up everywhere. I did all the washing and ironing. I was on my hands and knees twice a day, cleaning the floors upstairs and down. And the windows. And the kitchen and long hallway. I also served them breakfast, lunch and dinner and late night tea.

My day started before sunrise and went long after sunset.

For three days the only time I was allowed a break was to eat my meals. I was dead tired each night. I didn't have time to think. I was not allowed outside the iron gate. I ate whatever was left over after their meals. Sometimes the mother brought home small pieces of pork or ribs. She caramelized them with shrimp. Whenever she cooked this dish it was gone as soon as it reached the table. Sometimes the mother would save me one piece of meat and a shrimp. She would hide them under her bowl so her daughters couldn't see them and eat them.

At night I slept curled up in the corner at the back of the kitchen floor.

While I felt safe from the outside world, I wished my baby was with me. I cried. I wondered how long I had to be here to earn enough money to send for him? Then I realized I had not asked the family about my salary. I had been there for weeks.

It was Saturday breakfast. I had rehearsed my lines since the night before, choosing my words carefully. They must not know I was married and had a child. Now I was nervously waiting for the right time. The mother had made eggs and bought three small loaves of French bread. I poured the boiling water into their coffee tins.

Then, steadying my nerves, I spoke.

"Madame, and Misses, please excuse me. My mother sent me here to find work so that I could send money back home to help out the family. Could you please tell me what I get paid each month? My mother wants me to let her know."

They calmly ate their French bread dipped in fried eggs and drank their coffee. The girls looked at each other and laughed but said nothing. The mother ordered me back to the kitchen.

That afternoon, as I scrubbed the kitchen floor, the mother came and stood over me.

"Girl! We've decided we can't pay your salary. My daughters say you are not qualified to be a maid, that you are fortunate we even took you in. For now, your pay will be the food you eat and a place for you to sleep. They said they would think about whether they want to keep you. But for now, you are only temporary."

She turned to walk away.

Nga spoke up from the other room. "And you can't leave until you pay us back for the clothes you are wearing and all the food you have eaten! Mother, don't forget to tell her that for the past three weeks you have taken your time to train her, too." Another voice, Lan's, echoing "Yes, Mother! And what about my pajamas? She burned a hole in them when she ironed!"

I was dumfounded. I couldn't hear what else they were saying. My vision blurred with tears. I felt hopeless and helpless. In shame and fear I ran on bare feet from the kitchen to the front gate. It was locked. There was no way out. I went back to the kitchen and got down on my knees. I started scrubbing the kitchen floor over and over in my rage, scraping, scouring the beautiful tiles. My tears mixed with the soapy water on the tile floor.

That night as I lay awake on the floor, I thought I heard whispers around me.

Do I sleep or do I wake?
I do not know. I hear a voice whisper
Girl, do not cry, no tears or despair
No evil, no violence
Let the black pit close
Be still and remain yourself
Be moral and whole, not broken
Work harder and don't complain

CROSSING THE BAMBOO BRIDGE

Let Time use you wisely
Learn from evil how not to be
That the snake can never fly
Though your road is unknowable
Follow it, let it lead you to yourself
Be lost that you may be found
When detours invite and shade trees shelter
Rest but do not remain
      Take Time with you slowly
You are the journey, you are the route
You will arrive and remember where you started
Hardship heals, pain washes clean
You are the charm
You will see green pastures, you will see
Flowers, birds, bees and sweet honey
You will see

I rolled over on my side and opened my eyes.

Who is talking to me?

I looked across the floor. No one was there, of course. I shook my head and said harshly, mimicking the ugly sisters.

Girl, you are out of your mind.

And then I slept.

For three long weeks more, I worked as hard as I could without complaint. My hope was that they would pay me soon.

One morning after I had cleaned upstairs, I started down the stairway. My bare feet made no sound. I could hear them talking in a room.

"Mother, you should tell the maid to give you her ID."

"Why? What for?" asked the mother.

"That maid Ba no longer works for our friend. She left them. We have to make sure this one doesn't get away, too."

I didn't wait to hear more. I ran down the stairs, stepping lightly.

At midday, as I served them, the mother said,

"Girl, I need to have your ID."

"I'm sorry, Madame, I don't have it," I said. "I left it with my cousin in Phu Lam so I wouldn't lose it." It was a lie, of course.

The mother looked at her daughters, frustrated.

"Girl, you should have your ID card with you at all times! You must send for it."

"Yes, Madame, as soon as I have a day off."

They glared at me, but nothing more was said.

All morning I had rehearsed what I would say. I was still very nervous.

In Qui Nhon, after that woman tried to pick my pocket, I had rolled up my birth certificate and slid it into the hem of my shirt. With everything that had happened to me, the bus terminal, Hau, and slaving for these people, I had forgotten all about it. When I first came here the family had told me to throw my old clothes away, but I didn't. I saved them in case I returned to the country. I would give them to the poor, I thought.

Now I was in a cold sweat. Did I still have it? All morning I had desperately wanted to check my old shirt, but didn't for fear the family was watching me. When they went upstairs to nap, I ran into the kitchen and unrolled my shirt.

It was wrinkled, but it was still there, still readable.

My birth certificate!

I was so relieved. I had been so lucky! My charity had saved me.

Day after day I told myself I had to get out. And every day, the fear of being found by Binh, by Hau, the fear of hunger, would defeat me.

No, stay here. It is safe.

This couldn't go on, though. My baby was sick. He needed medicine. He needed food. Nearly two months had passed and I had not sent any money home. How could my mother take care of him? She had nothing.

He will die!

Night after night I had the same terrible dream. My baby lay on a straw mat. His head was turned from me. He wouldn't look at me. When I picked him up, he let me, but his body was limp. I cried out, "My baby is dying, please someone help me! Please, please help me."

In my dream, people came, but not to help. They carried spears and bamboo sticks. "You are a bad mother," they screamed. "You only think of yourself! *You* should die!" I tried to escape, but they dragged me on a rope out to the bamboo trees.

My kicking and screaming would wake me up.

Every night I lay soaked in sweat, crying.

No more, I thought. *I cannot take this anymore. I will take my chances outside these walls.*

"Get up, lazy girl! Four o'clock and you are still in bed? Get up! We need water. The floor has to be scrubbed. You are stronger now. You must go get water and bring it home!"

For the past week I had awakened to the same voice, scrambling up from my mat. Now I had to get water for them! The faster I worked the more duties they gave me. But my salary had still not been mentioned. Also, every night now the daughters demanded I give them a massage. Then they had the nerve to complain my hands were too small. That I was too weak to squeeze deeply into their muscle and bone.

Last night, rubbing them, I wished I could turn myself into a monster with huge hands and huge feet. In a book of legends, I had read of such a creature living on Sam Mountain in Chau Doc Province. A Vietnamese Yeti, or Bigfoot! I had imagined myself as this creature, squeezing the witches' shoulders, their necks, with my huge hands! In my daydream I saw their eyes pop and their tongues hang down to their navels.

In reality I was squeezing with all my strength and the ugly sister I was working on was yelling.

"Ouch, ouch, that hurts! Mother, make her stop!"

Now I stood in the dark at the gate, waiting, a bamboo pole across my shoulder. Big square metal tins hung from it, one at each end. With one hand I held the pole. With the other I carried a smaller round bucket attached to a long rope.

The mother inserted the large key into the lock, opened the gate, and let me out.

"Girl, I know exactly how long it takes to fill up these water tins. Don't linger! If you do a good job, I may give you some sweet rice. Now go, before the sun rises."

She shut the gate and turned the bolt.

I waited to hear her enter the house.

Last night, when she told me I had to get water, I knew that it was my best chance, my fear or not. Now, finally, I was outside the gate. What would be would be.

I slipped the pole off my shoulder and dropped it on the ground. I reached into one of the tins and took out a small bag containing my belongings

In my mind I saw my son lying on a straw mat, dying. I had to go. I had to find a job that paid. No more safe slavery.

I started to run slowly, and then faster.

Run, girl, run. And don't look back.

CHAPTER 13

My Saigon Angel

*R*un, run, don't walk.

I knew when they realized I was not coming back with the water that they would be after me.

The large flip-flops on my small feet suddenly tripped me and I fell on my face. I picked myself up quickly, deciding I could run faster barefoot. I took the flip-flops off and stuck them under my armpits. I didn't know where I was or even which street I was on. I just kept running as fast as I could. I didn't care who I bumped into. I ran through the streets and alleys to the point that I couldn't breathe. I had to stop.

I squatted at the curbside, gasping, my elbows on my knees, trying to catch my breath.

As I inhaled some new air, I could smell burning incense. I held my breath for a few seconds to release my other senses. In the pre-dawn hush I could hear chanting nearby, steady and strong. I lifted my head up and looked around. Down the street I could see the dim lights of a temple. Without thinking I began walking toward it.

I hesitated in the courtyard, peering in.

The temple was crowded with worshipers for early morning prayers. Everyone wore their nice clothes, kneeling and bowing low, their hands clasped in front of their chests. A group of monks in yellow robes were seated on the large mat with two monks in brown gowns seated on each side. Their left hands were on their chests, their five fingers pointing up to their chins. Their right hands held small handled sticks that they tapped lightly on small gongs. The monks' eyes were closed but their lips moved, repeating their prayers in a steady rhythm.

I bowed my head and bent my body. Slowly and quietly I walked into the back corner of the main chamber and knelt down. I closed my eyes in prayer to Buddha to help me to find a job.

The praying and chanting went on forever. I had been kneeling for a long time. I felt numbness and tingling in my right leg. It had gone to sleep. I began to fidget, unable to concentrate. I tried shifting my position and rubbing my leg. The noise disturbed the people praying nearby. They lifted their heads and looked at me with disapproval.

"Sorry," I said.

One woman put her finger to her lips, "Shush."

I didn't dare move.

The chanting stopped. Slowly, one by one, the monks quietly rose and left the chamber.

I had no place to go so I waited for the room to empty, but when this group of worshipers left another group came in. Some stayed awhile and others just knelt down for a few minutes. Some put handfuls of real money in the small boxes chained to posts at each shrine. I didn't have any money but I was tired of kneeling so I went around from one altar to the next. There were so many gods that I didn't know which was which. Some had many arms and some had many heads. Some of the gods were standing like warriors ready to draw their swords. Some of the statues had such hideous faces that I was afraid to look at them.

I was hungry.

Around me, altar after altar was covered not only with flowers but also with cookies, cakes, fruits and sweet rice, all the offerings people had brought with them for their favorite god. My mouth was watering and my stomach was making noises. People were looking at me.

I moved into the far corner. In front of a shrine was a bunch of brown rotting bananas and a few wrinkled oranges with dried leaves on the stem. Nervously I walked over to the shrine and bowed. I wanted so much to steal that old fruit but my hands wouldn't lift from my chest.

No one's watching! Take it. Hide it under your shirt.

At that instant I looked up at the altar. The angry god glared down at me. My fear and my shame overcame my stomach.

How will you ever explain this to your child? That you stole food from a Buddhist temple under the god's eyes?

Shamefully I went back to the main chamber. I knelt down and bowed low. I recited my sins. I asked the gentle-faced Buddha with the big earlobes to forgive me.

Outside the sun had risen and so had the noise. I walked out to the small courtyard. The streets were crowded with peddlers and merchants, with motor rickshaws and cyclos. I squatted on the cement, my back against a tree.

What do I do now?

Where should I go? Should I go and find Auntie Moi? I knew she lived in Saigon with her son. Maybe I should take my chances. Yes, she might bring me back to Duc Pho but right now I needed a place to stay. I needed food to eat! I was so hungry!

Stop whining. You are always hungry. And you've been living pretty high for the past month. You had three meals a day, little pig! Not even one day on your own and you are ready to give up? Auntie Moi caught you on your first escape, remember? Now you want to go looking for her?

Sitting under the shade tree, I argued with myself.

I had to get out of this mess. Should I take another chance with her? It had just been bad luck that she caught me.

In 1954, Auntie Moi's husband took their three older children and went north, leaving their baby son, Tinh, with her. With no land and no money, she asked my mother to care for her son and went to Saigon to find work. When she returned to Duc Pho to get her son she was very glamorous. It was just my bad luck she had come when I tried to run away.

That had been three years ago. Maybe it will be different now.

Somehow I doubted it.

I watched the people coming into the temple. They all carried gifts. Some burned pretend money or incense in the trays on the altar. Others put real money in the boxes.

That's why your prayer didn't work! You didn't bring any gift or even a stick of incense.

Still, I was better off than the beggars in the courtyard.

There were many more beggars than when I had arrived earlier. An old Indian woman across the courtyard made me especially sad. She lay on an old dirty mat. Her face was dark and deeply wrinkled. Her salty white hair was filthy. I could tell it had not been washed or combed. She had only one leg. Every time someone walked past her she raised her shaking hand and cried out, "Please sir, please ma'am, help the old lady! I have no money. I have no home!"

I felt so bad watching her lying there begging in the hot sun.

I got up from my comfortable spot and walked over to her. Her eyes were milky, almost blind. She gave me a faint smile and said, "Thank you, miss." She thought that I had money to give to her. Without thinking I bent down and started pulling her mat over to the shady tree.

Her expression changed from a smile to fear. She violently kicked at me with her one foot, crying aloud in a language I didn't understand.

I didn't know what I had done so wrong. I tried to get her to stop yelling. Then a male voice behind me said, "Leave her alone! Are you trying to steal the old lady's money?"

I looked up. Over me stood a nicely dressed Indian man, a cigarette in his hand. His eyes were furious with me. He grabbed me by my neck, lifted me into the air and tossed me like a rag doll. I landed on the cement, scraping myself, too scared to cry. He scooped up the old beggar and carried her across to his Honda parked in front of a café. He put her on the seat designed for her deformed body and they drove away.

Everything happened so quick that I was still in shock.

A well-dressed woman came to my rescue. She helped me get on my feet and took me over to a bench. She sat beside me and took out a paper fan. She fanned herself and then turned her hand and fanned me. I thought my secret prayer had been answered even though I had not brought any gift to the gods.

The cool breeze of the fan calmed my fear. I thanked her for her kindness.

"I saw what happened," she said in her northern accent. She opened her purse and handed me a piece of candy. "That man sent his own mother out to beg! Disgusting. You weren't trying to steal her money, were you?"

"No," I protested, "She was burning in the hot sun. I just tried to help her, that's all!"

"That's a good girl. You have a good heart. God will reward you some day." She smiled at me. "Where are you from? Do you have any family?" The sweetness of her voice and the sweet candy in my mouth made me let down my guard. I spilled out almost everything except that I was married and had a child. Then she asked to see my hand. "I want to read your palm," she said. So I stretched my hand out.

She told me to make a fist. Then she held onto my wrist, counting all the lines on the side of my hand. Without speaking she opened my fist and traced her finger over my palm, muttering, her head bobbing slightly.

I waited courteously but impatiently. I wanted her to tell me my bad luck was over.

"Please, Madam, what do you see? Is there any chance that I will find a decent job?"

She looked up from my hand.

"In your past, you had a very bad life. You had so much bad luck I can't begin to describe it. However, your luck is about to change. Not only will you get the job you want, you will also be rich, too. Very rich."

My heart was pounding with excitement. "Madam, you must have a lot of friends. Will you ask them to hire me? I will do anything! Please, will you help me?"

She looked at me carefully, from head to toes.

"Well, do you want to come work for *me*?"

I was on my feet, excited, "H-how much will you pay me?"

"Oh yes, I will pay you a lot of money."

"Oh thank you, so much! I will make enough money so I can send for my baby!"

Her eyes narrowed, her voice changed.

"You have a baby? You told me you were a country girl, that you came here to work to take care of your mother. You didn't say anything about having a child!"

"Oh, Madam, yes! Truly I am a country girl. But my mother forced me to marry when—

I was so happy I was babbling.

She interrupted, annoyed.

"I thought you were a virgin! I mean—" She stopped. "I mean— you are too young to have a baby." She tried to correct herself.

It was too late. Suddenly I remembered all the stories of young girls coming to the big city to find their dream, only to be wooed by sweet-talking madams and forced into brothels. If the girl was a virgin, the madam would sell her to a rich Chinese man in Cho Lon. I was in a panic.

Do something quick. But don't let her know that you know.

I said in a sad voice, "Oh, Madam, that means I cannot work for you."

"Oh, no, no," she said quickly. "You can still work for me. I am rich. I own a lot of businesses. I know a lot of people. If you don't work for me I will find someone that wants you."

She reached over to hold onto my hand, but I was already moving. I bent down to pick up my belongings.

Think, think.

I acted excited and eager. "Madam, should we go to your house now?" It worked. She relaxed her guard, dropping her hand.

As hard as I could I shoved her off the bench and ran.

And ran.

Like a dog, my nose soon began to smell fish, raw meat and rotten produce.

In the middle of a square was a large market building. In front of it and around it were rows and rows of food stalls. Crowds of people were buying and selling, bargaining. As fast as a cat I dashed into the throng, ducking and weaving my tiny body through them. Before I knew it I was inside the market.

I went from one aisle to the next, pausing to hide behind racks or between piles, fearfully looking everywhere. I kept moving slowly, always watching. Sometimes the women venders would yell at me to move, some of them kicking at me. Finally I was near the other end of the market, at the back entrance. Crouched behind a pile of cooking pots, I turned my head to look back. They were all strangers in the market, no help for me. I turned to run out.

The woman from the temple was standing in the exit.

She was not alone. A young man with black sunglasses was with her. They were searching the crowd.

I panicked again. Quick as a rat I turned back, running, crawling, between the rows of people, trying to keep my head down, not looking where I was going. Disaster. I ran full tilt into a woman shopper and fell to the dirt floor. Beside me her food basket lay strewn over the ground.

"Sorry, sorry," I said quickly.

The woman was hitting me hard on the head with a bunch of carrots. In a Southern voice she cursed at me. "What in your father's name are you trying to do? Are you a little thief? Are you trying to pick my pocket? I will smash your head open like a melon!"

As I lay on the wet dirt, I frantically tried to pick up what had fallen from her basket. All the while she kept whacking me with the carrots. *Whack, whack.* People were stepping over me now. I was using my shirt to wipe the dirt off her food. She yelled, "You will pay for what is on the ground or I will call the police on you!"

When I heard the word "police" I started whimpering.

"Please, Madam, I don't have any money. Please, let me work for you without pay. *Please, Madam, please.*"

She heard nothing I was saying. She bent over, grabbed my shirt and pulled me up hard.

"I will turn you over to the police, you little thief!"

On my knees I looked up at her, intending to beg her for mercy.

No words came out of my mouth. My jaw dropped. I couldn't believe my eyes. It was the woman I had met at the water well.

"Mrs. Ba," I yelled.

She apparently didn't recognize me.

Her eyes narrowed and her brow scrunched.

Oh no, I thought, *she has been talking with those wicked sisters!*

In a rush of words I said, "Mrs. Ba, It's *me,* the girl at the water well! You remember? Last month you helped me get a job with the mother and two daughters? I needed the money so badly for my mother! But they wouldn't pay me. I ran away this morning. It is true, Mrs. Ba! I worked for them for a months but they wouldn't pay me or let me leave. And they fed me like a dog. I was a slave, Mrs. Ba!"

Gulping air, I went on.

"I hid in a temple to pray. There was a woman there. She fooled me. She said she wanted to take me home, to help me, but she just wanted to sell me! I escaped. She and a man are chasing me! They are at the back door! I was so afraid!"

I looked back at the door. They were nowhere to be seen.

Oh, no. Please.

I looked back at Mrs. Ba. Her face had tightened even more.

I was crying. "Mrs. Ba! They were right at that door, honest! I was so scared. I tried to run away from them. I am so sorry I bumped into you and made you drop your food basket! I am so sorry, Mrs. Ba! *Please, don't turn me over to the police!*"

I was sobbing loudly.

She apparently hadn't heard a word I said. Her head was turning, her eyes scanning all the market entrances, looking for the police, I thought.

I scrambled to my feet, ready to run if I got the chance.

She gripped my shirt collar tighter, picking up her shopping basket.

"Don't run," she said. "You have to come with me."

Many of the shoppers had stopped to look. I could hear them whispering as Mrs. Ba dragged me out of the market. "Look! She caught the pickpocket. Now she is looking for the manager. Maybe she will bring the girl to the police!"

When we were outside, Mrs. Ba let go of me.

"Now tell me again, child. Where is your family, and why did you run into me?"

Once again I explained to her about the woman at the temple. Now Mrs. Ba was really angry, not at me but at that woman.

"Damn those filthy animals! They all go after the young and innocent girls," she mumbled.

She looked at me carefully, pursing her mouth.

"You are hungry."

I nodded, suddenly unable to speak.

"Come," she said.

Moments later, squatting down on the sidewalk, I slurped the last spoonful of chicken rice soup into my mouth. I had been too greedy in my hunger. I had stuffed many hot peppers and bean sprouts into my bowl. When the seller had seen what I was doing she had quickly moved the vegetable dish away from me.

Mrs. Ba sat beside me, drinking her tea and waiting for me to stop eating.

The heat from the soup, from the hot peppers and the sun, was making me sweat heavily. My nose was running and my eyes watered. Sitting in front of this woman that I was trying to impress I didn't dare use my shirtsleeves to wipe my dirty face. I was trying to act more civilized, not like a country bumpkin. I reached over to peel off a piece of brown paper from a roll to wipe my sweat. The owner put her hand on the roll. "One piece, not two." She gave me a dirty look.

Mrs. Ba smiled. "Use your shirt. You will wash it later."

She put her glass down.

"Tell me the truth. Do you have any family or relatives living here?"

Without hesitation, I shook my head. "No one I can trust."

I told her I had left my village because of my family history, that there wasn't enough food for all of us. I left out the part that I was married and had a child. I told her again why I had run away from the sisters.

She nodded and sighed.

"Things happen for a good reason, child. They didn't pay you, but they gave you a place to live. Maybe they fed you like a dog, but they obviously fed you. You are much stronger now than when I saw you last. Otherwise, you could not have run away from that gang. So don't lose hope, child."

The hot peppers were still burning my mouth. I blew the air out of my mouth, poured myself another glass of water and drank it down.

"What is your plan now?" Mrs. Ba asked me.

I looked down to my feet, but I didn't answer her. My tummy was full but my head was empty. I was too tired to think, so very tired. Tired of wandering on the streets. Tired of running away. Tired of being afraid, of getting caught by my family. I wanted this all to end but I didn't know how. I couldn't ask Mrs. Ba to take me home. She had no home. She was a maid who worked to feed her family. She had been kind enough to buy me soup. She had taken her time to sit here with me. I didn't want to add another burden to her heavy load.

"Child, tell me what is in your mind, if there is anything I can do to help you."

At the gentleness and kindness in her voice, I burst into tears. I told her what had just gone through my mind.

She said softly, "This time you come with me. My boss has a daughter who is looking for a nanny for her children. Her husband is an Air Force pilot. They have two small girls. They live in the Tan Son Nhut base. Tonight they are coming for dinner. I will introduce you to them as my country niece."

She smiled.

"Maybe she will hire you."

CHAPTER 14

Mrs. Ba to the Rescue

I finished the bowl of soup Mrs. Ba had bought me. She got up, hailed a cyclo and climbed into the seat. First she rested her heavy basket of food under her feet. Then she signaled me to get in. There wasn't much room, only half my butt fit on the seat. I held on tight to the rail. She gave the old driver his instructions and finally turned to me with a stern look.

She had a lot to tell me.

"We are going to see my boss. You must be very careful. I know you are a smart and clever girl but remember, the rich people don't want their maids to be too smart. So, just remember now, you have no religion and you know nothing about politics. Especially, you don't know North from South. You are just a simple country girl, understand? Your mother is poor, and you have come to the city to find work to support your family."

She scowled.

"Keep yourself clean, always, but don't wear any makeup, and don't steal your mistress's makeup when she isn't home. She'll know. And don't look directly at the men of the family and never flirt with them. That is a no-no, understand? Don't spy on your mistress either. If by accident you overhear something you weren't supposed to, keep it to yourself. Don't tell tales outside about what is going on in your boss's household."

Her scowl deepened.

"Do you understand what I am telling you? You have to promise me you will *not steal.* If you want to be my niece, you must promise me now that you will follow my instructions. I'm telling you now so you know—a good job is very hard to find, and I don't want to lose my job because of you. Do you promise?"

I nodded my head vigorously. "Yes, Mrs. Ba, I promise!"

The cyclo stopped in front of a large gate. Mrs. Ba put down her basket and rang the doorbell. While we waited, she used her shirtsleeves to wipe off her sweat. She took off her cone hat and fanned herself. The gate opened and there was a young woman, her hands fixing her long black hair. She looked me up and down.

"Who is this?" she asked Mrs. Ba.

"Oh, this is my niece, Cam. I found her waiting for me at the market. Is Madame home?" Not waiting for an answer, she reached down and picked up the heavy basket and walked casually into the courtyard. I followed her, but I only took a few steps inside and stopped. I stood there as if my feet were planted in the ground. I couldn't believe what I saw.

In my fifteen years of life I had never seen anything so grand.

We were standing in a large courtyard. The Ly flower vines crawled along the high courtyard walls and gave out the most wonderful fragrance. There was a magnificent garden with many special kinds of flowers. There was a water fountain and there were bright colored birds in cages. The birds were chirping, singing and one of them was even speaking.

I thought I was dreaming. I had to be dreaming. *What kind of people actually live in this kind of palace? Is this a myth? Am I in one of the fairy tale books I had read?*

I couldn't move.

"Silly girl, what are you waiting for? It's real," the young housekeeper with the beautiful black hair whispered in my ear as she pulled me by the arm. She led me to the back of the house into the huge kitchen.

"Hurry up, girl! Untie the chicken and the ducks and put them into that cage over there before you squeeze them to death!" I had forgotten I was carrying a live fat chicken and two ducks by their feet upside down. They didn't seem to be moving.

A beautiful Vietnamese woman came into the kitchen. Suddenly Mrs. Ba was nervous.

"Madame," she said, "This is my niece. She has just come from the countryside, looking for work. May I keep her here with me for a few days? I hope you don't mind."

I was standing slightly behind Mrs. Ba, my arms folded respectfully and my head bowed low, my eyes fixed on the beautiful tile floor. My heart was pounding, my palms sweaty.

A pleasant scent of expensive perfume filled the air as the well-dressed woman with the cultured southern voice spoke quietly.

"Come here, child. Let me look at you."

I took half a step and stopped.

"What is your name, child?" she said. "Why, you're not even as old as my youngest daughter! Mrs. Ba, you say she is your niece? Yes, of course, your niece. All right, she can stay a few days, but then you must send her home to her mother. Why, she is too small and too young to work."

I burst into tears and dropped to my knees. Mrs. Ba thanked her boss, grabbed me by my shirt and pulled me to the back to the kitchen, shushing me. She scolded me for my boo-hoos.

"Stop crying. You're not dead yet, child. A few days here is better than living on the street. Now wipe off the tears and help me with the meal! I've wasted my whole morning with you. Now I am late! If we don't get this food cooked by the time the family comes home, we will both sleep on the street for sure!"

I felt guilty, and worried that she could be in trouble. I calmed myself. *Mrs. Ba is right*, I told myself. *I have a place to sleep tonight. I'm not dead yet. With her help, I'll have another chance to find a job.*

I squatted on the beautiful kitchen floor. I peeled garlic and onions and chopped up the lemongrass. I cut up vegetables. I even volunteered to kill the chickens and ducks and pluck their feathers. I cleaned and trimmed the fish, peeled the shrimp and scooped out the squid. While I did all this Mrs. Ba was marinating pork and making duck blood soup. She rolled the *cha gio* and sliced the beef paper-thin. She wrapped barbecued beef and marinated pork in *lat lot* leaves and stuck thin wood skewers through them. There was also chicken curry in coconut milk. There were crispy egg noodles and so much more, so many delicious dishes. The tantalizing smell of fat dripping on a hot burning charcoal grill was spreading through the house.

We worked until our backs were bent, our bones aching. We served lunch to the Master, to Madame and to their young daughters who were not yet married. When they were finished the three of us, Mrs. Ba, the young housekeeper and I, ate what was left over. Then the housekeeper went back to her ironing and Mrs. Ba and I continued to clean up the kitchen. My legs were cramped from squatting on the floor too long. My hands were wrinkled from washing and cleaning all the meat and the vegetables, and now the dishes and pots and pans.

So many of the foods Mrs. Ba had cooked were new to me. As I helped prepare the food, as tired as I was, the thought of this delicious new food was so exciting. Especially all the leftovers I would eat! I had pictured all the food and my mouth had watered as I muttered to myself, "I will use my fingers to scrape the bottom of the curry pot. I will use my tongue to lick the chicken and pork bones clean. I will use the rice to mop up the caramelized fish sauce at the bottom of the clay pot!"

I thought about when I was living in the countryside. We never had much. Only a few times in the year did my mother make a feast, at Tet or on the anniversaries of the deaths of my ancestors. Even then my mother never prepared such food as this. It had all been special-made food to worship the ancestors' spirits. And when it came to actually eating, I was always last in line. After worship the men and boys ate first, then the older women and the people who had come to cook, and finally the young girls. By the time it got to us girls, there was not much left. But I always looked forward to those special events anyway. Mother always scolded me about food, about eating. She said I always got too greasy. It didn't matter. Something about food has always made me happy.

That day with Mrs. Ba I was so happy I dared not show it. But she knew. How could she not know? I babbled all afternoon as we prepared the food for the evening meal. I couldn't help myself. I babbled and babbled. "Mrs. Ba, what's this? Mrs. Ba, what's that? Mrs. Ba, how many children does this family have? What do they do for a living? The Master must be very rich! How many wives does the Master have? I hate men that have many wives—"

Mrs. Ba just shook her head and spoke firmly, like my mother.

"Girl, you have already forgotten what I told you this morning. You must keep your thoughts to yourself. Rich people don't like you to be nosy. You must listen because I will not tell you again. There is nothing the rich dislike more than smart mouth maids. They also don't like maids who stick their noses in their business. Even if you know your boss is having an affair you look the other way, you keep it to yourself. Do you understand? It starts now. No more questions."

I thought about her words.

If I want a job, I better do what I'm told. Especially now. The only person that will help me is Mrs. Ba. I had better shut up. If she doesn't trust my mouth, out I go.

It wasn't easy but I shut up.

Later that afternoon, all the cooking done and the pots and pans clean, Mrs. Ba made two glasses of salty lemonade. She handed one to me.

"Girl, the table is set, the food is cooked. You have worked hard. Now sit and rest your bones before the family arrives."

I wiped my hands on my pajamas. My mouth was watering, and my eyes were blinking, but I didn't dare reach for the glass. I bowed my head low to show her my respect. "Thank you, Mrs. Ba. I am sorry I almost got you in trouble."

"Take it, child, take it!" She pressed the cold lemonade into my hands.

Then she nodded. "You are a smart young girl. Remember, tonight when I present you to the entire family you must keep your eyes on the floor. It doesn't matter who is speaking to you, child or adult, you do not look at them. If you must answer, you make it short and respectful. When you are dismissed, you must back out of the room, you must not show your back to them."

The hour had come. The doorbell rang. The housekeeper ran to open the front gate.

I was stunned. So many people, adults and children, aunts, uncles and grandchildren. I hadn't realized we were preparing a feast.

Six of the family's children were married, four with children and two newlyweds. As they all entered they kissed their parents and their aunts and uncles. "Bonjour, bonjour, Papa, Mama." I didn't know what they were saying, but their voices sounded very happy. Two of the young families had brought the children's nannies with them.

I snuck from my dishwashing duties to peek through the door into the living room. Not only were they speaking a strange language, they also were dressed strangely. I knew nothing then about Western clothes. I asked Mrs. Ba what they were saying.

"Rich Vietnamese people send their children to French schools so they can speak French," she said coolly. "Get back to your work."

One of Madame's daughters came over and stood in the kitchen door. My stomach knotted as I watched her approach. I dashed back to the water hole and squatted down, pretending to be busy washing dishes but watching her out of the corner of my eye. She was very pretty. She came in the kitchen and went over to Mrs. Ba.

She picked some food off the serving trays. While she was eating one of Mrs. Ba's delicious *cha gio* she asked her in Vietnamese, "Mrs. Ba, can you find me someone to look after my children? My young *au pair* just quit. She just ran off with our gate guard. She didn't give me any notice. Now my cook isn't too happy about doing two jobs. Could you please find someone for me?"

When Mrs. Ba looked in my direction, the daughter did, too. I knew they were both looking at me so I tried to straighten my back. It would make me look bigger. "This girl is my niece," said Mrs. Ba. "She looks small but she is a very hard worker. You should try her out."

I scrubbed and scrubbed the pots but my ears were burning.

I heard them even though they were whispering. The daughter replied doubtfully, "I don't know, Mrs. Ba. She looks too small and too young for the job. Why, she's only a child herself."

162

Mrs. Ba said carefully.

"Yes, she is small for her age but she's strong and she learns fast. She's had some school, too. Please, don't let her size discourage you. She's a good girl. You should try her out first. What do you have to lose?"

The woman gave out a sigh.

"All right, you've talked me into it. I'll take your word for it and give her a try. But don't let her know that I am interested. Send her to me when she has finished working. I want to see how my girls relate to her."

The dinner was set on the table. The adults and older grandchildren were seating themselves. The younger children were with their nannies in another room. Mrs. Ba called me over, "Girl, come here. Auntie Co Moi needs your help to take care of her children while she has dinner with the family."

I wiped my hands on my pajamas and walked over. I bowed my head low to my future new boss, I hoped. Mrs. Ba handed me two plates of food already cut up. I took the plates and followed the daughter to the play room

"Mi Mi and Ly Ly, come here," she said. "This is Cam. She will help you with your dinner."

The younger girl, Ly Ly, ran over to her mother and held onto her legs, screaming. The slightly older girl, Mi Mi, yelled at her mother, "No! I don't want her to feed me. I don't like her! I want to have dinner with you!"

Although I had been rejected many times, each time it hurt badly. I wanted to cry but I told myself, *You need this job, your baby depends on you. Besides, they are just little children and you are a grown up. Do what it takes.*

But do *what?* These weren't the country children I was used to. These were rich city children and they were spoiled. *What should I do? Should*

I take them or just let their mother handle it? While I stood there debating with myself, the mother made my decision for me.

"Now, girls, you must stay with Cam. Mommy wants to have dinner with the adults. Besides, all your cousins are in here."

The mother's eyes looked at me. My turn.

Okay, Cam, do it.

I put the plates of food down in front of the older girl, Mi Mi.

"Mrs. Ba made this special delicious food just for you," I said. "If you wait for me just for a minute, I will help you." I walked over to the crying child and bent down. "Would you like to go outside and play for a while?" I firmly picked up the crying child from her mother's legs. The child screamed even louder, kicking her feet and hitting me with her hands. I turned and said to Mi Mi. "I will be out in the garden with your sister if you want to come with me."

I picked up Ly Ly's plate and walked out into the garden.

The little girl was still screaming. I took her over near the bird cages. The birds chirped as I pointed to them. As I walked through the garden I exclaimed about how beautiful all the flowers were. As I talked, I spooned the food into her little mouth. At first she refused but after a bite or two she began to eat, becoming more controllable. The older girl had brought her plate out to the garden. So I sat down with her and fed her too.

We were alone. I talked to the girls as they ate, telling them the myth of the tiger, making funny noises to go with the story. They were laughing now. Suddenly, from hanging vines, a small salamander dropped onto the older girl's leg. She jumped onto my lap, her mouth opening but no sound coming out. I held both girls tight to my chest. I could feel their hearts pumping fast. I told them there was nothing to be scared of. It was just a small salamander and it was just as scared as they were, I said. I told them the myth of the salamander's life and how it began. I made more noises. They thought I was funny. They went to the walls and looked for other salamanders, laughing and chasing them. Their laughter brought out the other children, their nannies following them.

Soon I was sitting with the nannies, all of us watching the children play, the noise rising and the gossip flowing. Although I was very curious about the family, Mrs. Ba's warning was still in my mind. So I didn't ask. The truth is, I didn't need to. They couldn't wait to tell me. One of the nannies pointed at Mi Mi and Ly Ly.

"Their mother, Daughter Number Ten? Her husband's family comes from the North. He is an Air Force pilot. He doesn't make much money. *She's* the one who brings in the cash. But she's not as rich as her brothers and sisters. I hear they live in government housing at the Air Force base at Tan Son Nhut. I've never been there but the maid who just ran off told me it is a row house. They can't afford a lot of things, especially when it comes to paying someone to take care of their children. The maid said the worst part was that she couldn't have any visitors. She could only meet her boyfriends outside the gate. That's too funny! Now she runs off with the gate guard! There are guards everywhere, you know. I tell you right now. It is a very strict area. No one can come in without a permit card. So if you have a boyfriend, just forget it!"

She turned to me. "I hope you're not thinking about working in there, are you?"

The other girl, with darker skin and a square face, pointed at me and laughed. "What are you talking about? Her, a boyfriend? Look at her skinny body! It'll take ten more years to fill her out! What man would be horny enough to want her?"

The first girl gave her a dirty look and said to me, "Don't listen to her. You'll have more boyfriends than her! You stay here for few days with your Auntie Ba, and I will help you find a job myself. Don't go in the Base."

I thanked them for their concern but I had already made up my mind. Besides, they were just showing off. How could any of them get me a job?

No, this was my chance. Tan Son Nhut sounded perfect. *No one could find me in there!* And the two little girls, Mi Mi and Ly Ly, were my pass through the gate. I definitely wouldn't let this opportunity slip away.

"Mi Mi and Ly Ly, my sweethearts, how are you doing? Are you having fun? It's time to get ready to go home."

Daughter Number Ten was standing at the door.

The older girl, Mi Mi, ran to her mother. "*Me oi, Me oi,* Mother! Mother! We want Cam to come home with us!" The younger girl echoed her, "Yes, Cam is *fun!*"

The mother knelt down to the girls and held them in her arms.

"Are you sure?"

The little girls bobbed their heads up and down.

"Well, then," said their mother, "Why don't you girls go over and ask Cam if she would like to come home with us."

The little girls came over, blinking their eyelashes at me, asking me so seriously to come to live with them. Inside me, the little monkey in my stomach was jumping up and down.

The mother was talking to me. "If you decide to work for me I will pay you three dollars a month, with room and lunch and evening meals included. I will also give you two cents a day for breakfast outside. If you are smart, though, you will eat leftovers and save the money. When the girls are in bed and your chores are done you are free, but no boyfriends hanging around. You will also have one Sunday afternoon off a month to go see your friends and family."

I stuttered my thanks but my thoughts were in a jumble as she walked away with the children. Everyone was moving towards the gate to go home.

One Sunday afternoon off. But where can I go? Who can I see? And how long will it take me to save enough money to send for my son?

Part of me was thrilled, but now that I had the job, suddenly I was unsure. So many things I didn't know. Where was Tan Son Nhut Base? The maids said it was a terrible place. What will happen to me in there?

The little monkey was getting annoyed.

Food, silly girl! Lots of food. We eat!

Yes! Oh, yes! Now I could eat the delicious leftovers Mrs. Ba had set aside for me. Good food, too, not like the place before. I calmed down as I thought of the future. And the mother is nice to me! That had never happened before. Someone to be nice to me.

Except for Mrs. Ba.

I went and stood before Mrs. Ba, my hands folded in front of my chest. I bowed my head low, my tears streaming down my cheeks. I had met Mrs. Ba twice now, had known her barely a day but somehow it seemed like a lifetime. There were no words to express my feelings.

"Girl, what are you waiting for?" Mrs. Ba scolded me. "Your boss is waiting for you outside. They are ready to go." She gave me a gentle push, "Never mind the food. You'll eat later. Hurry up, child, before she changes her mind."

Her eyes were soft and misted.

"Go on now."

"Oh, Mrs. Ba," I cried.

I ran through the gate and stopped.

The Vespa's motor was already running, the two girls standing between the seat and the handlebars, held in by their father's arms. The mother sat behind her husband, her legs crossed to one side. She held tight around his waist, her head lying on his shoulder.

The five of us ride on their Vespa? I didn't see how. I stood there, not knowing what to do, where to sit. My new mistress pointed behind her at the rack on the back of the Vespa: "Sit there, and hold tight."

I clambered on. Off we went through the evening streets of Saigon.

CHAPTER 15

Tan Son Nhut

That was how we drove, all the way to the Air Base at Tan Son Nhut.

I remember how scared I was and how exciting it was. All the bright lights blinking, the streets filled with motorbikes, scooters and cars, cyclos and bicycles, the heat from the exhaust fumes in front of us mixing with the hot air and blowing in our faces.

I was holding on so tight to the seat. I did not dare move up closer for fear of touching my new boss's body. From time to time I would catch a whiff of her expensive perfume mixed with the thick street air. I also tried to eavesdrop on what they were saying but their voices trailed off in the wind. At the Tan Son Nhut gate the guards saluted us and the father just nodded in return.

It was late when we reached the Vietnamese officers' quarters compound.

I don't know what I expected but it was a disappointment. As the road curved around and the quarters came into view, I saw that they were all alike, large cement row houses with tin roofs and cement floors. To me, an ignorant country girl, they all looked like big funny tents. Not very impressive.

Each row house had a long corridor down the middle with quarters on either side. The houses were divided for two to four families, depending on rank. Most were occupied by pilots and their families. My new boss's quarters were in the middle of a three-family house.

So this was a row house. I had not understood when the nannies had said a row house. Now I knew. Oh well. I thought about my new boss. The nannies had been right about her situation. Her house was nothing compared to her mother's home!

My only duty in their home was to care for the girls. It was natural for me to care for children. I had been doing it all my life. Except this time I would get paid for it. The only other difference was that these children were richer. They needed more pampering. Even so, the work was easy and there was too little of it.

As the days passed I quickly became bored. The nights were another story. As much as I felt safe inside the Tan Son Nhut base, when night came I would get very homesick. I missed my family and especially I missed my son. I decided I needed to be more tired at night. But I had too much free time during the day. So I offered to do the dishes and help the cook. Very soon I had won the cook's approval, too.

My new bosses were nice, especially the wife. She liked me to serve afternoon tea to the other officers' wives of the same rank. Some were a lot older. The first time I served them tea, my boss introduced me to them with a smile. "This is our new *au pair*. Her name is Cam. She is new to the city and it will take time to train her. So, please, gracious ladies, go easy on her, yes?" Because of her kindness I wanted so much to please her, but sometimes the comments from the other women in the group made me so upset I wanted to pour the hot tea in their laps!

I remember one older wife remarking about me to my boss.

"Nhu, you won't need to worry about this girl. She is such a hick, and a little slow, too. Honestly, Nhu, you had a nerve to bring a stray home. I bet she hasn't even had her period yet. And her skin is as dark as a Montagnard! Good thing she is still young, she'll be good for a few years. Anyway, I was glad you fired that other one before she stole your man!"

They all laughed and went on with their cat meowing. I could feel my blood rise, my face getting hotter. For my boss's sake I tried my best not to spill while I pulled the hot tea into their cups. But I wanted to pour it on that woman's head!

My new bosses were unusual. Although upper class, educated in French schools, they didn't make me address them as Master or Madame. They told me to address them by their rank in their own family's birth order. He was the sixth child born in his family so I called him Uncle Number Six, or *Cau Sau*. She was the tenth child in her family so I called her Auntie Number Ten, or *Co Muoi*.

Unlike most of the officer's families living in the Base, both the husband and wife were working. Five days out of the week, it was the same routine. Each morning after breakfast he put on his dashing white pilot's uniform. He kissed his beautiful young wife and his daughters. He kicked off the stand of his Vespa and walked it out to the street. He put on his sunglasses and fixed his cap, started his motor, and turned right onto the road.

Then it was her turn. While she was changing, I dressed the girls and then walked her oped out to the street while she walked out with the children. Sometimes they would cry and wouldn't let go of her hands. She always patiently told them how much she loved them. Sometimes I wished she were my mother.

Before she started her moped she tucked the back train of her *ao dai* in so it would not get caught. She covered her hair with her scarf, draping it around her neck twice, and put on her sunglasses. She looked so elegant, like a movie star. She would say, "Girls, be good now, Mommy will be back at eleven." And off she went like a dream. At first I couldn't believe it was real.

This only happens in the books, not in real life.

Such harmony and style in a family sometimes made me wonder, if my father hadn't been killed, what my life would have been like. Some days I just stood in the street watching her ride away, letting my mind imagine their love story. *How romantic,* I would think. As I tended the children, morning after morning, I dreamed of such a life. Beautiful dreams. In reality I was a nobody from the poor lower class countryside. My mother was right. I had read too many silly books.

My boss gave me a little money every day for breakfast, but I always saved it. A bowl of leftover rice and a cup of warm water was fine for me. Sometimes when the cook felt sorry for me she would fry the rice with a little bit of oil and soy sauce. When little things like that happened to me I would remind myself, *life is good. Don't mess up. Accept who you are and get on with life.*

Each morning after breakfast I took the girls to the officer's club courtyard. We would play hopscotch or jacks. Sometimes we would chase butterflies, trying to catch them with our bare hands. Sometimes other children would join us with their nannies. The nannies would sit together and watch the children play. More often we would gossip about our bosses and what they were like or things they had done. Sometimes I thought about making up stories to tell the other nannies but always a vision of Mrs. Ba's sharp glance warned me.

I would bring the children home before their mother returned. Then their father would come home for lunch. After lunch the family took their nap. After the nap the father went back to work, but the mother stayed home. Weekends were free for both husband and wife. More often they went to see his family but sometimes they went to see her family. They always took me with them to look after the children while they enjoyed themselves with the other adults. I very much enjoyed these family trips, especially the ones to her parents when I could visit with Mrs. Ba.

In my first three months with them, whenever I got my pay I asked my boss for my half-day off. I would take a pedal cyclo across the city to Phu Lam where I would send my earnings to my mother. The only money I kept for myself was my breakfast allowance. On my third trip to Phu Lam my life changed again. The woman who I used as a go-between to send the money took my money the same as always before she gave me the bad news.

"Cam, I have bad news for you. Your baby is no longer with your mother. Your husband's family came down to your mother's house and took your son."

I don't remember what I said to the woman. The only thing I remember is wandering the streets of Saigon for hours. I don't remember how or when I got back into the base. I knew I had been gone a long time because my boss was very angry with me. She told me that if I ever did that again she would fire me.

For about a month after that Phu Lam trip, I was obsessive with the girls. Sometimes I even pretended I was their mother. My foolishness caught the cook's attention. One day, after I gave the girls a bath, I put them to bed. As I kissed the girls on their forehead, I said, "Sleep tight, my darlings, Mommy loves you." When I turned around to leave, there was the cook.

She took me in the kitchen and closed the door. She slapped me silly. Then she pointed her finger at my face and screamed at me. "You're a stupid girl! Do you want to get killed? To go to jail? Do you want to get fired? If you ever do that again I will tell the bosses! Do you understand me? If you are lucky they will only throw you out!"

Her stiff finger was waving in my face. I didn't understand. She kept on at me. "And then where will you be? Standing on street corners, that's where! On the street! That would be great, wouldn't it? Face it, your son is gone! You left him there! *You* did, nobody else! You are not the saintly one! Don't you pretend you are! You want another baby? Go get yourself pregnant! But don't you mess around with other people's kids!"

She was so angry she was spitting now as she talked, the white foam from her lips dripping down her chin. "These people are rich. They have money! They have position! They will skin you to your bones if you mess with their kids! Do you understand me? And one other thing! If you think jobs are easy to find, you are a stupid, stupid girl!"

I was shocked and I was scared. This was so unlike her. She had always been so kind to me. She had looked after me since my arrival. She had spoken to the boss about how wonderful I was. She had gotten my salary raised. She saved food for me when I was busy and couldn't eat. She had taught me how to cook, how to shop for food, so many other good things. I trusted her. She was the only person that I had told about my son. Now she was angry with me. I felt helpless. I was terrified that she might tell my boss anyway.

In my sadness and fear I went to the Buddhist Temple and lit incense. I knelt down and prayed to my ancestors and the Buddha to guide me on the right path, to give me the strength to go on with my life.

Life went on. The cook never spoke of it again. But it was always there between us although we were still close. I never quite understood what happened that day. She never betrayed me, and I knew she had saved me that day. But something in me had broken. Something had left me. I let go.

I buried my past and covered it with rock. I no longer thought about my son or my mother. By the end of that year I was a stranger even to myself. I changed my direction and I changed my image. I cut my hair short, and learned how to wear makeup and high heels. I removed the Quang Ngai accent and learned how to speak with the Southern dialect. Mini-skirts were in, but I didn't have the money. And I know my boss would not allow me to wear them. That didn't stop me. When my boss gave me her old clothes, I sewed them into mini-skirts that would fit my small body and hid them at my friend's place.

I buried my past, but not my dream of an education. It seemed so far away, though. When I felt really down, which was often, I would tell myself, "Girl, the sun rises every morning. You can't turn back the clock but you are still alive. Tomorrow you will do what you set out to do."

Brave words, sad words. The life of the poor is terribly hard to change. There were times I felt there was no hope for me. I asked the Buddha, I asked God, I asked my Ancestors, "What have I done so wrong? Why does my suffering keep following me?" I hungered for an education but I was a girl, a poor girl, without family or support. And this was Vietnam, after all, where education belonged to the rich, not to the poor. Surely I was over my head to dream such a dream.

In Vietnam the rich made sure the poor stayed that way. And what did the poor need an education for? They were stupid anyway. No, private schools were for the wealthy and public schools were for the middle class, for people who had connections. If you had money or connections you could send your children to French schools. You could hire tutors or pay for extra classes in a different school, whatever was needed for your children. Especially for the boys.

A boy could become an engineer, a doctor or a lawyer, someone important in government. Whatever it took, you made sure your children were in the top ten percent of their class. For those students that fell below, if it was your son, you found someone to pay so he didn't have to fight in the war or you got him out of the country. Corruption was like breathing. It was everywhere. It was the way things were done. I knew all this from my own life. Why couldn't I accept it?

In the end my desire to learn, to be educated, took a different path. If I couldn't go to school, I would have to be my own teacher again.

In the mornings when I took the girls out to play, I made sure to return home before the cook came back from the market. I would hurry to help her unwrap the food. If any wrappings were scraps of newspaper I would quickly set them aside before she threw them out. Afterwards I would dry the scraps and then wait for after lunch when the bosses were napping. I would take them out and read them. The cook knew what I was doing, of course, but she pretended she didn't see.

Sometimes the papers were stained with blood or fish slime. Sometimes the stories had the beginning or the end torn off. Even so, I would read them over and over, often making up my own stories, but when a story about the news in the world had been ripped, there was not much I could do.

However, I soon realized that my real classroom was serving afternoon tea for the wives and beer to the husbands at their card games. It wasn't just their gossip I heard, I also learned what was going in the outside world. Fortunately in the eyes of my bosses and their friends I was nothing more than a stupid country girl. I was practically invisible.

More often the men got together on weekend nights. They played cards, drank, and smoked their cigarettes. They talked about what was happening in politics and in world affairs. Sometimes they debated over who would be the next ones in charge of government. In the beginning I thought it was interesting but sometimes it got boring listening to the big boys talk and brag. I also didn't like cigarette smoking, and the smell of beer, but when they weren't talking about themselves there was always something I could learn.

I enjoyed the afternoon teas much more, because the wives had all the juicy gossip. My eyes may have been downcast, looking at my feet, but my ears stuck up like a little mouse.

The gossip was nasty, it was catty, it was great. The wives talked about everything, but mostly about other wives. They also talked about movie stars, which was a revelation to me. Since I had never seen a movie I had no idea movie stars existed. I learned quickly. They also talked about the wives or mistresses of government leaders. The infamous Madame Nhu, sister-in-law of President Ngo Dinh Diem, was always a hot subject.

A dangerous subject. In our country it was forbidden to speak ill about our authorities. What was more dangerous was that Madame Nhu not only had power, she had a vicious temper. If she found out you were talking disrespectfully about her, she would make your life miserable. She could have you arrested if she felt like it. She was a notorious woman. Not that she could stop all the talking, though.

Listening to the wives, I learned how Madame Nhu got her power. It seemed that President Ngo Dinh Diem had been a priest before he became president and still lived a celibate life, which gave him much respect among the people. One day when Madame Nhu's husband, Mr. Ngo Dinh Nhu, was out of town. Madame Nhu sent a message to the President. She said it was urgent but that she was too ill to come to see him. As a good brother-in-law President Diem came to see her. She received him in her bedroom wearing nothing but lingerie. He came over to give her a kiss on the cheek. Instead, she wrapped her arms around his neck and pulled him onto her bed with the camera clicking. After that she blackmailed him and became the most powerful woman in the country.

From then on, according to the wives, Madame Nhu expected all the people to honor her like our famous heroines the Trung sisters, the *Hai Ba Trung* of the past. They said Madame Nhu also had her own army cadets. As much as the wives badmouthed her, though, I sensed that underneath it all they envied her. Like her, most of these women were highly educated. Many of these wives could do better for themselves, but they were all afraid to break out. All except one.

One of the wives lived across the street. She was a small woman of 4' 11," although in high heels and a beehive hairdo she might reach 5' 5." She also had a firecracker personality and cared less about what other people thought of her. As she watched more and more Americans coming into Saigon she saw an opportunity to make a lot of money. She wasted no time. She hired a tutor to teach her English. Shortly after that she opened a bar, which became the scandal of the base.

The other wives would whisper, "She has sold herself out to those devil Americans! She is worse than Madame Nhu! Why, the other day I saw her bring some Americans to her home. They had dinner with her family! Honestly, her husband is a wimp! Disgraceful. What will that woman do next?—leave her husband and children and marry an American? Oh!"

Her maid was another subject for their claws. The wives disdainfully called the maid *Hoa*, meaning servant. Hoa was a stunningly beautiful girl from Hue, with black hair that fell to her knees if she let it down. But Hoa could not read or write. Again, the women hated her beauty more than her ignorance.

The more the wives talked about this woman and her maid, always behind her back, the more curious I became. Shortly after the woman opened the bar and started making money, her husband was promoted to a higher rank. This infuriated the wives.

Oh yes, afternoon tea was a delight, listening to the cats meowing. As for me, the more I heard about this woman the more I admired her for her determination. She always stood up for herself. While everyone else talked, she acted.

This gave me an idea about how I could improve my life. It involved her maid, Hoa.

One day I saw Hoa in the club courtyard while the children were playing. I moved closer to her and casually took out a piece of old newspaper to read. After watching me awhile, Hoa shyly came over to me and asked if I would read her *Vietnamese* boyfriend's letter from the battlefield. After that we become friends. I read all his letters to her. Soon she wanted me to write back to him. She told me what to write but it was not too romantic. I decided to help her.

At first I just added a few lines to the letter. However, as time went on, I chose to write it romantically, the way I saw the lives of my bosses. When I read to Hoa what I had written she loved it. The more she liked it the mushier I wrote, to the point that, when I read it to her, it made my cheeks blush.

Hoa offered to pay me but instead of accepting her money I asked her to bring me all the scraps of paper that her boss's English tutor had tossed in the wastebasket.

At first I wanted the scraps just to see what was written on them. Then slowly I learned the words by matching up the English words with Vietnamese words. I would repeat these words over and over, again and again. I memorized these words but without knowing how to pronounce them

I felt if I could speak English I could get a better job, maybe with the Americans. As much as I tried, though, as hard as I worked, I wasn't getting very far.

Outside of Saigon the war was going on but Saigon itself was safe, especially in the Tan Son Nhut base. By this time, however, the government was facing not only the Viet Cong but increasingly the Buddhists too. Soon there were Buddhist demonstrations all over the south. The news that a young monk had burned himself to death in the heart of Saigon swept through the base like wildfire. Then came word of an unsuccessful coup at the presidential palace. After that, there was no more loud talk at the afternoon teas, just whispers.

Then came the coup itself, when President Ngo Dinh Diem and his brother Nhu were killed while Madame Nhu and her children escaped. Finally we heard in Tan Son Nhut base that President Kennedy had been assassinated. The pilots were sad and dismayed by Kennedy's death. As I served them, I listened to their discussions about all the changes in South Vietnam's government. I also heard their fear that the new President Johnson would withdraw the U.S. troops.

Then, on top of everything else happening, the cook left.

She told me she was just returning to the country to care for her sick husband, but she didn't come back. Often I thought of her. I missed her and wondered if she missed me. We had worked together almost two years. After she left, my bosses decided that the children were old enough now to go to school half days in the morning. When they realized the cook wasn't coming back they also offered me her job. I would manage the house and look after the girls when they were not in school. My boss suggested that I learn to ride her moped so I could go to market every morning before the family woke. My days became very busy. Actually, between cooking, shopping and caring for the children it was downright hectic. At the same time I definitely had more freedom. And my salary went up another dollar.

When my boss became pregnant with her third child, the afternoon teas became less frequent, which I didn't mind. I missed the gossip and the news but I didn't miss the wives. As my boss grew more tired and sick she wanted me to take over more of the housework. At first I felt overwhelmed, but eventually I became good at it.

Four o'clock in the morning. I was already up and out, the laundry washed, the shoes shined, with me on her moped putt-putting off to market. I used my new freedom profitably. Sometimes I would just run errands for her but sometimes I would take in other jobs at the market to get extra pay. I also got very good at bargaining. And I still kept for myself the money that my boss gave me for food. Everything I did was on schedule. The laundry on the line, the market done, and breakfast made before the family got up. Then I got the children dressed and ready for school. The parents took turns taking the children to school.

From eight to eleven every morning, after they left, the house belonged to me. The first thing I would do is put on the radio I wasn't allowed to use. Then it was down on my hands and my knees washing floors. The bedding was changed every day, cleaned and dried and put back. Then I prepared their lunch. During the two-hour family nap I would iron and get ready for the girls. If there was time, I would secretly practice my English and read my papers. My boss began to tell me how thrilled she was with my work, especially my cooking. I worked very hard to please her.

Then one day I overheard her tell the neighbor's wife I was stupid and a slow learner.

"It has taken patience and time with her," she said. "For two years I've tried to teach her how to cook and she still can't cook as good as our old cook. At least she is a good girl, though. She doesn't run around with the guards like my last maid."

I didn't speak to her for a few days after that. I was crushed. I took her orders and did what she wanted and politely answered her when asked. But there was no chitchat, no small talk. I thought about leaving.

"Cam, what is wrong?" She stared down at me with concern. My hands were scrubbing hard on the bottom of a pot. "Nothing, Auntie," I said, the tears dripping down my face. I wouldn't look at her.

And then, somehow, she knew.

"Oh, Cam," she said, "I never meant for you to hear that. Yes, I did tell her you were stupid. But it was because I didn't want her to lure you away from us. I want you to know that I never think you are stupid. Even from the beginning, I knew you were smart!"

I felt better, but it was another reminder.

I was a servant, nothing more.

It was true that I had come a long way since the day I ran away from home. Here in Tan Son Nhut base I was safe from everybody. I had a full belly, good clothes on my back, and a clean bed to sleep in.

But now I thought about owning my own business.

In nearly three years I had saved all my earnings, buying myself a little gold from time to time, which I sewed inside my old clothes. The only thing missing in my life was my son, but it was just memory.

I thought I was ready to move on.

My plan was to rent a bed with a family I knew. Then I would buy myself a street vender cart to sell cigarettes or food at the markets or on the streets. I knew I wouldn't have a comfortable life like I had here but it would be my own life, on my own terms. I would pay for English classes at night. I would go to school.

CHAPTER 16

An is Wounded

Once again, it wasn't to be.

An had been wounded. He was in a nearby hospital. The woman in Phu Lam told me about him.

"Your brother has been shot. He's not dead, but he was wounded in the legs. He was sent to Cong Hoa Hospital. Your mother sent me the message from Duc Pho. Everybody is looking for you."

She gave me the address of the hospital.

I was shocked. *My brother is wounded and I didn't even know? How could I be so wrapped up in myself? It's all my fault! He might be dead and buried, for all I know!*

I just stood there feeling sorry for myself.

"He was shot over two months ago, but we couldn't find you," she reminded me.

I thanked the woman and took a cyclo back to Saigon, to the Tan Son Nhut base.

In the crowded streets I felt so alone. I wanted to cry, but there were no tears. The thought of my brother lying wounded, or maybe even dead by now, numbed me. *Oh, Buddha, what has my family done to deserve such grief? First it was my father, killed at twenty-seven, and now my brother?*

The following weekend I asked my boss's permission to find my brother. She said yes.

Walking into Cong Hoa Hospital overwhelmed me.

It was like a scene from the movie *Gone With The Wind*. There were large rooms, all filled with hundreds, a thousand, of young men lying on small cots, bandaged. Some were badly wounded. Some with blood soaked through their white headbands. Some without arms, some without legs, some with no arms or legs. Some of them didn't move, their wounds covered with flies.

The terrible smell made me want to throw up. I had prepared myself for a hospital but not for this. I didn't expect to see this many injured young men in one place. They all looked so gloomy, so depressed.

Many decades have passed, but I have not yet forgotten that day.

It must have been my short mini-skirt, my high heels, or my cheap perfume. Whatever it was, I sure woke up those sleepy men. As soon as they saw me they started howling, whistling, and banging on the floor.

"Sweetheart, are you looking for me?"

"Where have you been, darling? I've been waiting for you."

"Oh no, pal! She's my honey! I'm over here, love!"

They were so bold, so loud. I didn't know what to do. I was embarrassed and a little uneasy about their behavior. I gave them all a friendly smile and awkwardly went up to the nurse on duty.

In a little voice I asked her, "Miss Nurse, could you please help me? I am looking for my brother. His name is Tran An. He was brought here a few months ago. I'm not sure if he is still here."

She gave me a gentle smile and pointed to the corner of the room. "He is over there. What is your relation again?"

I didn't answer. I hurried anxiously through the ward to the corner.

There he was, my big brother, still in one piece, his arms and his legs all intact. However, one of his lower legs and ankle were wrapped in a plaster cast.

"Anh Ba," I said.

He stopped what he was doing and looked up at me. He looked like he had seen a ghost or had been shot again. His jaw dropped down to his chin, his mouth was open, and his eyes were large.

Then they narrowed.

"Is it really you?" He wrinkled his brow. "No, it can't be you. It must be some hot movie star coming in here to disturb this hellhole. Yes, that explains it."

He was more angry than pleased to see me. He looked down at his leg and tapped on the plaster.

"I have to go to take a shower," he said coldly.

I just stood there.

I wanted to cry but not in front of all these animals. I was so upset at my brother's reaction. Here I had taken the day off without pay, I had taken two different cyclos to get here, I had snuck around my boss to dress up pretty to cheer him up! And now he was acting like I was a stranger off the street!

"Hey, An! An, old man, you dirty dog! You still got it, hah?" The voices yelled out so loudly he couldn't ignore them.

"She is my *sister*!"

Hooting.

"Oh, yeah, sure, we know. We've got one at home just like her!"

Loud, coarse laughter.

An looked up at me, frowning. "What are you doing? And those clothes! What, you didn't have enough money to buy a few more inches of cloth for the skirt? And what is that on your face?"

Obviously my brother didn't like how I looked or how I was dressed.

Instantly I reached down to my skirt and tried to pull it down.

"It's the new fashion. All the girls in the city wear them."

"You are not a city girl," he said.

I wish I had worn a long ao dai, I thought. *I wish the floor would crack and I could go under it.* I had to get out of there.

I handed him the package I brought with me.

"Brother, I brought you some cigarettes and some candies. If you like, you can share them with your friends. I am glad that you weren't hurt badly. I will leave so you can get to your shower."

My tears were about to burst. My brother reluctantly accepted my gifts and pointed to the end of the cot.

"Go on, sit down. Don't bring more attention to yourself than you already have."

After that I came to the hospital at least once a week to visit my brother. I always brought cigarettes. A few months later, my brother was discharged from the hospital, and from the South Vietnam army.

The South government didn't give him any pension or back pay.

An didn't want to return to the countryside. But unlike many men who had come to the city, his leg injury meant he couldn't drive a *cyclo mai* - motorized rickshaw - or even pedal a cyclo. And he didn't yet have a high school diploma. He found work in a factory, but was soon laid off.

My brother was on the streets with no money and no job.

Every month for three years I saved my salary to buy small bits of gold. I had stitched them all into my clothes so no one knew I had any money. Instead of using my savings for English lessons, I would pay for him to get his diploma and buy him a job.

The day I was to give him the money he was waiting for me in a small café in Phu Lam.

A young woman about my age sat at the table with him. She was beautiful, young and sweet. Instantly, I didn't want her there. She stood up and bowed her head when my brother introduced her. I didn't catch her name because my brother was stuttering.

He was nervous, very nervous.

When he lit his cigarette, his hand was shaking. His shirt was wet under his arms. This is not like him, I thought. I tried to be calm but I asked myself, *what is this pretty girl doing here? Why is she is here at our meeting?*

Looking at him I thought, *He is up to no good!*

I wanted to scream at the girl and tell her to get lost.

I wanted to tell her, *Foolish girl, did you know my brother is a married man. He has three children and no job! If you think he is a rich man, you are a fool! Find some rich old man to gold-dig, and don't waste your time!*

As for my brother, my thoughts were boiling.

Brother, so help me, if she is your second wife or girlfriend I am leaving! I put my education on hold to pay for your high school diploma. I paid for your driver's license so you could make a living driving a taxi. So you could support your wife and children at home! And here you are. Just like all other men! Just like our father, our grandfather! One wife, two wives... I don't want any part of it! What did you tell this young girl? Are you going to get this girl pregnant and go home and ask your wife to accept it? That's the way our father did it. Didn't you learn anything? I can't believe you are doing this!

My head was about to explode. I took a sip of cold, salty lemonade and cautioned myself.

Be calm. Don't say anything. Calm.

"Sister, thank you so much for coming. I have met with a man who is helping me to find a job. He has said the job is mine. It is a government job. You know, sister, if I get this job, I am set for life. I will be the driver for the Director of Taxes out of Tuy Hoa, near our home. However, I have to pay him tonight or otherwise he will give it to the next person. That is why I asked you to meet me here."

He was very nervous. His stuttering was worse. He reached across the table to hold the girl's hand.

My heart was pumping and my head was buzzing.

Part of me was ready to fight for my sister-in-law, for my nieces and nephews. Part of me was jealous of the girl. It was hard for me to explain the fearful sadness that I felt then, as if I was being left out by my brother, being used.

I could not put up with this.

I got up from the table and grabbed my cone hat. I went out to the street curb and waited for a cyclo to come.

My brother had left the café and followed me.

"What's wrong?" He asked me.

I looked back at the café. Between my tears and my whimpering I said, "Brother, if you want to destroy your own family that's your business! But I won't help you do it! You should think about your wife and your children before you take a mistress!"

I flagged down a *cyclo mai*. It stopped in front of me.

I took money out of my pocket, shoved it at my brother, and got in.

"Sister, sister," he called after me as the cyclo roared into traffic. "I will not do anything stupid that will hurt my children!"

I raised my hands in the air and shouted back at him.

"Tell that to your wife and children!"

The loud noise of the cyclo carried my voice away.

CHAPTER 17

Cinderella at the Officers' Club

I cried, knowing I had to put my dream on hold again.

It had broken my heart as a child when I had to stop going to school so my younger brother Ming could get his education. It had broken my heart that my mother had chosen him, not me. Now my older brother was taking my dream.

Yes, this time I did it willingly but I couldn't stop the tears, the despair, the heartache. In my grief I asked myself if my brothers would ever know how much I had given up so they could have their future? Probably not, because I would never tell them.

I reminded myself that they were my family, my brothers, my blood, that I should not be selfish. But I couldn't stop the pain. And I had no one to share it with. Worse, even though my boss had been good to me, the thought of being her servant for another three years made me ill. My pain, my anger, changed me.

And not for the better.

To escape my misery I worked harder at my job during the day. But at night, after the family was asleep, I began to sneak out and go over to the officers club. I would sit outside the chain link fence in the dark and listen to rock & roll music.

Sometimes I would peek through the fence and watch the rich girls and officers dancing their way through the night on the club veranda. Sometimes I tried to copy their moves, trying to twist myself as they did. All the while the sounds of Chubby Checker and Elvis Presley were pounding, drumming through the night air. In spite of my not understanding the words, their voices and their music made me forget my troubles. Sometimes I would hug myself like a partner, dancing alone in the dark. I let my thoughts run free. Free to dream.

But dreams were not enough. I wanted to be like those rich girls, if only for one night. I made up my mind, and my nerve. I had found a break in the chain link fence, large enough for me to squeeze through. I would sneak into the next dance they held at the officers club! I would stand on the dance floor and let the music blast my eardrums! If I got caught, I would lose my job but I didn't care. I was sick of being good. I was tired of doing the right thing.

A few nights later there I was in the dark, sneaking through the hole in the fence, my tight mini-skirt, high-heeled sandals and makeup rolled up in my hand. The night was hot. Soon I was at the back door of the club near the ladies room. *Everyone is drunk,* I told myself. *No one will see you.* Like a mouse I was in through the door and into the ladies room.

I had done it. My stomach was woozy and my knees were about to buckle. *Hurry, hurry.* Quickly I pulled on my lime green mini-dress and stepped into my sandals. Sweat was dripping off me, the mini-dress sticking to my tiny body. I rolled my black pajamas in old newspaper and shoved them under the sink. Slowly I moved to the mirror and looked at myself. My mini-dress was hanging just right, above my knees. My long hair was up like Madame Nhu's. I started to put on my makeup.

Oh, God what am I doing? I suddenly thought. *Why did I let myself do this? What if my boss or his friends are here? What if they find out? I should have listened to Mrs. Ba!*

I struggled for control.

You chicken, never mind Mrs. Ba. She's gone back to the countryside. Forget her. Just do it! Once in your life, do it. No one will recognize you.

Do it!

This was it. Three years of listening, watching. Three years of copying the officers' wives. Weeks of practicing in high-heeled sandals at home. This was it. *This night belongs to you. You are not who you are. Your bosses are home with their new baby son. No one will know you. Go on, girl, soon the dance will be over! You're not even on the dance floor! No one will know you.*

I couldn't move. I was scared to leave the ladies room.

Suddenly the door was flung open. A young girl in a pink dress rushed into the bathroom. She threw her purse on the counter and went to the toilet. When she came out, I was still standing there. She looked at herself in the mirror and fixed her hair. She opened her purse and took out a small bottle of perfume. She daubed a little on the back of her hands and on her neck and her chin. She turned to me, "You want some?" Before I could speak, she touched her fingertip to my neck.

"Why are you in here and not out there dancing?" She laughed. "Come on. Come with me. I'll show you how to have a good time!"

She grabbed my hand and pulled me out the door. She held on and before I could even find the words we were on the dance floor. She laughed and started to do the twist. Suddenly everyone around us was twisting. So many people were jumping and twisting I didn't know what to do so I just kept moving to keep from being hit. With my eyes still frantically on the girl I was unaware that one of my boss's friends was headed straight for me.

By the time I saw him it was too late. I tried to move away but he blocked me and began to twist. I had no way to avoid him. Awkwardly I began twisting my knees and my ankles. Boy, it was a lot different from doing it by myself! At first I nearly fell on the floor, but the beat of the music made my body loose. Without knowing how, my body started moving with the rhythm.

And just like that I was one of *them*, one of the young beautiful people as they twisted and shouted! They howled. They squealed. Some were twisting forward, some backward. Some twisting sideways with one foot on the floor, and some so low down they were nearly flat to the floor. They seemed to be having so much fun. It was wild! At that minute I didn't know or care who I was dancing with. *I was dancing.* Fortunately, my boss's friend was too drunk to recognize me. *It didn't matter.* I felt so alive. My heart was pounding with excitement. I just did what the others did. I was having an amazing time.

Then came a slow dance and everybody seemed to have a partner. I tried to move off the floor because I didn't want to dance that close but my boss's friend grabbed me and pulled me to his body.

His speech was slurred. He breathed heavily into my ear.

"Where did you come from, my beautiful girl?" I could smell the alcohol on him. I tried to get away from him, but his grip was too strong. When the music stopped I quickly went into the bathroom, grabbed my things and let myself out the back door of the club.

No one noticed.

I took off my high heels, changed into my black pajamas, squeezed through the small hole and ran back to my boss's house.

I lay on my bed and relived the night, still excited. How amazing, how magical it had been! *Thank God, he was so drunk,* I thought, *otherwise how could I explain it to my boss?*

Then I must have fallen asleep because I didn't hear someone moving in the kitchen. A voice was saying, "Cam, Cam, make me a cup of coffee." At first I thought I was dreaming but when I opened my eyes there he was, my boss's friend.

He hadn't gone home after the dance. Well, that was nothing new, because my bosses treated him like a younger brother. My heart was pounding. Quickly I slid out of bed and went over to the table to make him his coffee. I tried not to look at him but I could feel the blast of his eyes on my body.

"Cam, do you have a sister?" he asked.

"No, sir," I replied.

"Hmm," he said, "I thought I saw someone who looks like you at the club tonight."

My hands were trembling when I handled his coffee.

He wasn't as drunk at I thought. Oh God, I forgot to take off my makeup! He will tell my boss! At the same time I told myself to relax. *He was a gentleman, a fun guy,* I thought. *He had always been nice to me.* I leaned over the table to give him his coffee without looking at him.

Instead of taking the coffee from my hands, his hand went right at my breast.

In my horror I dropped the hot cup of coffee in his lap. I backed off to the kitchen wall. I covered my chest with both of my hands. Everything happened so fast. I didn't know what to do. My mouth was open but I was speechless.

At the same time he gave out a loud yell. He kicked the chair back, jumping up and down like a monkey. In a panic he was trying to unbutton his pants. His loud yell had awoken both of my bosses. They were at the door in no time.

"What is going on here?" the wife asked. He pointed at me, "She spilled hot coffee on my legs. It was an accident." The husband looked me up and down and fixed his glasses. In a strange voice he ordered me, "Make Uncle Tuan another cup of coffee and bring it out to the living room. And this time be more careful."

"Tuan, are you all right?" the wife asked. He nodded his head. She turned to me "Luckily for you I had boiled that water last night so it wasn't too hot. Otherwise he would be badly injured and you would be in a lot of trouble."

After that episode things weren't the same in the house. Although I was still the cook, my bosses hired an old woman to care for their new baby boy. I still served the teas and the beer for the card games but I could tell from my bosses' attitude that they didn't believe the coffee spill was an accident. And in any question between me and their friend, I was bound to lose. I was only a servant.

After the accident, my boss's friend tried to avoid me whenever he came to visit. But soon he became bolder. Whenever I served them beer at their card games, he always asked me to light his cigarette. And he would stare at me, so much so that the other men began to comment on me. Another time he came in the kitchen and asked me to iron his uniform. As he handed it to me he whispered, "Don't spill coffee on it. There's a dance coming up at the officers club."

He thought it was very funny.

I thought it was time for me to leave.

BOOK THREE:

Hopeless City

CHAPTER 18

My Godmother

I knew there was no future for me in Tan Son Nhut.
Although the wife had been very good to me, I knew she would not
be unhappy if I left. Even if she didn't know what had happened the
night of the dance, which I doubted, their friend's interest in me had
become obvious to everyone.

I'm also sure the wife thought that I could become a problem for
her with her husband's friends, maybe even with her husband. And
finding good help wasn't difficult in their circle. When I finally told her
I was leaving, that I wanted to try different work, it was a quick
conversation and I was gone.

I didn't think it would be hard to find a new job. I had experience
and I knew a lot of people from different places. I also knew the wife
would give me an excellent reference. I could have had a good steady
job. Except it didn't work out that way.

I had been in a cocoon, a fantasy. Now it was broken. After Tan Son Nhut, all my demons came rushing back into my life. My life suddenly seemed so worthless, so aimless.

For whatever reason, I couldn't stay in one place too long. It seemed as if I was always running away. I would take a job for a month, other times for a week, and often just for a few days. Always I would quit. From job to job I moved constantly, all over Saigon and from city to city all over the south, from Nha Trang to the Delta down to Ca Mau.

Then one day I couldn't take it anymore. I packed the few belongings I had left and became a drifter. I stopped trying to work. I moved in and out, staying with acquaintances, friends, relatives—anybody willing to take me in for a few days or a week. Finally, about the time I had gone through all my savings, I also ran out of places to stay. When people saw me coming, they closed their doors and quietly told me to go away.

I knew it had been wrong to use other people like that, but I didn't know how to pull myself together. I couldn't get going again. I was sinking in the quicksand. Even though I was the problem, every time other people rejected me I went ballistic. I would rage, "I have two hands, two legs. I am a strong girl! I don't have to beg!"

But each time I was rejected I went deeper into depression.

You are no good. You are a worthless bum. You are selfish. You are a lousy mother. The list of my shame went on inside my empty head. I cried, I begged for my ancestors' forgiveness. There was no answer.

I continued to live my life without purpose.

One day I showed up at the job of my Aunt Moi, hoping that she would take me in for a night. She said she had no room for me, that she was tired of me showing up without warning. She was still family, though. She gave me money and directions to go see her friend, Mrs. Hue. "My friend Mrs. Hue has worked for a family a long time. She might help you find you a job." As I turned to leave she said, "Cam, don't come back here until you find some work!"

Outside, I climbed into a motorized cyclo. Except for the clothes on my back, all my belongings were in my hand.

When the cyclo driver pulled to a stop on a corner of Hai Ba Trung in Phu Nhuan, I got out and paid him, looking doubtfully up at the second floor of the address. Hesitantly, I climbed up the long staircase. When I reached the top there was an open space with a small wooden sleeping platform, a divan, next to a window. On the divan was a pillow, a straw mat and a blanket neatly folded. I put my belongings down on the divan and used my hands to straighten my shirt and comb my unruly hair. Then I took a deep breath and knocked softly on the door.

A woman in beautiful white pajamas opened the door.

"Yes, are you looking for someone?" she said.

"Mrs. Hue...?"

"No, I am not Mrs. Hue. I am Vu Linh. Mrs. Hue went to the market. Would you like to come in and wait?"

I gulped down the saliva in my mouth. "No, thank you. I will wait out here."

"All right, then, if that's what you want."

She was about to close the door when a loud noise came from my stomach. The woman looked at me for a minute then said, "I am in the middle of my breakfast. Would you like some?"

I was embarrassed. I could feel the blood rush to my face. "No, thank you," I lied, "I just ate at my aunt's house."

She nodded politely and closed the door.

I sat on the platform and smelled the French bread toasting and the coffee and my mouth watered. My stomach kept making loud noises. I had a bigger problem than my hunger, though. For the life of me I couldn't remember what Mrs. Hue looked like.

Like my Aunt Moi's husband, Mrs. Hue's husband had gone to North Vietnam. He had taken their son with him, leaving Mrs. Hue and a daughter a few years younger than me to fend for themselves. Mrs. Hue had come to Saigon to make money not only to support herself and her daughter but also her mother. She had been very fortunate to land the job with Vu Linh.

When Mrs. Hue arrived at the top of the stairs she didn't know me, nor I her. But when I told her who I was, she knew my family and my life story. She definitely was not thrilled to see me show up at her job but, with the pride of one countrywoman to another, she didn't kick me out. She brought me inside and introduced me to her boss.

"This is Vu Linh," she said.

The words *Vu Linh* normally meant Wet Nurse Linh. Clearly, however, this woman was no wet nurse. When I had talked to her earlier I had been too nervous, staring at my feet when I spoke, but now I had a good look at her.

I liked her instantly. Actually I had liked her from the moment she had offered me, a stranger, part of her breakfast. She was an unpretentious woman, down to earth. She wore her hair pulled back in a bun. She didn't wear any makeup or lipstick, but her faced glowed, her skin even and smooth like soft brown eggshell. Her lips had a natural pink gloss. She had a slight overbite that made her look so charming. Her white, almost ivory, pajamas gave her the look of an angel.

When she asked me what I was doing and where I was going. I told her I was between jobs. Which was true, sort of.

"Is that why you are here? To look for a job?" she asked. "I can't give you one, but you can stay as long as you like," she offered. I don't know how Mrs. Hue felt about that but I was so grateful not to be on the streets tonight. Actually Mrs. Hue was happy not to lose face with her boss.

That night, as I lay under the mosquito net on the divan with Mrs. Hue I didn't ask any questions. No matter. Mrs. Hue was happy to have a countrywoman to talk with and also she was dying to gossip.

When Vu Linh married her husband he was already married to Vu Linh's half-sister, who was ten years older than her. According to Mrs. Hue's version, the second marriage was the older sister's idea. She didn't want to share the wealth with an outsider woman, of which there were many, since the husband had many concubines, any one of whom could have ended up as a second wife.

I listened to Mrs. Hue but I'll never know the true story.

As for her being the second wife, Vietnamese men with authority had all the power they wanted in society. If they could afford two wives they had them, whether in the countryside, like my mandarin grandfather, or in Saigon like Vu Linh's husband. Sometimes the first wife could not give the man a son. Sometimes it was just because the man wanted them.

According to all the stories, including his own, Vu Linh's husband was a northerner from a wealthy family well known in the North. He was educated by the French. As the Communists under Ho Chi Minh rose in the North, most of his brothers and sisters joined them. He didn't. He left his family and escaped to South Vietnam. He had twenty dollars in his pocket when he arrived in the South. He landed a job in construction and quickly made enough money to start his own company. He was a brilliant and instinctive businessman who never doubted his instincts. He grasped concepts intuitively and acted without hesitation. It was about this time he met and married Vu Linh's sister. She was seventeen.

Soon his business was booming and, by the late 1950s he was, by some accounts, the richest man in South Vietnam. He owned many rubber plantations up in Dalat. He owned shipping lines. He built tall office buildings, hotels and airport runways, both in the north and the south. He even built schools for underprivileged children, one for boys and one for girls. He was fluent in several languages and French was his second natural language. He served for a time as the Trade Attaché to France. Another time he served as Ambassador to SEATO. He traveled to many countries on business and government missions. Always, it was Vu Linh who accompanied him.

His only mistake was one that many self-made wealthy men have made. He thought his instincts in business would make him a success in politics.

In 1958 he campaigned for the Presidency of South Vietnam against Ngo Dinh Diem. Luckily, or unluckily, depending on how you look at Vietnam history, he lost. During the campaign Diem had offered him a high position if he withdrew but he had refused him. To the victor go the spoils. After the election Diem's government confiscated eighty-five percent of his wealth. Even so, he remained a wealthy man; a fascinating, charming, wealthy man. He didn't just have two wives, he also had many concubines, and he had many children by his first wife and these concubines. The first wife had thirteen children with him. I also knew some of the children of his concubines. Vu Linh, however, never had children of her own.

Before his political campaign, Vu Linh's husband had owned many homes. When I met Vu Linh, though, he only owned one house in an alleyway off Truong Minh Giang Street. It was a big house, though, four floors high with about thirty rooms. It was almost a small hotel to accommodate his large family and all the servants. Most of the first floor was the large living room where the father held court. The dinner areas, the kitchen and maids and nurses quarters, were in the back. Above the first floor were hallways with rooms off to each side and balconies. Each child had a private bedroom. For himself and Vu Linh, however, he rented a small apartment in Phu Nhuan. It was a very strange relationship. Every night he would go home with Vu Linh, even though it was the first wife who had borne him their thirteen children.

After he lost the election to Diem, he didn't bother to work for about twelve years. Gradually his close friends and followers left him as he sank into himself. Unfortunately the bad ones hung around. He grew more and more depressed over those years. As he lost heart, the ones leeching off him began to lure him into experimenting with drugs and gambling. By the time I met him he was nearly broke. For a rich man, that is.

This was the situation when I met Vu Linh.

Whatever Mrs. Hue or anyone else thought about her, I liked Vu Linh as she was. She was not only beautiful she was kind and gentle with everyone I saw. My reaction to her was simple. I was happy to have a roof over my head and a warm bed to sleep in. I was happy to have someone truly care about what happened to me. During the time I stayed with Vu Linh she took me with her everywhere she went, shopping, playing cards or visiting the first wife.

To Vu Linh, I was her foster child, but to the other members of the family I was little more than one of the staff. When they noticed me at all they looked at me as one of Vu Linh's charity children that she had taken in off the streets. When we visited, most often it was to help out in the kitchen with the meals. Even though they had many people working for them, family meals were always a major production. For lunch and dinner, it was not unusual to have thirty people or more to serve. And Vu Linh was a gifted cook.

Vu Linh was the kind of second wife every Vietnamese man dreamed of having. She always treated the first wife with respect and as someone with authority. She was beautiful and gentle. She loved all the children as if they were her own. She wept hard when the oldest girl died in a car accident. She moaned when her husband abused another girl. She was so proud of them for all their success.

Even though she was a second wife she went to church daily. She spent hours praying for everyone she loved, including me. She served her husband and his family with dignity. I never once heard her complain about anyone in the family. She loved her husband with all her heart. By then she knew she would never be able to bear children. So she took in children like me to give us a second chance. Sometime she even took in her husband's illegitimate children and cared for them, too.

For all the months I was with her, when we visited the first wife I was never invited up to the higher levels of the house. I listened to everything, though.

When the children in the family spoke with each other or with their father, they spoke in French. When they spoke to their mother, however, or to Vu Linh or to a servant, it was always in Vietnamese. As I watched them communicate with each other, I felt a yearning to learn another language. One day I mentioned to Vu Linh my wish that I could speak French like the first wife's children. Vu Linh scolded me.

"You are too poor to speak French!" she said.

Then a few days later she asked me a question.

"You are a poor girl with no education," she said. "If you had the choice, what would you like to do with your life?"

Carefully I chose my words. "I would like to learn a trade to support myself. Then, when I had enough money, I would like to go to English class."

She took a long look at me. "Why *English* class?"

I said, "Because more and more Americans are coming to Vietnam. The better I speak their language the more chances I have to work for them and earn better pay."

She said nothing more. A few days later, after dinner, she called me into her room.

"Would you like to join this household? What I mean is, the owner of this building, who lives downstairs, also owns a sewing school. I've asked her to admit you as a student. Since you don't have money to pay, in exchange you can work for her to pay for your lessons. If you do well in sewing, I will loan you the money to open a small shop some day."

Listening to her, I was happy and afraid at the same time. I mean, why would she want to help me? I didn't understand. In my experience the only person who ever offered me anything was Mrs. Ba. Even then she actually only fed me once. But now, this woman was not only offering me a place to live and food to eat, she was offering to send me to school to be a seamstress. Did my ancestors' spirits feel sorry for me? Was my bad luck finally over because I had suffered enough? Or did the spirits want to punish me, because lately I had been thinking selfishly, and lazily. I didn't really want to work. Did Vu Linh know that? Was she that cruel? She knew my dreams. Was she teasing me? This couldn't be true. Good things didn't happen to me. What did she want from me? Was she really a kind and good person? Could I trust her? I was so confused.

Vu Linh must have known what was going through my mind.

"Child, I am doing this because I see something good in you. You have a good heart and an intelligent mind. I just want to give you a chance to be what you said you wanted to be. Hopefully, some day in the future you may help someone else as I am helping you. I took you in as my foster child because I like you and I care about you. Go on now, go and think about that."

I joined her household and I went to school.

Vu Linh may have thought I was intelligent but the owner of the school didn't. Very quickly she made it clear to me that I wasn't smart enough to be in the same class with her other students. She made me clean the toilet and sweep the floors. In fact, she treated me worse than a servant. She also knew I wouldn't tell Vu Linh.

However, her staff and the other students in the school felt sorry for me. When the owner was not around they secretly taught me how to thread the sewing machine and how to hem and stitch.

For three months I worked hard and hoped she would have a change of heart. She never did. I learned as much as I could from the students but the owner refused to teach me anything. She continued to treat me like dirt. One day Vu Linh asked me to show her my work from the school. I didn't want to create trouble but I had nothing to show her. So I told her the truth. She was so angry she went to the school to confront the owner.

The owner told Vu Linh I was stupid. "The girl doesn't know how to do math! How could I teach her? She didn't know how to add or subtract or divide! How could I let her cut material? Material costs money! I let her stay because you are my tenant. I only took her in as a favor. So take her home with you."

Staying with Vu Linh was a special time in my life. I had love and I had security. I wanted it to last forever but I was not the only child she had taken in. I particularly remember one man named Quy.

Quy was from North Vietnam. He was much older than me. Vu Linh had taken him in and had raised him from the time he was a child. Some people said Quy was her husband's illegitimate child from before he came South. Others said Quy was from the disadvantaged boys school her husband had opened before he had lost the election. I didn't know. When I first met Vu Linh, Quy had grown to manhood and was long gone.

After Vu Linh took me in, however, Quy returned.

During this time Mrs. Hue had gone back to the countryside. I had become Vu Linh's daughter and her personal companion. She took me shopping, and bought nice things for me. She paid for my English classes, too. We spent a lot of time together. When Quy returned I guess he expected to be her favorite. When he saw her pay more attention to me he became jealous. He began to torment me when Vu Linh was not home. When I mentioned this to Vu Linh she told me not to pick fights with him.

"I cannot throw him out, Cam. Like you, he had no family. I am his only family."

One early morning while Vu Linh was at the church I was doing the laundry. Quy came home after being out all night. He was very drunk. He lurched through the door, his shirt unbuttoned, his pant leg torn, his face red like a rooster's comb. He growled at me with contempt and started towards me. I knew I was in danger. Slowly I backed away from him into the bathroom and quickly shut the door and locked it. I prayed that Vu Linh would come home soon.

"Hey stupid girl," he yelled. "Fuck your mother! I am hungry! Come out here and make me some food or I will break down the door and beat the hell out of you! Open it! Open it, you fucking girl! I am really pissed! Open the door now!"

His fists were pounding on the door. It made me scared that the door would break. My heart was pounding so fast I had to put my hands over my chest. This went on for some time, then the pounding grew weaker and finally it stopped. I heard heavy footsteps moving away then a thump, more cursing, and a moan. Then nothing. I waited and still heard nothing. Finally, keeping the chain on, I opened the door and peeked through the crack. Quy was sprawled on the floor passed out.

Carefully I unlocked the door and tiptoed around him. Then I gathered most of my things and went out the door.

I was on the street again.

Later, I came back to the house to apologize to Vu Linh. She was kind and understanding but Quy was still there. It was a painful meeting.

"Cam," Vu Linh said softly, "I was very sorry to see you go." Her eyes were sad. "But I understand. It was your choice and I respect that. Some things I cannot change but, please, if there is anything I can do to help you, come see me. My door is always open for you."

I walked away lonely. Vu Linh was out of my life. Or so I thought.

CHAPTER 19

My Brother's Nanny

The morning I ran out of Vu Linh's house I had taken shelter with my distant cousin, Song.

When I say distant cousin, I mean very distant, fourteenth or fifteenth removed. Maybe even further. Actually, the only things we both knew were that our last name was Tran and that we were related.

Song had come to Saigon long before I did. He had married a woman from an orphanage. They owned a small electric supply shop. It was not much of a shop, much less a home, one square room built next to a water wheel. During the day they used the room as the shop. At night they stacked the supplies in a corner to make room to sleep. By then, they had already taken in four boys from the countryside. There really was no room for me, but they were kindhearted people so they took me in anyway. At night, for themselves, they had a small wooden divan to sleep on. For the boys they built a loft of plywood over the piles of supplies.

I shared a straw mat with the dog. In the doorway.

Song suggested I should invest in a small business of my own. A small business to him meant a pole, two baskets, a few pots and pans, and enough bowls and chopsticks to serve people. I didn't like that idea too much. So I went back to see Vu Linh. With her help, and Song's, and my own meager savings, I bought an ice cream cart.

I set up my stand next to Song's shop.

Even though Song and his wife were nice to me, sleeping in their doorway night after night made me feel so nonhuman. So I worked like a dog to make enough money to move out. Every day I was up before anyone else in the house. I did my chores and rode my bicycle to the ice cream factory. Because I was new to the business, at first I only went to the factory once a day. My cart wasn't large and if the ice cream melted I lost my money. As I learned how to sell and started making money, I went to the ice cream factory two, sometimes three times a day.

Every night I closed up my shop carefully and counted my money. I set aside a payment on the money I owed to Song or to Vu Linh. Then I set aside enough for the next day's purchases. What was left I sewed into my clothes. I didn't want anyone to know I had money. Eventually I made enough money to pay a first month's rent. I happily left the doorway.

Truly, nothing can smell as bad as a Vietnamese slaughterhouse on a hot summer day. And living next to one, as I now did, should have been the most terrible punishment. It smelled wonderful to me, though. It was my own place.

Finally, I was my own boss.

Such beautiful words. *My own. Mine.*

Now that I had my own business and my own place, I worked from early morning to late in the evening. I didn't just sell ice cream. What little skill I had learned in sewing school I put to work between ice cream customers. I knitted, I hemmed, and I stitched, taking the overflow work from a shop nearby. It didn't pay very much, but it filled spare time and with the extra cash I earned I could pay for English lessons sometimes. As for my stand, if I had to go away for any reason, even for a day, I would rent it out to someone. When I returned I took it back.

I thought life was beautiful. Life was great! I was no longer hiding from my ex-husband or afraid that he would find me. I wore my mini-skirt. I went to nightclubs if I had the money. I did what I wanted, when I wanted. For the first time in my whole life I thought I was free. But in the back of my mind, in my superstitious way, I didn't believe it would last.

Then my older brother's letter arrived.

It had been almost a year since An got his government job in Tuy Hoa up the coast. He had brought his wife and his three young children there to live. From time to time he would write to me. In every letter he asked me to come live with his family.

This time, he asked me for help, but not for money.

"Dear, beloved Sister." he wrote, thanking me sincerely for all that I had done for him. It was very sweet of him, I thought. Yes, I was his sister but I also had helped him because I loved my nieces and nephews. I did it because it was my duty to our family.

Love and duty.

His wife Thuong had to return to Duc Pho to care for her sick mother, he wrote. Being the only child, the burden had fallen on her. He asked me to come to Tuy Hoa and take care of his children while she was away so he could keep his job. I wasn't too happy about it, but I loved my brother. So I rented out my ice cream stand and off to Tuy Hoa I went. I stayed up there with him for three months until his wife returned. Then, my duty done, confidently I went up to him.

"Brother, please, I would like my ID card back and a bus ticket to Saigon."

He sat on the wooden bench and drank his tea, his t-shirt draped over his shoulders. He picked his teeth with a toothpick but said nothing.

I was getting impatient, and annoyed.

"You know, Brother, I spent all my money on your children. I don't have money for a ticket. If you can't buy me a ticket, that's fine, just give me my ID back, please. I will sell my jewelry and buy a ticket myself."

He took another sip of his tea.

"Sister, I have a good job now, thanks to you! Now, let me return the good deed. Stay here, Sister, with us. Let me take care of you. It's not good, a young woman living alone in a big city."

He nodded solemnly at me.

"There are many good men here. You will find a good husband. You need a family of your own. I don't want any trouble to happen to you! You need someone to look after you."

I couldn't believe what I was hearing.

"Brother, I don't need a husband. I don't want a family! I especially don't want anybody to look after me. I can take care of myself. I want to be free! And just for the record, Brother, I have never gotten myself into trouble, ever!"

"There, you see?" he said. "That's the point I'm trying to make, You say you want to be free! Sister, there is nothing free. The way you come and go as you please? It is nonsense. And you never get into trouble, you say? Let's see now—you've been married once, engaged twice and you are not yet twenty years old! What do you call that?"

I was angry now.

"That's not fair, Brother! You know I only married because Mother forced me. As for Vien, that was a mistake. Yes, I promised Vien I would marry him. I thought I liked him. But I changed my mind the same week, so that doesn't even count! Tell me, how many girls do you like, Brother?"

I pointed my finger at him.

"As for that Ban Me Thuot guy, just what did you tell him?"

My brother was as calm as could be.

is a good man, just what she needs. She is one lucky girl! He is a strong man. He will manage her. She will thank me someday!"

I muttered to myself.

"You think so, Brother? I will thank you someday? Just you wait and see."

From that moment on, it was a game to me, nothing more.

Phuc was a big pain in the butt. After our engagement he was at my brother's house day and night. If I wanted to go down to the beach, he wanted to come with me. If I wanted to go to the market, he offered to take me. And always he bragged about how many girls in Tuy Hoa were in love with him. About how many girls he had already had sex with, and who was still a virgin and who wasn't. What a stupid man! I tried not to show it but my patience was wearing thin.

I was also getting anxious. A month had gone by already! I had to get back to Saigon. I had been waiting for the right time to come. Now I realized I had to make the right time.

Always before, when I asked my brother and Phuc for permission to go to Saigon, no matter how I pleaded, their answers were always the same. No and No. I knew Phuc didn't want to lose face. I also knew he liked money a lot.

This time when I came to them, I told them to keep my ID card. That I wouldn't need it. I wasn't going back to my old life, I told them. All I needed was for them to go to the town hall and get me a seven-day travel permit.

"I mean, really, what kind of a job could a woman find in a big city in seven days? You guys are smart men but even you couldn't get a job in seven days. And where can I go without my ID card except to come back here? I don't have any money! What are you so afraid of? I have to come back. I don't want to get caught in Saigon without my ID. I don't want to go to jail!"

The way they looked at each other I thought, *Almost there.*

"Look, I haven't been very clear about this. I've been confused. The reason I need to go to Saigon is to sell my ice cream stand and gather my belongings! Don't you think it's a shame to waste all the money I invested in my ice cream stand? Also, some people there still owe me money!"

I looked at Phuc.

"Phuc, it's my only dowry!" I pleaded. "There is one other thing. I also owe money to some people. I want to settle with them. I don't want them coming up here after my husband!"

I paused and then gave them my throwaway line.

"Of course, if you don't think I need to go, that you can take care of all this for me, well, that would be fine with me, too! Here are the people's addresses." I picked up a pencil, jotted the names and addresses on a paper and handed it to them.

And held my breath.

Please, please, this time be in my favor!

And so it was.

Within days I had a seven-day travel permit, a round trip bus ticket, enough money to eat, and two changes of clothes. The morning I left Tuy Hoa, as I waved goodbye to my brother and Phuc, I promised them I would return soon. Well, of course I would, they thought. They were so smug. It was wartime. Everyone had to carry their ID or travel permit with them at all times or risk prison, probably a beating, or even being tortured to death. Of course I would come back.

When seven days went by, and then several months, they finally realized that they had been taken. Months later, when Phuc finally came to Saigon to find me and bring me back, the me he was looking for was no longer there.

That was all in the future, though.

CHAPTER 20

The Fortune Teller

On that crowded bus from Tuy Hoa I clutched my permit. I was still so angry with my brother I promised myself I would never speak to him again. Because of him, my hopes, my dreams, my life, might have all slipped away again. I was angry with myself, too, for not taking charge of my own life.

It took two hard days to reach Saigon. When I stepped off the bus, it reminded me of the last time I had escaped. The difference this time was that I knew the city now and a lot of people. Having no ID was a serious problem, though. In five days my permit would expire. Then what?

As much as I didn't like it, the only person who could help me was Song. The thought of sleeping in the doorway again was so shameful. How humiliating it had been for me. But I didn't have another choice. *You have to survive*, I told myself. Life is hard when you are born with nothing.

So I went to see Song.

Song not only welcomed me back without question, he gave me the money he had collected from the rentals of my ice cream stand while I was away. I was very grateful. It wasn't much money but it helped me get started again. So, like that, I had my ice cream stand back. Staying out of jail was another story. My travel permit quickly expired.

I still didn't have enough money to buy a fake ID.

The local police routinely searched homes and shops, often at night, supposedly looking for Viet Cong. I didn't know how many Viet Cong they ever caught but one thing I knew for sure—they caught plenty of innocent people like me without proper identification.

Countless nights, I lay on my mat half awake, waiting for the police to come. When they did come, pounding on the door, Song would try to delay and fumble unlocking the door, giving me time to grab my mat and crawl inside a small supply box under the boys' loft. The fear and intensity were so great that, after each search, my body would shake. Even so I was caught twice. Luckily, Song lent me the money to bribe them so I didn't have to go to jail.

Then came the young street gangs. They chose my ice cream stand as their meeting place. They told me never to tell anybody about them or I would be punished. They also had the nerve to charge me dues and eat my ice cream without paying. At first I was scared but the more I thought about it the more I became angry. I'd be damned if I would let them use me as a base to terrorize the other small businesses! My first thought was revenge. But what could I do? I could pull the rug out from under those punks. I would sell my ice cream cart, that's what! That way I could protect myself, and Song, too. I thought I was being so smart.

Before I could sell it, I was kicked out of Song's house.

That evening I had planned to see the policeman's wife who wanted to buy my ice cream cart. We had not yet agreed on how to do it. I wanted her husband to get me a permanent resident ID but she didn't want her husband to get in trouble. We were still negotiating.

Song came over to my stand that afternoon. He couldn't wait for me to close, he said.

"It is urgent. I need to talk to you."

I had been about to close anyway, so I did. I thought it was about him and his wife. They had been fighting a lot lately. We went to a soup stand a block away and sat on low stools. Song was quiet and not very friendly. He ordered two bowls of soup without asking me what I wanted. He started eating in silence. The situation was so awkward I couldn't stand it. I asked him, "What's up with you, big brother Song? Have I done something wrong?"

Instead of answering me, he started to lecture me, not giving me a chance to speak.

"What's up with you! Yes, there are things in life we must do to survive. But we know there is the right way and the wrong way. I know you had many difficulties in your life. You have tried very hard to make it on your own. Because of who you are, what you were doing, I tried to help you. However, sometimes things don't work out. Your bad omen seems to travel with you. Lately you seem to have chosen a wrong path, to take the easy way out. You chose to join those devils, that gang! Well, that is your choice you make, the people you associate with, but I don't want to get involved! I want you to move out of my house."

I was shocked. I was angry at him.

"What are you saying? Have you been... spying on me?"

Song would not look at me. In a hard voice he said, "I didn't have to spy. You right there outside my shop. I saw you. Those boys are bad news. You let them hang all over you. You give them money. You give them food. You flirt with their leader!" His voice was rising. "I saw it with my own eyes! I don't want them making trouble for me now. I don't want you in my house."

He stopped talking and waited for my response.

I was stunned.

I wanted so much to tell him, "Song, I thank you so much for helping me when I was in need. If you had asked me I would have told you. I am preparing to move out. To protect you and your family! I am selling my business to a policeman's wife in exchange for my ID card."

But the words out of my mouth were different.

"What are you saying? You want me to leave? For your information I had nothing to do with those rats! They force my money same as everyone's!" I got up from the table quickly, mumbling, "Thanks for the soup. My time is up. Yes, I am sorry that I overstayed!"

I walked out onto the crowded street without looking back.

All the good things he had done for me suddenly vanished, replaced now with anger at his injustice, his cowardice. He had judged me before he asked me. The rage inside me combined with the heat, the noise, the terrible smell of the slaughterhouse. Inside my head I was screaming.

One of these days you will see! You hypocrites! You will see! I will get even with you all!

I wandered through the streets, thinking about how hard I had tried to do the right things, and how the right things always deceived me, leaving me helpless.

Why, Buddha? Why?

I stood in front of the steel gate and pressed the doorbell hard.

A tall, deeply tanned American man in shorts, his hairy chest shirtless, came to the gate. He took one look at me and yelled loudly over his shoulder for his housekeeper.

"Hey, Mama-san, get out here! *Mama-san!*"

A middle-aged Vietnamese woman scurried out.

"Why do you come here now?" she hissed. "You know the Americans are home during the day and weekends!" The Americans worked nights. This was a weekend.

"Moi! Can I come in?" I asked.

"No, you can't! The Americans are waiting for their women. I also have to leave soon."

"Please, can I wait for you out here?"

She hesitated, and said, "No, go back to your ice cream stand. I will meet you there." She turned and hurried inside. I didn't want to go back to my stand. I didn't want to see Song. Instead, I just crossed the street, squatted on the hard ground, and waited for her.

Moi was one of my ice cream customers. Sometimes I would visit with her at night just to get out of Song's house. Sometimes she would come and hang out at my ice cream stand when she was lonely, which was often.

When Moi came back that night, I told her what had happened. She snuck me into the house while her bosses were too drunk to notice.

The next day I went to the policeman's wife and told her that she could have the ice cream cart for nothing. That was my revenge on that gang. The thought of those punks trying to extort money from a policeman's wife made me laugh. Also, I didn't care anymore. At that time of my life, when anything bad happened to me, I just walked away from it, not looking to the future. I never went back to see Song, either.

For the next few weeks I woke up early and left before the Americans came home from work. I spent my days wandering the streets, or visiting the zoo or markets. I also started dropping in again on people that I knew. My aunt, my cousins, my friends. Each night I waited for the Americans to go to work before I came in and took shelter.

As much as Moi pretended everything was fine, I knew she feared her bosses would find out about me. If that happened she knew she'd be fired but her kind heart couldn't tell me to leave. One day I caught her vomiting in the bathroom. I didn't need to ask what was wrong. I told her I had brought her the bad luck. I promised I would leave as soon as I found work.

Moi put in her two cents worth. "Go see this fortune teller in Cho Lon. She will help you," she said. "Maybe she can give you some magic to take away your bad omen."

Cho Lon was Saigon's Chinatown, although many Indians lived there as well. Cho Lon had many temples and many more fortune tellers. I was always going to see them. I decided to see the one Moi had recommended.

Heavy curtains blocked the sunlight from entering the fortune teller's chamber. Inside, the smoke of incense was thick. Pictures of terrifying gods hung on the walls. The shelves were crowded with exotic knick-knacks and temple statues. In the center of the room a middle-aged Indian lady in bright robes and dark makeup knelt on a rich rug behind a low teak table. She wore gleaming long gold earrings, a bright scarf covering her forehead. Gold teeth shone between dark red lipstick. Her long fingernails were painted black.

She watched me approach. Her eyes were powerful and penetrating. In her dark palm she held a huge deck of cards. Nervously I knelt and waited for her to tell me how bad my life would be. I told her the year of my birth. Not taking her eyes from mine, she slowly lay cards down on top of the table. Finally, she dropped her eyes to the cards and in a cracking voice, spoke in perfect Vietnamese.

"You say you were born in the year of the monkey. That is not a good omen. Your future does not look promising. There are dark forces overshadowing your life. You have tried but you cannot get out from under them because many other evil spirits are following you, trying to pull you down to them! Child, the cards never lie. If you do nothing about this, if you give up, you will be dead before you are thirty years old!"

She stopped talking. She stared at me with those deep, sinking, dark, dark eyes.

I was shivering and tears were rolling down to my cheeks. She took a deep breath and closed her eyes, mumbling something I couldn't understand. Suddenly her hands were waving in the air, her eyelids fluttering, her eyes rolling. Her body jerked and stiffened. She moaned loudly. I thought her soul was leaving her body. I thought she was dying.

I was no longer crying. I was frozen in fear.

I wanted to run outside and call for help but I couldn't move. A few minutes later she seemed to be back to normal. She shuddered and opened her eyes and took a sip of her tea.

"Child, I have made contact with your ancestors' spirits. Your omens are very dark but your ancestors say there is a way to restore your luck. This what you must do to save yourself – if you do not do this, you will be dead by your thirtieth birthday – you must purchase a pretend coffin here. You must pay the fee for my services, of course. You must also purchase with gold a white paper outfit. I will get it for you. You will dress in the white paper clothes, climb inside the coffin and lie down and pretend you are dead. I will conduct the ritual to send your dark soul away. Then I will give you the magic for your new soul."

She paused and leaned forward.

"If you do what I say your luck will return to you. You will be a new person with a new life. You'll make a lot of money. You'll get all the luck I have promised you. But, child, if you *don't* do these things...."

She sat there, her eyes boring into me.

I wept uncontrollably.

"Oh, Madam, have pity on me! I have no money. I have no family. Is there any way you could help me? Can you not perform the magic to send my dark soul away? My luck will come as you have said. I will make my money and return to pay you many times over—!"

She cut me short. Angrily she said, "Child, who do you think I am? Someone to fool with? Without payment, there is no cure! If you are mocking me, I promise you, you will be dead long before you are thirty! Then it will be too late to come back here and cry about it!"

"Madam, please," I begged. "Let me work for you for nothing. I will be your servant, your maid. Please, I want to live. I don't want to die!"

"Get out!" she ordered furiously.

I ran out, my pockets empty. The fortuneteller had taken all the money that Moi had loaned me.

Sick at heart I stumbled through the busy streets, mumbling to myself, "The year of the monkey. What year is this? How many more years do I have to live?"

I tried to remember how many Tets had passed since I had left my mother's home. I couldn't think. Days, months and years were all jumbled together, meaningless. One year went and another year came, that was all. Then I tried to recollect all the events of my years in Tan Son Nhut. When had the young monk burned himself? And the coup when Ngo Dinh Diem and his brother were killed. When was that? And who were the leaders now? I didn't know.

Suddenly I missed my life in Tan Son Nhut base. I missed the afternoon tea gossip.

I thought about why I had come to Saigon, about my goals to make money here and get my son back, about being independent. My life was rushing past me and I had done none of these things! Everything I had touched had turned to ashes. Now an angry fortune teller had just told me I would die before I was thirty. I couldn't even remember how old I was!

Deep in my despair I stepped out onto the street.

Cho Lon streets are death traps. Whatever the hour, the streets were jammed with bikes, jeeps, trucks, Hondas, rickshaws and motorized cyclos, all of them going too fast, all of them acting as if they were the only one on the street. The noise of loud horns, screaming engines and curses was deafening.

I didn't hear any of it. I didn't notice most of the curses were directed at me.

CHAPTER 21

Ham and Cheese Sandwiches

I didn't stop. I was in a daze. It was all a strange dream, One foot in front of the other I kept walking. I was nearly to the other side when a young woman just missed me, yelling, "Fucking moron, you! Watch where you're going! You stupid woman! If you want to kill yourself, fine! Just don't involve me, you—"

"Sorry, sorry," I mumbled, my cone hat covering my face. I stepped up to the curb.

IThe young woman was so mad she pulled her Honda to the curb beside me, grabbed me by the arm and turned me toward her. The anger in her face turned to surprise.

"Oh, my god! Cam, it is you! What are you—? Cam, you almost got us killed!"

I didn't know who she was or how she knew me. I just stared at her. In her excitement she babbled, "Don't you remember, Cam? When we worked in Tan Son Nhut base together?" She paused, "No, I guess you would not recognize me now. I am Hoa!"

I looked at her, but my mind was a blank.

"Sorry, I don't- *Hoa?*"

She didn't look anything like the girl in Tan Son Nhut base. Her nose was sharp looking like a foreigner's. She wore heavy makeup. Her big dark lovely eyes now had thick false eyelashes. Her fingernails and toenails were long and painted. Her hair was cut short in a boyish hairdo. Her mini dress barely covered her hot-looking body. She had on tiny high heels. Large dark sunglasses sat on top of her head. She looked just like the girls that Moi's bosses brought home.

"Come on," she said, grabbing my hand. "We'll have coffee." She pulled her Honda onto the sidewalk and locked it.

Sitting on the chair, I took off my cone hat and fanned myself. Hoa ordered a Vietnamese iced coffee for herself. I said I didn't want anything even though I was very thirsty, but Hoa wouldn't hear of it. She ordered me a Coca Cola with ice. I loved cola but I couldn't remember the last time I had one. I drank it greedily. The fizz made me belch loudly. Hoa laughed and then said, "So, Cam... what do you think, huh? I know you must be wondering why I dress like this. Right?" She laughed again. "I'm a bar girl, Cam. I work in a bar now and I sell tea." She swept her hands down her body. "I have an Australian boyfriend now. He likes me to dress this way."

I stared at her. "You are very stylish and very beautiful. I hardly recognize you."

She laughed out loud.

"Why don't you just say I dress like a tramp! It doesn't bother me. Life is funny. How hard we try to be good and do the right thing, and yet we always end up wrong. Do you remember when we worked in Tan Son Nhut Base?"

"Yes, I do," I said. "You had a soldier boyfriend."

"Yup. Him. And you wrote all those love letters. It was fun to live in that dream world. But real life is cruel and painful." Her eyelashes were wet. "Cam, we were so young, so ignorant." Her soft voice was lost in the noise of the street.

I hesitated before saying, "You quit your job before I did, right? To go to Ban Me Thout to be with him."

"You have a very good memory, Cam. Yes, I did. I wanted so much to be married, to have someone to protect me. I wanted so much to have a family, have children."

She sounded somewhat sad.

"And...." I said.

"And, he was married."

She sipped her coffee, looking out over the street.

"You know what? I didn't care! I thought if I did what he wanted he'd leave his wife and marry me. It sounds so selfish, doesn't it? I would be a home wrecker, but I didn't care! I loved him so much. How stupid I was. I gave him my virginity. Then he persuaded me to work in a bar. At first it was wonderful. I learned to speak English. I just sold teas and talked. After hours I was home with my man in the flat he got for me. And then I got pregnant."

Her long fingernails lightly scratched the tabletop.

Her eyes were far away.

"It was his baby, no one else's! He was the only man I slept with. But he denied it. Then he said if I wanted to be with him I had to have an abortion. I said no, that I wanted to have his baby. A week later his wife came to my flat. She beat me up so bad I miscarried. I packed my bags with a friend and returned to Saigon. But I couldn't go back to being some pilot's maid. It was hard enough keeping their hands off me in Tan Son Nhut. So, here I am, a bar girl. At first I was so angry at that man I would have hurt him if I could. But now I think he did me a favor. I have a wonderful Australian man now. He loves me to pieces."

She looked at me closely.

"How about you? Why weren't you paying attention crossing the street? You scared me half to death, Cam! I got so angry because I thought you were one of those people who try to cause accidents to make money!"

"I am sorry about that. I was so confused and depressed."

I told her my life story since our days at Tan Son Nhut base. I also told her about the fortune teller. She looked straight at me and said, "Cam, no one gives a shit about who we are or what we do. If we vanish from this earth tonight no one will give a shit for very long. It just makes more space for them. We all live for ourselves, no one else. So I don't plan to give up my life so easy, and don't you either! However, if you're serious about killing yourself, please, try to have some fun first, huh? Come on, let's go."

I sat on the back of Hoa's Honda, holding her waist, looking down at her bare beautiful legs. A group of youths on flashy, powerful new Hondas drove up on both sides of us. They all flirted and whistled at Hoa before roaring way. She turned her head, "Did you see that? Those son-of-a-bitch rich kids! I hate them!"

She dropped me at the corner of Truong Ming Giang and Nha Tho Ba Chuong, near Moi's house. It was still too early for the Americans to go to work. I would walk the streets for a while. As if reading my mind, Hoa said, "Cam, why don't you come see where I work?"

I shook my head. "I don't think so."

She said, "Why not?" Then, "Oh, very well. If you change your mind here is where I work." She gave me a card. "Oh, I have a new name now. I am called Ly Ly." She revved her motor, quickly made a U-turn and in seconds was lost in the street crowd.

Moi had been waiting for me at the gate.

"Don't come in," she cautioned. "One of the Americans is sick. He is staying home. You must find some other place to stay."

That night I returned to take temporary shelter with Vu Linh. After the fortune teller, though, I was scared to cross a street. I was scared to go out at all. I feared the fortune teller had put a hex on me. I was scared Quy would kill me. I was scared of sharp noises. I was scared of my shadow. This couldn't go on.

The more I remembered how safe I had felt at Tan Son Nhut the more I wanted to go back there. But without any ID papers I couldn't work for the military again. Instead I took a job as a housekeeper for a family living on the civilian side of Tan Son Nhut Base.

This side of the Base had no gate and no guards but these people lived in beautiful, big villas on large landscaped grounds with garages and cars. Their homes and grounds being so large, few people lived on this side of the base. The home of my new bosses, the Nings family, was decorated in the modern French style with a long veranda separating the large main house from the cooking and laundry areas. Like their isolated neighbors, the Nings were definitely rich.

The father, in his sixties, was retired. The oldest son was an engineer. The son's young wife was the most beautiful woman I had ever seen. She was so elegant and classy, like a china doll, it was easy to see why the whole family practically worshiped her. She didn't have to lift a finger at home. All she had to do was go to her job, which she loved. She was a teacher. She taught French at the Chinese school in Cho Lon.

Every morning the old man took his daughter-in-law to work. Then he took his two younger children, a boy and a girl still in their teens, to school. Then he took his old fat wife to market or to her engagements. While they were out, the main house was locked. I could not go inside.

The old lady controlled every aspect of their daily schedule, from entertainment to shopping to tailoring. She also did all the cooking. Although I was the only servant, my work was not that difficult. As housekeeper my duties were to clean the house and the family courtyard, do the laundry, change the beds, wash the dishes and do whatever else the old lady wanted. The Nings were okay, neither nice nor nasty. They were my bosses and I was their servant. I ate after they were finished. At night, they slept in their comfortable beds and I slept out in the garage on a rough bamboo loft reached by rungs tacked to the wall.

People are so strange. With all their money, though, what I remember most about the Nams was their passion for American ham and cheese sandwiches.

It seems the old lady had a friend who worked in the American Base. Sometimes this friend collected the American food left over from the weekend and sold it to the Nams. One Monday night they bought five-and-a-half ham and cheese sandwiches, all wrapped in cellophane. They were so excited as they set up the table on the veranda and put on some music, French opera I think. Then they all sat down for their feast.

The engineer was away on business that night so the old lady gave me the half sandwich, telling me what a privilege it was for me.

"One must have special taste to appreciate the American food," she said, "But I want you to acquire it."

I was so excited that I hurried out to my quarters in the garage.

I pretended I was them.

Carefully I unwrapped the cellophane, opened my mouth wide, took a bite and chewed. I nearly choked. The funny taste from the cheese made me gag. The yellow stuff on the bread had soaked through and the bread was so mushy it stuck to my mouth. I went outside and threw what was left in the bushes for the birds, if they wanted it.

Now I knew why Moi's American bosses loved her cooking.

It was very lonely for me.

The newspapers they read were all in French. The family language was also French. The only time they spoke Vietnamese was to give me orders. No one came to the house when they weren't home so I was alone all day long. I was also locked out of the house most of the day and there was no electricity or lights out in the garage.

Life was so calm it felt like death.

Actually, lonely doesn't quite describe what it was like. The Nams seldom spoke to me. I was practically invisible. With no electricity or even oil lamps in the garage I could not read or listen to a radio. With no officer's club or officers' wives, there was also no gossip or excitement. Because of my fear of the fortune teller's curse I didn't dare leave the grounds, much less go near the road, so nobody knew where I was. So I had no visitors. My only entertainment was watching my friends the salamanders as they skittered on the stucco walls trying to mate or catch bugs.

After four months of this isolation, I made up my mind that life was too short to live in fear. I would take my chances. I would try my luck. The next day I told my bosses that my mother was dying and I had to go back to the countryside.

They seemed sorry to see me go.

"You are a good worker," they said. "Only a young girl like you and you didn't cause us any trouble. You learned fast and you did a good job. We're sorry your mother is ill. If you return to Saigon, if you work for us again, we will give you a raise."

Before I started to regret lying, the old lady asked me to lie out all my belongings. She said she just wanted to make sure I had enough to get home but she really wanted to make sure I hadn't stolen anything. When she saw nothing except my clothes, she handed me my pay. I rolled up my stuff, shoved it into my bag, bowed my head and I was gone.

Did I have a plan? No, but once again I didn't look back.

A few days later, I stood in front of the full-length mirror in the bedroom of Moi's boss. My new green *ao dai* and white pants nearly touched the floor. In my new high heels I was almost 4'11." As I put on my makeup, Moi sat nervously on the corner of her boss's bed, looking out at the front door.

"Hurry up, Cam! We're not supposed to be in here. They'll be home soon!" I took a last look at myself and we walked into the courtyard. Moi, a plain woman, looked wistfully at me.

"You look so beautiful," she said. "I envy you. If I were ten years younger, I would go with you!"

I reached for her hand and gave it a hard squeeze.

"Thanks for everything, Chi Moi. Please, don't wait up for me. I'll be all right."

Outside the gate I flagged down a Honda driver. When we agreed on a price, I tucked the flares of my *ao dai* to prevent them getting caught in the wheels, and climbed on the back. I held onto the driver's waist and off we went, the wind blowing in my face, my hair streaming behind me. I looked straight ahead, my nervousness and fear mixing with my excitement. In my head I could hear Hoa's voice.

"Cam, if you plan on dying young, have some fun first!"

I thought about how shocked she will be to see me!

CHAPTER 22

The Country Mouse

"Miss, this is Tu Do Street."

The Honda driver had stopped.

A thousand neon lights were blinking. People everywhere, the crowds flowing in different directions. All the beautiful people. The women in pastel, scalloped mini-dresses, gold jewelry and heavy makeup, or in long *ao dais* gracefully fluttering in the breeze. The men all in stylish pleated trousers and silk shirts. Only the poor street peddlers wore traditional *ao babas*.

They strolled in couples past the fancy shops, the upscale hotels, the restaurants and nightclubs, the bars. Single men and women held hands freely. They pointed. They laughed. They seemed so happy, as if the world belonged to them, not to the war. I heard music blending with the motor engines driving by. I heard no bombs, no gunshots, no screams.

As I walked down the street, in the midst of this beauty, this gaiety, I was suddenly afraid, a lost country girl.

What am I doing here? Where, who...?

All the lights, the people. It was chaos. So many blinking neon lights. So many bars. The Hong Anh Bar, the My Lan Bar, the Than Linda Bar, the Ly Ly Bar. I could feel the sweat slicking my armpits. I was nervous and confused. Which one had Hoa told me?

I couldn't think.

Down the street I went, poking my head in bars.

"Please, is Ly Ly here? Ly Ly...?"

I found many girls named Ly Ly but none was Hoa.

I stood motionless on the sidewalk. I didn't know what to do. Should I go back to Moi's and get another job? Should I go back to the Nings and tell them my mother was dead and buried before I got home? That I came back because I liked them so much and wanted my job back?

I would at least be safe there.

No, I thought stubbornly. No more sleeping on hard bamboo poles. No more living alone and friendless without lights. *No, thank you.* No more eating scraps off other people's plates or sleeping on the floor in other people's doorways. I wanted to be one of the sleek, elegant women who walked this street as if they owned it. I no longer cared what my next life would be.

I wanted this one.

Cam, you are pretty. Use it. Hoa or no Hoa, go in there and get a job.

I ordered my body to move. Forcing myself, I reached out, opened a heavy door and stepped inside.

It was dark. It was hard to see. The smell of whiskey, of beer and cigarettes, was thick. It was cold. The air-conditioning was quickly cooling off my face, my body.

"Close that door, stupid girl!" someone yelled at me.

Another voice yelled, "Hey, girl, who you looking for? You looking for your husband? He's not here." Everyone was laughing hard. My courage vanished. Nervously, I looked around, hoping for a familiar face. Then a middle-aged woman came over to me.

"Honey, don't mind them. Who are you looking for?"

"My friend Ly Ly," I said.

She cupped her hand to her mouth and yelled, "Anyone know where Ly Ly is?"

The answers came out of the smoke. "Which one? Tall Ly Ly or short Ly Ly? Tall Ly Ly isn't here yet. Short Ly Ly doesn't work here anymore." From the back another voice, laughing, "Yeah, her Vietnamese boyfriend came looking for her and she ran away!"

I tried to make my voice heard. "Do you know where she went?"

More laughter.

"Hey, girl. Her mother's dead! We're not her keepers!"

I didn't know what to do. Hoa wasn't there. Should I ask for a job anyway? The cold air-conditioning was making me sniffle. I was on the verge of crying. I turned toward the door.

What do I do now?

The door was flung open, a blast of hot night air entering. A young woman in tight white bell-bottoms, low-cut red shirt and red heels stood there, her hip cocked. She looked around as if she owned the place, a tough smile on her lips.

I almost fell over. It was my first cousin, Lan.

When she saw me she froze.

For a timeless moment we just stared at each other.

She recovered quickly. Grabbing my arm, she dragged me to the back corner of the bar. There was no welcome in her eyes, only suspicion. And fear.

"Who sent you here?" she asked me harshly.

I protested, "Nobody sent me. I came to find my friend Ly Ly. She's not here."

"Why are you looking for her?"

I didn't know how to answer her. Before I could try, a group of American GIs came in and stood by the door. They made a lot of noise.

One of the girls called back to Lan, "Susie! Your boy is here!"

She pushed me down into a seat. "I have to work. Sit here and wait. We need to talk." All smiles now, she walked toward the Americans.

I sat alone in the corner, thinking about Lan, remembering my Auntie Moi always going on about how wonderful Lan was compared to me. "Lan has a good job working for the Americans. They pay her a lot of money. Lan bought her mother a small flat in Phu Lam. Lan is much smarter than you. Lan."

Well, now I know, I thought.

By this time my eyes had adjusted to the low light. I saw some girls sitting on the GIs' laps in booths while other girls sat with them at the bar counter. In front of the jukebox a group of GIs and girls were dancing to the loud music.

It all reminded me of the night I had sneaked into the Tan Son Nhut officers club. The only difference was here all the men were American men and there all the men there had been Vietnamese. I did have fun that night but it seemed so long ago.

I sighed, then sucked my breath in.

Lan was walking toward me with a GI.

236

She said to the GI, "This is my baby sister. Talk to her. She knows a little English. But don't buy any tea, OK?"

A tall, clean-shaven, baby-faced young American stood looking down at me. His Army uniform was starched, ironed and spotless.

He sat down carefully as Lan watched.

I didn't know what to say, what to do. I had seen many American GIs on the base or on the streets, and at the house where Moi worked, but I had never before spoken with any of them. My nervousness made me giggle.

The American asked me slowly. "What is your name?"

Before I could answer, Lan said quickly, "Her name is Mai."

She had given me a new name! Up to then I had been Can, Thu, Bon, or Cam, whatever fitted the family occasion.

In Vietnamese, I blurted out to Lan.

"Oh, Cousin! I have always wanted to have that name!" I was so thrilled. Lan didn't take me seriously.

"Whatever," she sniffed at me. "Just talk to him. He is a nice boy and poor."

That night Lan took me home with her. As we lay in bed we talked about our lives.

When Lan was growing up in our village, her dream was to marry her childhood sweetheart, the boy next door, her sister-in-law's younger brother. Sadly, when he became a teenager, he joined the Viet Cong and was killed. Her heart broken, Lan fled to Saigon. My Auntie Di Moi found her a job in a rich family. Lan hated it but stayed with it. Then as the war grew fierce back home, her mother came to Saigon with Lan's young niece. Lan's oldest sister had gone north with her husband back in 1954, leaving her baby daughter with her mother. They had never returned.

Lan bought a small flat in Phu Lam for her mother to live. For herself, she secretly rented a tiny space just big enough for a small bed. The owner was kind enough to let her use their kitchen. But Lan was desperate. Her savings would quickly run out. She had no way to provide for all of them from her meager salary. She sold her virginity. She went to work in a bar to support her niece and her mother.

"*Cousin,*" Lan begged me, "Please keep this between us. If my mother knew what I was doing she'd die or she'd leave! I owe her my life. I must take care of her. Our home was burned to the ground, our farmland destroyed. She will die if she goes back to the countryside!"

Lan was sobbing as she spoke. "You are the only one who knows. Promise me you will keep this secret until I die. Promise me, Cousin, please!"

Lying there silently, listening, there had been no words of comfort I could give her.

Now I was crying and I didn't know why.

Because she was a woman? Maybe. Because she was my first cousin on my mother's side and we both carried the same blood? Not likely. However suppressed, there was bad blood between our families. I knew that Lan's father had come to our home that night to lure my father out of hiding. Then our Viet Minh neighbors had come and killed my father. Listening to her now, though, the bad feelings somehow vanished. The only thing I felt for her was pity. She was another victim of the forever war. Whatever her father had done, she had nothing to do with it.

Growing up, as filled with grief as she was, my mother had clearly instructed us, "Whatever has happened to us, they are still your aunts and your uncles, your cousins. They are family. Whatever they do, do not do it back to them. Never let outsiders tear your family apart. Remember what I say."

Over the years, this lesson was constantly imprinted in our lives. Family comes first. When I became of marrying age, Lan's mother had been one of the matchmakers. My mother always said that Lan's mother had looked out for my interests. That it was me who caused all the trouble.

Now Lan herself lay beside me sobbing and begging. What was I to do? Get up and leave? Tell on her? No, I thought, my mother was right. Whatever family does to you, do not do it back. Lan and I are family. She is my cousin.

"I promise," I said.

The landlord agreed for me to move in with Lan. We paid extra for more electricity and water and for the extra use of the kitchen. Lan and I shared the bed. For a few weeks we lived in harmony. Every day I went to the bar with Lan. I wasn't good about asking men to buy me tea. Mostly I just sat in the corner.

I didn't make a lot of money but I was content. My English improved rapidly. I tried to make friends with the other girls and the bartender. Whatever needed to be done, I always volunteered. At the time I thought the girls liked me, but all the time they ridiculed me behind my back. One day Lan and I had a big fight and everything spilled out.

Lan had been in a foul mood all week. That morning she had gotten up early. I tried to stay out of her way, so I pretended I was sleep. She went outside to take a shower. When she returned I was still in bed.

"You going to lie there all day?" she scolded.

I sat up. "Lan, do you want me to do something for you?"

"No," she snapped. "Do something for yourself for a change!"

I thought she was nervous about her Scottish civilian boyfriend. He had been pressuring her to move in with him, but she was afraid her mother might found out.

I said, "Lan, if you like him why not move in with him? The other girls do it. I won't tell your mother."

Now she was angry. "Who are you to give me advice? As for moving in, when are you going to start working for a living?"

I looked at her with surprise. "I work," I said.

"Oh, really, where? You've been hanging around me for a month and you haven't sold one glass of tea on your own! I don't call that working!"

"But, but...."

"But what?" she yelled. "Cam, do you know you are the laughingstock of the bar? Every day you come into the bar waiting for a handout. Waiting for the girls to tip you to bring them food, to do their shopping! To clean up their mess! Don't you have any pride?"

I was stunned.

"Lan, I work. Not selling tea doesn't mean I'm not working. It just that I don't... I don't like men pawing me."

It was the first time I ever saw Lan go crazy.

She threw the hairbrush at me and then everything else she could reach. I ducked and ducked, pulling the covers over me to protect myself. She was raging.

"You think all the girls at the bar are whores, don't you! You think I am a whore! You are wrong, you... spoiled brat! You know why I work there! To support my mother, my niece! Who do you support? I bet you are too selfish to care about anybody else."

Her eyes turned mean.

"You think you're better than us, don't you? I bet you don't even know your son is here! As for your working, I will move out of this place. See how long you last then!"

I kicked off the covers and jumped out the bed. I grabbed her arms.

"Lan, what did you say? My son... I can't believe you are that low! You—you're no different than the rest of your family!"

Lan jerked herself free and slapped me hard across my face. She hit me so hard I saw lights. The last time I got hit that hard was by the cook in Tan Son Nhut. I backed away. I was speechless before Lan's rage. *She's really gone crazy,* I thought.

Her finger was pointed at my face, shaking.

"You leave my family out of it!"

The pain of the blow still traveled in my body. I just looked at her. "You ... hit me."

A look of horror crossed her face.

"Oh, my god. Why do you say things to make me so angry!"

I looked at her in disbelief.

"You... tried to hurt me."

She said nothing. Her hands were trembling as she reached out for me. I pushed her away.

She stood there a moment and then she turned. As she walked away she said, "Your son is here. He is in Phu Lam with his grandmother, your husband's mother. If you don't believe me, go see for yourself."

I didn't trust Lan, but the yearning to see my son was so strong I had to go.

I didn't have the money for a taxi and it was too far to walk. I had to take the cheapest bus. There were no seats or bench. People jammed together with their live animals. In the hot Saigon sun their stinking chickens, ducks and pigs almost made me puke. By the time I reached Phu Lam it was noon. I was drenched with sweat, dirty and smelly.

No time to care what I look like, I thought as I half walked, half ran, to their alley. I took off my hat and entered into the hut of the address my cousin had given me.

The tiny boy, all skin and bones, was squatting on the dirt floor eating noodle soup.

Like two strangers we looked at each other. It had been six or seven years since the night I left him. Without a thought I ran to him. He abandoned his soup and ran and hid behind the old lady's legs.

In the shock and pain of rejection I sagged to the dirt floor, my hands covering my face and tears. Sorrow took over my heart and soul. *I am a bad mother*, I thought. *Even animals didn't abandon their babies. I am a disgrace to our family.* When I lifted my head and looked at my son and his grandmother, I wanted to ask forgiveness.

But the look on the old woman face reminded me of all the pain and suffering she and her family had caused me. I raised my hand and touched the deep scar on top of my head. How could I forget the gruesome attack by her husband and son when they left me by the road to die? The acid taste in my mouth and detestation for the old woman brought me back to my feet. I looked at her, and looked at my son. The anguish in his eyes broke my heart.

I stayed all afternoon. I wanted to be with him, to hold him if I could. I also tried to convince the grandmother to let me take him home with me. I didn't win either one. Han would have nothing to do with me. The grandmother wouldn't let him out of her sight. As for taking him, her answers were quick and harsh.

"No, he is the only grandson, the only heir. His father was killed, did you know? Hah! Because of you! Do you even care how he died? After all he was your husband! You should wear the white turban to show some respect for his soul! You do not deserve to have this child."

I even knelt on the floor to beg her, but the answer was still the same. Finally I struck a bargain with her. I asked her, "If my landlady will let you and my son move in with me, will you come?" She said yes.

242

On the way back I worried about what Lan would say about them moving in with us. How could we possibly fit four of us in that tiny little bed? When we arrived, I discovered that Lan had made good on her threat. She had moved out. I felt relief, and then fear. How was I going to pay rent and support all of us? It didn't matter. I had no choice if I wanted to keep my son.

However, the thought of sharing a bed with my ex-mother-in-law was scary.

As it turned out, I wouldn't have to.

When I asked the landlady, she refused. "No, you only rent space for one bed, that's it. They cannot stay." But then she said, "There is a way for you to be close to your boy. My sister needs someone to look after her three children while she sells at the market every day. If the old lady will work for her for room and board, no pay, the child can stay with his grandmother at night. But during the day you must take him."

The old lady agreed to work. The arrangement seemed to benefit us all. They had shelter and food and I had time to spend with my son. At first, the old lady was suspicious. To see my son I had to come to where she worked. I had to help her care for the children and play with Han at the same time. Eventually she gained some trust. She would let me take him with me to my place, but at noon she would come over to check. In the evening I had to bring him back to her.

For a few weeks life was grand. I spent most days with Han. He came to love to be with me, and I loved to be with him. We had so much fun. Everything seemed to work out to my advantage. The only annoyance was the old woman asking me to find her daughter Truc for her. Day after day the old lady asked me, "Did you look for my daughter?" I told her "Yes," but I lied. I had no intention to ever find her daughter.

One morning when I came to get Han, full of hope and joy, the landlady and her sister were waiting for me. They charged at me, their fingers pointed at my face.

"You are a liar, you can't be trusted," they screamed. "Your so-called mother ran off and left my children home by themselves. Luckily my husband came home early!"

I stopped dead at the entrance, my heart pounding.

"What do you mean? W-where is my son?" I asked the women.

"She took him with her, my children told me," the landlady said. "They saw them both go in the taxi with a very pretty woman."

I was shaking. I clutched the landlady by the shoulder.

"No, please, it's not true, tell me it's not true!"

The thought of losing my son again made me sick to my stomach. It's my fault. I should have kidnapped him when he was with me.

I thought I was smart, but I was not. The old lady had one-upped me. I knew who the pretty woman was.

"Truc," I mumbled.

I panicked. I searched Phu Lam and also Phu Nhuan and Da Dinh to look for them. All day I searched but no one knew where they were.

The only person who knew where they were was my ex-sister-in-law Truc. But the thought of facing off with her sent fear through my body. Suddenly the memories of her last visit were in my head. Her voice, her image, especially her threats. I had still owned the ice-scream stand then. I was always talking about making money and getting my son back. At the time I hadn't fully grasped everything she had said to me but now it all came back.

"Hello, Sister Number Two," she had said. "I am your younger sister-in-law Truc. Do you remember me?"

There she stood in the dirty street, so sophisticated, so clean, compared to me. Her beautiful *ao dai* hugged her slender body. Her

244

black hair flowed down to her waist. Her fingernails and toenails were freshly painted. Her face was carefully made up, her long eyelashes thick and curled. Her pink lips were covered with gloss. Her high heels made her even more sexy.

She looked so elegant, so rich, so grand. It was impossible to believe we came from the same district. And there I was, dirty and smudged, my head inside the ice cream drum as I tried to clean it.

"What do you want from me?" I coldly asked her.

She smiled and I felt a chill.

"Oh, Sister, I come as a friend, a younger sister, as woman to woman. I have just come to invite you to go out with me to have a bite to eat."

For whatever reason, courtesy or fear, I closed my ice cream stand and went with her.

She took me to her house and showed me where she lived. She took me shopping and bought the material for a new outfit for me. She treated me to a very nice dinner. She smiled and chatted and told me a lot of things I couldn't remember later. The only thing I did remember was what she said after the dinner.

"Sister Two, I know what your plans are, what you are thinking. People tell me what you say. I have come to tell you it will not happen. My older brother is dead. My younger brother doesn't have a dick—he can't have any children. Do you understand what I am telling you? Han is not only a first son of a first son—he is the only heir of the Thach clan. I don't know what my brother did to you but I promise you, if you ever try to take your son away from the Thach family, what my brother did to you is nothing compared to what I will do to you!"

I stared at her like a rabbit.

"Do you know what I do for a living?" she said.

I shook my head.

She leaned closer.

"I am a taxi dancer. I know many powerful men. They are not only rich, they have power. And they all want me. All I have to do is to flick my finger and you will disappear without a trace. No one will ever know what happened to you. I tell you this because you are my Number One Nephew's mother. If I were you, I would not take my words lightly. I mean what I say."

She took me outside, hailed a taxi, put me in it and paid the driver. She knew exactly how much to give him. The taxi drove away.

When I had asked Lan once if it was true about Truc, she had replied quietly, "That's the rumor. I believe it. I know I wouldn't mess with her. So don't you go looking for trouble, not with her."

She looked hard at me.

"You are no match for that gal."

CHAPTER 23

The Birth Certificate

For over a week after losing Han I lay in my bed. I didn't bother to take a shower or go to work. I lost my job and had no money to pay for the rent. My life had turned upside down from bad to worse. At the time, as I looked at it, I had two choices: give up and die or choose a different way of life.

I thought long and hard.

Even if I was brave enough to go against Truc, how could I win? More importantly, should I even try? I was illegal, moving from place to place, no forwarding address, barely able to support myself. What kind of life could I give my son? How could I take him from a family? He was better off where he was than with me. I had no future. If I took him, he would have no future. Still, I had hoped and dreamed. Now I had lost him again. It was the end of hope for me.

I had always worried about my next life, what I would be. Now I no longer cared. I would take my chances. I decided that if life was going to treat me like a criminal, I might as well be one. So I bought and sold goods to American GIs and civilians without guilt. I put my son out of my mind. I began to live only for the day, without thought or care. Fear of being caught was always with me but it no longer stopped me. I no longer felt inhibited by the rules of how to be a Vietnamese woman. I wore makeup and dressed in short mini-skirts and high heels. I had no bones about who I dated. I dated young, handsome Americans. I also let it be known that I had no desire to date Vietnamese men.

I was not a goody two shoes, but any time a guy began to pressure me my son's face would always emerge. The pain of losing my child scared me away from any kind of long-term relationship.

Although I didn't drink, didn't smoke and wouldn't do drugs, I loved to party. I needed the noise and the mindless gaiety. More to the point, going to parties and bars, dancing at night clubs and hanging out with the hot crowd was now my livelihood. It was how I did my black market. In fact, Saigon's bright lights were what kept me going. The glitter filled my empty hours and I met people from all walks of life, the innocent and the eager, hustlers and wastrels, the rich and the poor. And always, of course, the middlemen.

One evening a photographer, Mr. Bao, came up to me.

"Hey, Mai!" he yelled, "I've got something you really want. But it's going to cost you!"

I thought he was talking about my son. Instantly I was wary.

"How did you find them?" I asked.

"Find who?" he responded.

"My son and my ex-mother-in-law! Who else?"

He looked at me strangely.

"What are you talking about? What kind of trouble are you in? You're... married? I didn't know you're old enough to be married. You've got a son—?"

Now I was upset.

"Mr. Bao, what are you talking about?"

He came closer and whispered in my ear.

"A birth certificate. A real one!"

I put my hands on my hips.

"How much? And how do I know it's real?"

"You'll just have to trust me," he said smugly.

Trust him. Fat chance.

Truthfully, at that point in my life I didn't trust anyone. No way would I trust him. Still, I had to take a chance.

"I want to see the paper first."

A week went by before Mr. Bao came to see me.

Without the paper.

"Sorry, girl, this is how it has to be. If you want this paper you have to meet its owner." He waved his hands. "This is for real! But she has other buyers. You have to move fast."

In the end I agreed to meet the owner. The date was set.

That night I unstitched the hems of my clothes where I had hid all my savings. I also pawned what little jewelry I owned. Now I had to pay the owner as well as Mr. Bao.

As the time drew near my nerves were raw. More than nerves, I was plain scared. So many unanswered questions about this. Was it a trap, a set up? Was my ex-sister-in-law out to get me? I knew if I got caught I was as good as dead. But—what choice did I have?

Oh, Buddha. Oh, God, please help me. Please let this to be true.

That morning I sat on the back of Mr. Bao's Honda motorbike in my dark sunglasses, my baseball cap pulled low, my black bellbottoms fitting snugly, my loose blue cotton blouse fluttering. I was trying hard not to show my nervousness but inside I was a wreck.

We rode without speaking through the Gia Dinh district and onto the highway headed north for Bien Hoa province. I didn't know this area.

"Mr. Bao!" I yelled over his shoulder, "Where are we going?"

All he said was, "You'll see."

It was midday before he turned into a small alley in Bien Hoa city. By then I was tired, sweating in the heat, and terrified.

He works for Truc. She warned me. He brought me out here to kill me.

When Mr. Bao stopped and shut off the engine I couldn't move. I was petrified.

He turned to me and said softly, "We're here. Be very careful when you talk to this old woman. She is very sentimental about this. The only thing she has left in her life is her daughter's birth certificate. I've taken people out here before but she wouldn't sell it to them."

He's not going to kill me? She—wouldn't sell? What...?

I stuttered, "S-she—won't sell? What? I don't—where is the girl?"

He answered calmly as we walked. "She died a long time ago. Didn't I tell you?"

I shivered suddenly.

"No, you didn't tell me and I don't want a dead birth certificate. It is bad luck."

He stopped short.

"If you talk to her like that you will walk out of here with nothing. And the police will catch you! You are living in the city illegally. *I* know it, and other people know it. I'm doing you a favor, girl. If you don't do this, you will go to jail. You will die before you are thirty!"

I whispered in shock,

"How did you know that?"

He raised his eyebrows in surprise.

"Know what?"

"That I will be dead before I am thirty."

He blinked and said carefully, "It is just a phrase I used. To express my thought. That's all. What makes you think I know you will be dead before you are thirty?" He frowned. "Do you plan to kill yourself?"

"No, b-but—the fortune teller in Cho Lon told me...."

After a moment he nodded.

"Yes... I see. Well, we will talk about this later. Now pull yourself together. Maybe today is your lucky day, yes? If we get what we came for, your luck can change. Hopefully the curse will be broken. Enough, let's go inside."

Mr. Bao opened the door, cleared his throat and called out.

"Mrs. Giang , this is Bao. I have brought my new friend to see you. May we come in?"

As we waited he told me her daughter's name had been Giang. In our country many people, after the birth of their first child, no longer used their own name. They were addressed either by their birth rank or the name of their first child.

An old woman's voice invited us in.

As we entered her hut the heat was like a pressure cooker and the stench turned my stomach. I took out my handkerchief, wiped my sweat, and covered my nose. All the while my eyes were searching for the trap. I was paranoid. It didn't matter where I went. I always inspected the location, looking for the way to escape. This time there was no ex-sister-in-law, no police, no murderers behind curtains.

Only an old woman in dark pajamas sitting on her bed.

Her legs were dangling almost to the floor. She must have been waiting for us. Her hair needed combing but it was pulled tight to the back of her head. I could see that the roots of her hair were white but the rest of her hair was black. Suddenly I felt pity for her helpless vanity.

Poor thing, I thought, *she doesn't know her head looks like a skunk. She'd be better off to let all her hair go white.*

Her face was deeply wrinkled and the skin under her chin hung loose like a rooster's wattle. In her hand she held a bamboo cane as old as she was. She tried to stand up but Mr. Bao quickly came over to her.

"Mrs. Giang, please don't get up for us. This is the friend I told you about. She has heard so much about you. She wanted to meet you."

Instantly I stepped forward and bowed deeply to show her my respect.

"What is her name?" she asked Mr. Bao.

"Oh, her name is Mai."

"That is a lovely name," she said. "If I had another girl I would have named her Mai."

Unlike her appearance her voice was strong and sweet. They kept on talking small talk. After half an hour of it, in the heat and moldy stench of the thatch, my patience, never plentiful, was running thin. Neither Mr. Bao nor the old lady had yet mentioned what we had come there for. I gathered all my courage.

"Mrs. Giang, Mr. Bao has told me that you had a beautiful daughter."

She turned her head toward me, annoyed at my interruption. Clearly, she seldom had visitors. With irritation in her voice she said, "Yes, I did have a beautiful daughter, but she is no longer with me. She is dead. That's why you have come here, isn't it? How much will you pay me for her birth certificate?"

She was so direct it threw me off balance. Luckily, Mr. Bao was there.

"Oh, Auntie," he said cajolingly, "We agreed about that before. I have what you wanted right here." He patted his pocket.

She looked at me, still talking to him.

252

"Did you tell her that my daughter is half French?"

"Oh, yes, Mrs.Giang. I did."

I gave him a look. *Are you crazy? Do I look half French to you?* He avoided my eyes.

The old woman studied me.

"No, no, she is too small to be half French."

Mr. Bao sucked his teeth.

She went on.

"Fortunately I didn't list the father's name on the certificate."

Her head swayed. "I am not yet determined whether to sell this or not. If I do, this young lady must promise me she will take good care of my daughter's good name."

She chewed her cheek as she talked about me.

"She seems to be a very polite young lady. I like that."

Finally she addressed me directly.

"What will you say if I tell you I want to adopt you? Will you be my adopted daughter? Will you light the incense for me and pray for my soul when I leave this world to join my daughter? It won't be long now."

I almost laughed. I was so giddy. In addition to the overpowering heat and the terrible smell and her rambling talk, I was going crazy with anxiety. Sweat was pouring out of every part of my body. *This woman is nuts*, I thought. *Now she wants me to be her daughter?*

The old woman was no longer looking at me, but Mr. Bao was. He saw my expression. He glared at me in warning, pointing to the floor. I bowed low, and struggled to speak calmly.

"Oh, yes, Madame, I will! As you know, I have no family. I will do as you wish."

"Good, good." She sighed. "I like you already."

Slowly she turned her back to us and faced the wall. She unbuttoned her shirt. It seemed like an eternity before she turned to us again. In her hands she held up a small red bag. She reached into the bag with two fingers and pulled out a wrapped parcel. Then she unwrapped several layers of paper and held the certificate. She was crying as she said, "Virgin baby, I am so sorry that I have to do this to you. I know you understand. You are not here to take care of me. I have to do this to pay for the doctor. Virgin baby, forgive me."

She wept quietly.

I felt sorry for her, my own eyes full of tears. I wished I didn't have to do this. At the same time I wanted her to give me the certificate. I wanted to get out of this depressing place.

Finally she put the certificate in her pocket, reached for her bamboo cane and slowly got up from the bed. She shuffled, dragging her feet, to the small shrine in the corner of her shack. She lit three sticks of incense, then turned her head and signaled me to come to her. Instantly I moved to the altar, knelt down before it and bowed my head.

She laid her old shaky hand on my head. She whimpered.

"Oh, virgin spirit, forgive me to let go of you. Oh, virgin spirit, protect your new sister. Oh, virgin spirit, give her permission to use your name for as long as she lives."

She removed her hand and gave me the sticks of burning incense.

"Pray for your sister's soul and for her spirit. Ask your sister's spirit for her blessing. She will protect you always." I bowed ritually with the incense sticks and stood up.

The ceremony was over. The old woman looked exhausted.

As for me, I was beside myself with impatience. As the old lady's hand reached into her pocket my heart pumped faster. As she reached out her hand with the certificate, Mr. Bao took a step forward to intercept it for me. Quickly she drew her hand back. She put the certificate back into the red bag, and held the bag to her heart.

Mr. Bao was frozen in mid-stride. So was I. We looked at each other, speechless.

My chest felt so tight it hurt. At that moment I wanted to jump the old lady, take the small red bag with the birth certificate in it, and run away. My feet were planted on the dirt floor, ready to lunge. Luckily for me, my mind and my mouth were quicker than my feet.

"Mrs. Ngoc," I said. "I understand how hard it is to give up something you love most. I have the same sorrow. My child is still alive but I no longer have him. My family has disowned me and the family of my ex-husband took my son away from me. I had to escape to Saigon without my papers. Madame, please help me."

The old woman blinked her eyes. She was trying to hold back her tears. Her mouth was twisted with grief. "Oh, Ngoc baby," she said softly, "It is time for me to let go of you. It is the right thing for me to do." She looked at Mr. Bao. "You are witness. This girl is my daughter in spirit. This paper is for her, and for her only."

Slowly she handed me the red bag.

A strange sensation ran through my body as I received the red bag. I closed my eyes and let the indescribable feeling enter my veins. In tears I knelt at the old woman's feet.

"Thank you so much, Madam, for sharing this with me."

She patted me on my head.

"You take good care of that paper, child. Do you know I was not always this old, this ugly? During the French time I was a beautiful woman. Yes, I have had my share of good times. Giang's father was a Frenchman. Did I tell you that? He didn't even know that I had a child with him. She was all I had and when she died it was so hard. I just... and now...."

She stopped talking, her hands fluttering in the air.

"Go. Go now. You have my blessing. Giang's virgin spirit will protect you. Go now."

Mr. Bao signaled me to leave.

I got to my feet, bowed my head to him and to the old lady and backed out of the hut. In a few minutes Mr. Bao came out and we rode back to Saigon.

Mr. Bao cautioned me to wait, to make sure there would be no problem from anybody about the birth certificate. Finally, when we were sure it was safe, I went to Gia Dinh City Hall and filled out forms for my new ID card.

I was Tran Thi Giang. My mother was Tran Thi Thuy.

My father was Unknown.

BOOK FOUR:

A New Life

CHAPTER 24

Looking for Myself

Overnight I transformed myself once again.

My new security made me restless. My black market business was growing rapidly, taking most of my time, but I wanted more. I wanted new challenges. Up to then I had mostly traded in goods but now I did mostly money exchanges.

I watched as the very rich sent their children abroad to be educated, sometimes in France but mostly in the United States. Those children carried with them satchels filled with American dollars. As soon as they landed, the children opened illegal bank accounts for their parents and relatives to hide the money. When they needed more American dollars they bought them in Saigon from black marketers like myself.

About this time, I rented a new, roomy house with another girl. We hired a housekeeper to look after us. We hired college students to give us English lessons. We went to Taekwondo classes to learn to protect ourselves, from what I wasn't sure, but I discovered I was good at it. Soon I was going up for my competition brown belt. It still wasn't enough for me. It seemed that I wanted everything, and nothing.

As our student friends talked about us on campus, our house became known as a popular place to hang out. Most days the house was crowded with young college students, which was fine with me. I wanted to learn about politics, about the world, not because I expected to use it but because I wanted to learn. We welcomed students who needed to crash but we weren't pushovers.

Our house rules were firm, and enforced. No drinking, no drugs and no sex. If the students didn't respect the rules, out they went. It seldom happened, though. Most of our friends were from well-to-do families and they worked hard for their degrees in law or medicine. Student bums weren't welcome.

I'll never forget how much I learned from them. About the war, about the government, about politics and the world outside Vietnam. I didn't need lessons in corruption, though. I had always lived with corruption wherever I was. To me it seemed everybody was corrupt. It was a way of life. And now everybody used the war as their excuse. Everybody looked for an edge to survive.

I was no different. I worked the money black market with the Vietnamese because I had to, but I preferred doing it with Americans because they wouldn't cheat me. Oh, I ran into a few who did, but not often. But then Auntie Moi gave me an idea. Instead of buying risky American dollars, she said, buy American checks.

From birth to death, there is no fairness in the world.

A third of the Americans who came to Vietnam, military or civilian, never experienced life outside the huge U.S. bases or Saigon. They never got shot at. They never even got dirty. They lived very comfortable lives in barracks, compounds or outside in villas. They had barbed-wire walls, MP guards and *mama-san* housekeepers. Their clothes, their uniforms, were always clean and pressed. Their boots, their shoes, shined like black mirrors.

Even those who didn't have it good mostly had it safe, unlike those American GIs who fought out in the countryside, often living filthy, eating canned food and sleeping on rivers, or in swamps and mud or sand. Those GIs, if they weren't snake-bitten or diseased, or killed or wounded, were lucky if they slept in tents or hooches.

Back then I didn't know this but, sadly, I might not have even cared. My job and my life was buying and selling American dollars, not making peace.

The American GIs in Saigon were my business.

Most GIs only had MPC ("Military Payment Certificates") to spend. Many of the merchants in the countryside would honor MPC and redeem it at the bases. However, in the cities and on the black market, GI money had little to no value.

Because of the war and general corruption, Vietnamese people did not trust the banks. They felt their money was not safe and could be taken away at any point in time. People wanted the American dollar since it was a more stable currency. The idea of check trading and acquiring American dollars on the black market became widespread.

GIs would bring me their American dollars or checks and I would give them Vietnamese dong (our local currency) at a higher exchange rate than the banks would. Then I'd take the dollars or check to the richest and highest-ranking government officials and sell it to them for a greater value than it was worth. With the help of family overseas, they opened illegal bank accounts in the U.S. to hide the money there.

In the beginning I was afraid of getting caught. It was risky business, but I told myself, "Money, I will live among the rich." It was war, after all.

Looking back, it was terrible way to make a living. All I can say is that war makes heroes and also brings out the worst in many people. War is a kind of madness. Some people lose their hands, their legs, their eyes. Some lose their minds, their families, and their lives. Some people take other people's lives. For me, war and the hatred in war had taken my father, my childhood, and my baby. I had lost my dreams and I had lost hope. I lived a life without any tomorrow. Yes, I made money. I had a warm bed, food in my belly, and I had surrounded myself with people. But I had nothing inside. I had become worse than cynical. I believed in nothing and no one, least of all myself. Vu Linh had been my guardian angel, but I hid even from her when I saw her. Deep down inside my soul I believed I was dirty. I believed no one could love me. It wasn't just that I believed I would die before I was thirty. I no longer cared.

Why bother to live?

One morning, after a night's party at a friend's house, I was coming home at 5 a.m. When the cyclo stopped at the curb I stepped out onto the sidewalk and paid my fare.

When I turned around, Vu Linh was there beside me.

I was totally unprepared. I didn't know what to say to her. Mostly I was ashamed. For so many months I had avoided her. Now here she was, cheerful and happy to see me. She didn't ask me where I had been all those months or what I was doing out at this hour. She just took me in her arms and gave me a big hug. Then she patted my face and hugged me again. Standing back, she looked at me from head to toe, smiling.

"My daughter, I am so glad to see you! I miss you so much."

Still smiling, Vu Linh started to turn away. "Come, I am late for church," she said. She grabbed my hand and pulled me down the street and into the church.

"First, I have to thank God! Then we will go have something to eat. Do you want to wait for me here or come up front with me?" All the people in the church were near the front. I pointed to the back pew and said, "I will wait here." She hurried up the aisle as I sat by myself in the pew. I was nervous, embarrassed and filled with regret.

I shouldn't have let her pull me in here. I should have stayed at my friend's house. I should have come home earlier. Church is a place for good people to come and pray. I don't belong here.

I looked out the open door behind me.

You don't belong here, I scolded myself again. *Get up and leave.*

I was powerless to move. All the eyes on the wall statues and in the stained glass windows were staring at me. I looked up at the altar in the front of the church. Above the altar hung the body of a man nailed on a cross. His head was tilted over to one side.

A cold chill ran down my spine.

This was the first time in my life I had actually been in a church. I knew nothing about Jesus Christ or the Catholic religion or what any of this was all about. All those months ago, when I had lived with Vu Linh, she had faithfully gone to church every day but she never invited me to go with her.

Now something strange was happening to me, a feeling in my soul I couldn't explain.

If you had asked me then what religion I was I would have shrugged. My grandfather and father had been Cao Dai, so I was a Cao Dai by birth, although I knew nothing about it. My mother was a Buddhist so I went to the Buddhist temple because I wanted to make her happy. Also, many of my uncles and aunts on my mother's side were Buddhist. I wanted to fit in so I went where they all went, although I knew nothing about that either. God or Buddha, I only prayed when I was afraid.

Someone was talking to me from far away.

"My daughter, are you ready to get something to eat?"

I must have fallen asleep. Vu Linh was leaning over me, smiling. The church was empty. There was just Vu Linh and me. I sat up straight.

"I'm sorry," I mumbled.

"Sorry for what?" she asked.

"I fell asleep."

She shushed me. "It's all right. A lot of people do it."

"But ... "

She sat down beside me and held my hands.

"My daughter, now tell me. Why didn't you come to see me?"

How sweet and how gentle it was to hear her speak. My tears started to drop.

"I – I am ashamed," I stuttered.

"Ashamed of what?"

I could hardly talk, I was crying so hard.

"Vu Linh, I am a bad mother! I'm not even looking for my son any more. I am empty, nothing inside me. I bought someone else's birth certificate, a dead person's. I work in bars and now I am doing black market. I am not worthy to be loved. Vu Linh, I am no good!"

She pulled me into her arms and held me tight, rocking me like a baby.

"My daughter, don't cry. God forgives you. God loves you. Don't you see? He sent his only son to save us? Don't cry."

I cried even harder, understanding only that her arms were holding me.

"I was so ashamed," I cried. "So afraid that you would despise me, hate me. That if you found out what I was doing, after all your help, that you would send me to jail. *Oh, Vu Linh—!*"

She put her finger over my mouth.

"Hush... don't talk, just listen. There is nothing secret about what you are doing. My friends all told me. They are all amazed how clever you are to find the way to make a living. And I have always known where you lived. I just waited for you to come see me, but you didn't. So I started coming to this church hoping to run into you."

She looked at the altar.

"You see, everyone has secrets of shame. We are all sinners. I do not go to church to be a saint. I go to church to find help to wash my soul. Our soul has windows. We look through them. If we don't clean them often they will be covered with dirt, and everything will look dirty to us. I am not a saint. I come to church just for me. I want to clean my soul. Every day I try to do good things, but not always. God knows that. God does not punish me for trying. God doesn't judge us in life. While we breathe, we can hope. God forgives us when we try. So who am I to judge anyone?"

She looked at me.

"You do what you must to survive—as long as you don't steal or cheat or hurt people or sell yourself. Our government says it is illegal to do black market or date foreigners. That's what the rules are. But whose rules are they? Not God's. So, you will be all right by me, too."

She smiled. "I am hungry. Let's go get something to eat."

She turned her face to the altar and made the sign of the cross. When she turned back to me there was a handkerchief in her hand. She wiped the tears from my face.

Then she held it over my nose and said, "Blow."

CHAPTER 25

The American

Needless to say, I was no longer a meek country mouse. I lived like a typical, rich Saigon kid, rebellious and self-destructive. I cared about nothing. I lived day by day, hour by minute. I had no future, no dreams and no hope. I did what I had to. Bars, movies, parties and nightclubs—I came and went as I pleased. And I dated only Americans. There were a lot of guys in my crowd of student friends but I wouldn't date them.

We lived the life of the carefree, the careless. War was everywhere, even in Saigon, but we didn't care. We used any excuse to party. If a friend got drafted, we had a party. If a friend was discharged after he got wounded, we had a party. If a friend got killed, we had a party to send his soul to the other side.

We lived in fear but no one would admit it. We drove motorbikes, Hondas, as we called them. On our Hondas we went round and around the city, night after night. We dared each other to do things we weren't supposed to do. We were young and shining, like ripe fruit. Nothing could happen to us. We thought we were invincible.

I was fortunate that I had my guardian angel, Vu Linh. Her love, her guidelines, her prayers and her strong faith were starting to reach me. She kept telling me God made me for a reason, that I should not waste my life.

One day she surprised me.

"I know you don't think much of me, the way I live my life," she said. "You think I'm just a second wife to a rich man, that I have no purpose. You are wrong and so are the people who say to me, "God will punish you for stealing your sister's husband!' God has punished me. He didn't give me any children of my own. But I didn't steal my sister's husband. I married him because my sister asked me to. He had so many women. Any one of them could have taken him away. My sister knew he was interested in me. She said she needed my help. So I married him. I kept him with his family so he didn't leave them."

She looked at me.

"And if God didn't give me my own children it was so I could take care of other children, like you. You must think about your life, Daughter, and use it wisely. God only made one of you, not two!"

I was trying to change my life, but somehow I wasn't getting very far.

December 21, 1968, the darkest night of the year.

That December night, like most other nights, my crowd had decided we would go out and party. We chose the Queen Bee which was, along with Maxim's, one of the two hottest nightclubs in town.

We weren't there very long when a group of young American officers walked in. One of my friends knew one of the officers so we decided to put our tables together.

One officer was stiff and uncomfortable. His shirt was buttoned up to his neck. While everyone else rearranged tables and chairs, he just stood there. He didn't know what to do.

So I went over to him and said hi to him.

He gave me a shy smile. I told him he had a very nice smile. He thanked me and smiled again. When the tables and chairs were all laid out the way we wanted, I asked him to sit down. Then I pulled out a chair and sat down next to him. In Vietnamese, my friends started to tease me.

"Mai, he is very handsome. You always fall for that type."

"No, thank you," I retorted. "I already have a boyfriend. He comes to town once a week from Long Binh Base. He adores me."

Bill was an American I had met in a nightclub. He was a good man who treated me well, and I had no complaints.

They laughed. "That never stopped you before! Say, this guy is really handsome and he knows it. He's kind of conceited. He's just playing hard to get." They dared me, "Get him to go to dinner with you and we'll double the bill!"

"Hah! No thanks, not interested." We kept teasing and laughing, in Vietnamese and English. Then the floor show started, a Vietnamese woman singing old French songs. Soon it was so loud we had to shout at each other. Finally, everyone got up and began dancing. Everyone except this officer. We were the only ones at the table. I asked him what his name was, what he did.

He told me he was a Navy Lieutenant, a Dai-Uy, that his name was Bernard Donohue but in the Navy everyone called him Bernie. In the states, though, he was known as Brian. It was the nickname his mother gave him because he, his father, and his grandfather all had the same name.

I asked how long he had been in Vietnam.... Was his family sad to see him go.... How was his mother, father, etc. We talked and he started to unwind.

He had come to Vietnam many months ago, during the Tet Offensive, to fight in the war. He had spent long months on the rivers and in the swamps, from Cua Viet on the DMZ to the Rung Sat killer jungle near Saigon, down to the Delta and up to the Cambodian border. Long months of death. Months of hell.

Now he was in Saigon. Admiral Zumwalt had ordered him into Saigon and given him the command to train the Viet sailors to take over and operate the combat craft—the Swifts, the Riverines, and especially his own boats, the PBRs—of the Brown Water Navy.

When he first arrived, he told me, he hated Saigon. He wore khakis and he was saluting every time he turned around. Worse, he was in a big hotel with air-conditioning and MP guards while his men were out on narrow rivers and tiny canals getting shot by the Viet Cong. He also was disgusted with Saigon's PX mentality.

I didn't realize it right away, but he was exhausted. He had been working days and nights to put his staff together, find equipment and instructors for the main classrooms and set up the three separate boat training sites. His headquarters was a nine-story building in an alley off of Hien Vuong Street near Hai Ba Trung. His Boat School was to open tomorrow.

"Tomorrow!" I said. "Why are you here?"

He laughed. He had been sitting by himself in his office, he said, totally exhausted. Delayed battle fatigue was pulling him under. He was at the end of his rope.

Some of his staff had come looking for him. When they found him at his desk mumbling, they told him he needed a night off, a night out. But he had no clothes except his uniform. A friend lent him a brown civilian shirt and he used his own khaki uniform pants. His staff wanted to take him on a wild binge down Tu Do street but he knew he was too tired and too uptight.

Yet here he was at the Queen Bee nightclub.

At one point he told me that, after his tour of duty, he was going to enter a monastery and become a monk. I smiled and nodded but I thought it was funny.

When I told my friends what he had said they all laughed. I remember making a joke. "He's too handsome to be a monk, to waste what's under that habit!" Then, when he told me he was very poor, I felt ashamed that I had laughed. His father was ill, he said, and he had to send his pay home to help his mother.

I felt so sorry for him then. I even offered to buy him a drink, but he said no. I told my friends they were wrong—that he wasn't conceited, he was just sad.

"His father is sick," I said. "He misses his family. He is lonesome."

They hooted at me.

Before he left, he wrote down his full name and an address and gave it to me.

I stuck it inside my bag and thought nothing of it.

Since that early morning meeting at the church, I had gone to see Vu Linh more often. By then, she and her husband had given up their own apartment and had moved into the big house with the First Wife. One husband, two wives and thirteen children, all under the same roof. And Vu Linh's "children" were coming and going, too.

From Vu Linh I began to learn about the Catholic faith, but I was afraid to commit to it.

Vu Linh herself never pressured me. Either I wanted to be Catholic or I didn't. She said I was her Godchild, her daughter, even if I was not Catholic. When her husband heard her say that, he announced that I was *his* godchild, too. Then the First Wife decided that, since I was her husband's godchild, I should call her *Mama Tien* and call her husband *Bo*. I didn't know what *Bo* meant, but it sounded nice, so I did. The First Wife was always sweet to me.

As a godchild, I was free to come and go anytime I wanted. It was casual; no one in the house ever stopped me or invited me although the First Wife's daughters were nice enough. Eventually I became friends with one of the younger girls. She was young, sweet and innocent.

I didn't have a father so I adored my godfather. Whenever I came to visit I always brought him a small gift of cookies, fruit or cigars. This particular morning, the day after the Queen Bee nightclub, I brought him some big grapes. He lay on the mat smoking his opium. I sat on the teak divan peeling skin off the grapes. His eyes were closed. He took a deep drag on his opium pipe. When he opened his eyes I handed him the grape. He sucked the juice and spit out the seeds.

I watched him prepare his pipe. He heated a needle in a lamp. When it was hot enough he dipped it into the opium jug. The heat would melt enough opium to stick to the needle. Using his thumb and little finger, he rolled the opium into a tiny ball. When the ball had some consistency he injected it into the pipe and burned the opium over the lamp. Then he closed his eyes and took a long drag.

My godmother was busy cooking on a small stove, preparing his breakfast.

I peeled another grape, waiting.

"*Bo*," I said casually, "I met a young American guy last night. He is a Navy man, a *Dai Uy*. He is kind of nice. He just opened a Navy school on Hien Vuong near Hai Ba Trung. A tall building, he told me."

Bo dropped his opium pipe on the tray.

"Vu Linh's Daughter, tell me more about this American. Where did you meet him?" He looked at me carefully. "And why are you telling me this? Do you like this American?" His eyes were alive. "Do you know the building you talk about? I built it! I used to own it. Vu Linh, you know the building I'm talking about?"

For the next half hour we talked about this young American.

On the way home it occurred to me that I had never mentioned a boyfriend to my godfather before. There was something about this young American that made my head spin. Try as I might, I couldn't get the vision of his face, his smile, out of my mind. His smile made me want to see him again, but I felt silly and embarrassed at the thought of going out and looking for him.

Don't go looking for him! Girls don't look for boys. And he is a foreigner!

I was still arguing with myself when I got home. I was still arguing with myself that night. The next day, I mentioned it to my roommate, Thuy. She was all over me. "Mai, are you crazy? He is a foreigner. It's forbidden! What are you thinking? You can't go looking for him—It's too bold to go looking for a man you just met! Besides, you have a boyfriend! Don't be foolish!"

The more she talked, the more I wanted to see him again. I rummaged through my purse until I found the piece of paper he had given me and showed the address to her.

"Thuy, bring me over here on your Honda."

She objected but in the end she gave in.

The place was not hard to find.

The building towered over the street front shops, its lower levels hung with barbed wire. At the alley entrance and on street corners stood barbed wire barricades, sandbagged sentry posts and MP guards with machine guns.

I told Thuy to turn around and go home but she refused.

"No way! You made me drive you here, and now you're scared? Well, get off my Honda and go in there and get it over with! Otherwise I'll never hear the end of it. Get off my Honda. Now."

272

"Thuy, what if he doesn't remember me?"

"Didn't I ask you that before we drove here? You said he would. Go on, before the MP guards shoot us both."

"But I didn't know he is this important." I whimpered.

"Who cares! He's probably just a low-life trying to impress a girl. Go find out."

Reluctantly I slipped off the seat and walked up the road. Inside my head I was arguing with myself. Should I do it or shouldn't I?

Don't think. Just walk.

A stocky MP guard wearing thick glasses stepped out from his post and stopped me.

"Hold it. Where do you think you going, Miss?"

While he asked me, his rifle was pointed straight at my chest. My heart started jumping crazy. Nobody had ever pointed a gun at me before. I was so scared and nervous I nearly wet my pants. I tried to talk but the words didn't come out, just sounds.

"Beat it, Sister," he said firmly. "There's nothing here for you."

Somehow his order gave me courage.

I said, "I want to see *Dai Uy* Donohue. I know him."

His brown eyes were traveling up and down and all around me. He was looking at me, over me and around me, his eyes always moving. Then he took off his Coke-bottle glasses, took out his handkerchief and wiped the sweat off his forehead.

"I don't believe you," he said.

I took out the piece of paper with Brian's handwriting on it. He held the piece of paper up to his eyes and his jaw dropped. His face went from authority to surprise. He turned and looked behind him, his gun never leaving my chest.

"Hey, mate, she wants to see Mr. Donohue. Should I let her in?"

"She have any proof?" came the reply.

"Yes."

"Take her inside and go get the boss."

"Come with me, Miss," said the stocky MP.

I followed him into the building. He handed me over to two other guards and walked through a wide door, leaving it open. I sat on the bench in the waiting room, the guards on either side of me, guns in their hands. Through the open door I could see a stairway beside a large open space. Americans and Vietnamese men in Navy uniforms were walking past the door, eying me.

I wondered what they thought about me.

Do they think I am Viet Cong? Do I look that suspicious?

One of the guards shut the door. Now I felt really uneasy. The MP guards made me feel like a prisoner. *I have made a big mistake to come here,* I thought. *What did I think I was doing? Why did I go looking for him anyway? Oh, this is so embarrassing. How will I explain this to my godmother?*

He must be important. All these guards.

I told myself to get up and walk out before he saw me but I was so afraid of the guards I couldn't move an inch. It seemed a very long time before the door opened. There was Brian in uniform with the stocky MP. The guards saluted when they saw Brian.

"Sir," said the stocky MP, "She showed me this paper with your handwriting on it, so I let her in."

Brian was speechless.

If I hadn't been so scared and embarrassed I would have giggled. I don't think in a million years he would have thought I would show up at his headquarters like this. I had to say something, quick.

"My girlfriend and I were just driving around when her Honda broke down. So I thought I would come to see you while it was fixed."

Oh, you liar, liar!

Brian looked at his men and then at me.

"It is nice to see you, but I have to get back to work."

He walked me outside and through the sentry post. Everybody was watching. Neither of us spoke.

That was it.

I was so glad to get outside, I half walked, half ran, down the street. I didn't look back. I jumped on the back of Thuy's honda. "Hurry up, get out of here," I ordered her.

"What happened? Tell me!" she said.

"Nothing happened!" I said. "*Go, go.*"

On the way home, Thuy kept asking me what had happened beyond the gate. I told her that nothing happened, but she didn't believe me. She said, "If nothing happened why are you so upset?"

"Thuy, could you please just drop it? There is nothing to talk about."

She was angry with me and now I was annoyed with her. In silence we drove through the busy Saigon streets, the sun beating down on us.

I was enraged at myself.

How could I have done this, let myself be humiliated like this? It is embarrassing for a woman to go looking for a man! Where is my pride? I already have a boyfriend who loves me and cares for me very much. How can I tell him about this? Am I a two-timer or what?

My head was spinning like a dog chasing its tail.

I had no answers for what I had just done.

CHAPTER 26

My Two Boyfriends

Sure enough, that afternoon Long Binh Bill surprised me with a half dozen sweaters.

When we met downtown, he said, "Mai, I missed you so much that I traded my day off and borrowed a jeep to drive into the city to see you. I hope you like the sweaters. When we walked on Nguyen Hue Street last week I saw you look at them, but I wasn't sure which color to buy so I bought them all."

Instead of being happy, I felt guilty and sad. I started to cry. Poor Bill, he thought he had done something wrong.

"Mai, I am so sorry, I didn't mean to upset—"

I didn't let him finish.

"Presents, presents, you always bring me presents! You shouldn't be that nice to me because I'm not that good. You should be looking for a girlfriend who appreciates you—"

His big brown eyes just looked at me.

"—and please don't say that you love me!"

Our visit was short and awkward. We went to see a movie and then to eat. Always a gentleman, Bill treated me with respect. He dropped me off and returned to Long Binh.

I tried my best not to think of Brian. I told myself that Bill was a good man. He had nothing but love for me. We had dated for three months. He didn't know where I lived. He didn't pressure me to go to bed with him. He is a proper boyfriend, I told myself. That Navy guy doesn't even know you exist. Forget him. Never talk to him again.

Three days had passed since the morning I had seen Brian.

I was doing my routine, including English classes. My student friend who had taught me English was now in the South Vietnamese Army so I had signed up for English classes at Dien Hong School. That day, after class, I didn't feel like going out or doing anything so I took a taxi home.

Brian, in uniform, was sitting in a beat-up jeep outside my house.

He smiled and said, "Hi, my Jeep is broken."

I was so nervous, so excited, that I had forgotten I was never going to talk to this man again. All I could see was his smile. *But how did he find me? Had I broken our house rule? Had I given this man my address? What do I do now? He is here.*

I sat beside him in his Jeep without doors.

"Let's go eat," he said.

As he drove, I held the flares of my *ao dai* so they wouldn't flap. The wind blew on my face, on our bodies. I was too nervous to ask how he knew where I lived. I couldn't tell what was in his mind because he was driving on busy congested streets.

From time to time Brian glanced at me and smiled.

At the restaurant, he ordered simple fried rice. I don't remember what I ordered. I was so nervous. I was trying to be dignified, to sit up straight and be calm. We started to talk. On the table was a dish of limes and peppers. Without thinking, I sliced off a sliver of a tiny, bird's eye pepper and handed it to him.

"Try?" I teased.

Instead of refusing, which I expected, he popped it into his mouth. Suddenly his face turned very red. His eyes watered. He couldn't speak. He reached for the glass of water and gulped it down. I couldn't help it. I started to laugh. It was a nervous laugh. I felt sorry for him. Here he was so young, so poor, but he had asked me out to eat and now I was poisoning him.

He objected but I paid for the dinner.

We started to meet almost every day downtown. The next time I saw him he confessed he had lied to me. "I'm not poor," he said. "I'm not sending money home either."

I asked him why he lied.

He said, "The guys told me never let a Vietnamese girl know you have money. They will strip you to the bone, make you fall in love, and then dump you. So I made it up."

The truth was that I had fallen in love with him. I had fallen for him like a typhoon, like thunder and lightning. I couldn't see beyond him. In my heart and mind he was a god. Rich or poor, I didn't care. I was glad he had told me the truth, though.

A few days later we went to the International House for dinner. It was my first time ever in such a fine place. The red carpets, the cooks in white frocks and chef's hats behind the long serving tables, the huge sides of beef, and the waitresses in their uniforms.

Brian pulled out my chair, holding it for me. I sat down. Even in my high heels, my feet barely touched the floor. I swung my feet. Brian looked at me and smiled. "Need any help?" I was trying hard to act sophisticated but I was still a country girl.

I was amazed. Since I had met Brian everything he did amazed me.

After we sat down, Brian ordered a bottle of wine. The wine bottle was brought to the table and showed to him. As a small amount of the wine was poured in a glass, Brian ate a small piece of bread first. Politely the server waited while Brian tasted the wine. Brian nodded his head slightly in approval. I was so impressed.

Two new glasses were put on the table and the wine was poured. I didn't know what to do. Should I wait for the food? Drink it with Brian? I looked around to see how other people did it. When I turned back, Brian had his wine glass in his hand and raised high.

"Cheers," he said.

It was my first glass of wine. I didn't like the taste but I couldn't spit it out. It took me the whole long meal to finish that one glass. Luckily the delicious roast beef helped me to swallow it. By the end of the meal I saw two of Brian. I was happy, very happy.

He had to help me down the stairway.

I hung onto his arm and I laughed. I was not supposed to do that, hang onto him. Or even be with him in public. Vietnamese women dating foreigners were looked down upon. If we did date foreigners, we had to have papers to travel together.

As we walked down the stairs, I remember the eyes everywhere looking at us, some smiling but many with disapproval. Some people were whispering.

Whatever, either the wine had made me drunk or my happiness had overcome my fear. I didn't care what anybody thought of me.

When we reached the sidewalk, we were confronted with a crowd of street vendors. Merchants rushed at us, holding up their goods and screaming,

"*Ong My, Ong My* American gentleman' you buy, you buy?"

We walked through them to the curb and Brian flagged down a taxi. He held the door for me as I got in.

I smiled up at him. "Where do we go now?"

He touched my arm as he closed the door.

"You are going home," he said gently.

He was so proper.

I remember how upset I was to be sent home.

For me, at that time of my life, there was no one I wanted to spend time with except Brian. All I could think of was Brian, and Brian only. I no longer went out with my friends or cared to go to work. All I did was eat and sleep and dream of Brian.

Soon it was New Year's Eve. All of my crowd went out to Maxim's. I don't remember much about it except that I didn't drink anything. My housemate, Thuy, would not be back until very late. We left early. Brian took me back to my house.

He stood by the taxi, waiting for me to go safely inside.

Not tonight, I thought.

I broke our house rule. I invited him in. Then I invited him up to my room. Even though it was still December, the heat was intense that night. Upstairs, we walked down the narrow hallway to my room. I turned on the light and the ceiling fan. I felt the heat rushing to my own face. I didn't know if it was because Brian was in my room or because my room was so messy.

Earlier that day, after my shower, I had walked out of my slippers and my lounging pajamas. They were right there in the middle of the floor. My bed was still unmade, the unfolded mosquito net still hanging loose. I apologized to Brian for my messy room.

I kicked off my shoes, pulled out a chair, and asked Brian to sit down.

Brian didn't seem to care about the mess. He also didn't sit down. He reached for me and I didn't resist. Our lips touched and we kissed deeply. We could no longer control ourselves. Without a word I was in his arms, my heart pounding. Brian picked me up and carried me to the unmade bed.

Under the mosquito net we made love. For the first time in my life I felt free to express my womanhood. Like two over-excited teenagers we failed the first attempt. Not too surprising for a man who had lived almost like a monk. No matter, our next try was magical. My body's responses were intense, explosive. His touch, the warmth of his body, was pure physical pleasure. We lost ourselves. I wanted it to last forever.

But Brian's curfew was near. We knew what would happen if he was caught on the street after eleven or if he didn't return to his compound. At the door, his blue eyes looked down at me. "Mai, I promise to come see you tomorrow after work." I was choked with tears but reluctantly I had to let him go.

After he left I went back to bed. I held the pillow where he lay and dreamed of him. I sniffed the bed for the scent of his body. His scent made me want him back so fiercely. Everything had happened so fast I didn't have time to think. All I could think of were his blue eyes looking at me and his incredible smile. I searched my soul. *Do I really love this man?* My heart told me yes.

I mumbled to myself, "Love is wonderful, love is romantic. Love makes my stomach tremble...."

I closed my eyes and let the memories of our evening together fill my head.

Tomorrow, tomorrow he will come for me.

I was into my dreams when I heard gunshots near the house. I jumped out of bed, quickly put on my clothes, and hurried out on the balcony. Lights were flashing in the sky over the city. The thought of last year's Tet offensive was still fresh in my mind.

Oh my God. Where is Brian? Is he still on the streets? How long did I lay in bed? Are the Viet Cong invading Saigon again?

What should I do? Should I hire a driver and check on the streets? But I didn't know where he lived or which road he had taken. The thought of him being killed because of me made me sick to my stomach.

"I shouldn't have invited him into the house!" I moaned. "I shouldn't have hung onto him when he wanted to go! *I've killed him!*"

Before I met Brian I had seen many girls in love with GIs. I had seen them crying, angry, destructive, the things they did when their boyfriends left them and went back to America and never returned. I used to tell myself what a waste of time to cry over a boy. That night, in the same situation, I was not any better. I paced the room and up and down the stairs. Finally, I lay down again and cried myself to sleep, only to awake, scared that Brian would never return. I blamed myself.

Thuy came home late and found me still awake.

She stomped into the room. "What's happened? The maid's scared to death! Did your mother die?" Between my sobbing, I confessed what I had done. Thuy looked down at me and began to laugh. "You've really got it bad. You're in love! Do you even know what day it is?"

I shook my head.

"You've lost it, Mai. Did you forget you went out with your new boyfriend tonight? Do you remember why? It's the French New Year! People are celebrating; crazy American GI's are shooting guns or setting off firecrackers to make noise, to have fun! There's no Viet Cong invasion! Silly girl, I thought *he* was the one supposed to get the love potion, not you."

She walked out singing *Love Potion No. 9.*

The next day I prepared a lovely private dinner and waited for Brian.

Six o'clock went past, then seven o'clock. I was sure he would not return. Part of me wanted to go out and forget about him. Part of me didn't want to leave the house for fear he might come. Tired and sad, I went back to my room, closed the door. Pitying myself, I let my unwanted tears flow onto the pillow.

The door opened quietly.

I didn't bother to look, thinking it was Thuy coming to tease me again. I felt a big, gentle hand on my back. "Hi," said Brian. "Thuy let me in." I turned around and draped my arms around his neck. "You are back."

He held me quietly. He was nervous.

"What is wrong?" I said.

Still holding me he said, "Mai, we can't make love again."

"Why not?" I asked. "Because I am not a good girl?"

He shook his head, "No, no, not that—It's me, I am Catholic. It is wrong. It is a sin."

"Oh," I said. "I understand—you want to be a monk."

He blushed. "Not that either."

"Then why not?" I asked.

"It is... complicated," he said. "I – you—It's a sin to have sex with a woman who is not your wife." Before I could say anything he went on.

"Do you know why I am late to come here?"

"No. Why are you late?"

"I went to a church, a priest, to make my confession. To ask God to forgive my sin."

"Did he forgive you?" I asked.

"He forgave me," he said, "but I can't keep on sinning again."

I started to cry. "That's it. You don't want to come see me."

"No, no, I still can see you." Gently, he kissed me. "But you have to promise to help me not sin anymore, ok?"

"I promise," I said.

We had our cold dinner and went upstairs to my room. We went out and sat on the balcony. I sat under his arm, cuddling. We talked as we looked down on the streets. There was no breeze except the fan in my room so we went inside. We sat on the bed playing cards. Somehow we started playing strip poker. Brian was a good card player, but I was better. The game always ended in my favor.

So Brian continued to go to confession.

And I continued to lie to Bill.

Every time Bill came to visit me, I begged off going out with him. "Auntie Moi is sick," I said. Or, "Auntie Moi needs my help today."

Bill would just nod, "I understand."

For the first time in my life I knew what it felt like to love and be loved. I waited for Brian's visits. I didn't go out and I didn't care what my friend said. I stopped going to work and conducting my business.

One afternoon Brian came to see me. We just talked. He couldn't stay long.

After he left I stayed seated in the living room. There was a knock on the door. I didn't bother to get up. I thought it must be one of my friends coming to see me. But the knock got louder, so I asked Tu, the maid, to open the door.

It wasn't one of my friends. It was Bill, with two dozen red roses in his hands. He walked over and stood before the couch.

"I came to see you many times downtown, but you weren't there. I got worried. Today one of your friends gave me your address and said you were sick. I hope you don't mind me coming here."

I got off the couch as fast as I could. I pulled him to the door.

"No, no, you're not supposed to be here! I am waiting for my aunt. Please, you must go. I will meet you downtown. I don't want her to see you here! Please...."

He handed the roses to me and walked out with a sad face.

The maid was as scared as I was. She was running around the house, incense sticks burning in her hands, moaning, "*Mo Phat, Mo Phat!*" Oh, Buddha! Oh, Buddha! The strong incense was giving me a headache.

Then Brian walked through the door.

I almost passed out. The maid gave a shriek and ran into the kitchen. I just stared at him. He came over and gave me a kiss. "I forgot my cigarette lighter."

It was on the table. I handed it to him.

"Bernie, please don't go," I said.

"I wish I could stay but I'm already late," he said. "I'll see you tonight, promise."

After he left I decided to go upstairs and get dressed.

I was bothered about Bill, that I was being dishonest. Once I thought I might have loved him but nothing like the way I was in love with Brian. It's not fair to Bill, I thought. He's a great guy. He deserves better.

I was halfway to the stairs when the door slammed open.

Bill stomped into the room, his face as red as a pepper. He went to the coffee table and pulled the roses out of the vase. "Bill, w-what you are doing?" I stuttered.

"Who was here with you?" he glared at me.

"No one, just me. You have to leave, please. My aunt is coming. I will get in a lot of trouble!" I begged him, holding onto his arm, pulling him out the door.

I shut it and locked it this time.

When I turned around the maid was right behind me. I jumped, pressing my hands to my chest. "You should not scare me half to death," I whined. She gave me a look that said, *You did this to yourself. I had nothing to do with it, lady.* Then she turned and walked into the kitchen without a word.

"That was close," I whispered.

My heart was still jumping fast. I thought how lucky it was that Brian had left. Then I remembered their guns. Bill carried his under his arm and Brian carried his on the hip. The more I thought about their guns the more scared I became. I couldn't just wait for Thuy to come home. What if Bill was out there waiting for Brian to come back?

Now I was terrified. I had to get out, to warn Brian.

I didn't bother to look for my pocketbook. I went into the kitchen and asked the maid to lend me the money. I opened the side door and slipped into the alleyway, thinking I was safe if Bill was out front. It didn't work. As I stepped out from the alleyway, Bill spotted me. He started to jump out of his jeep, but I was quicker. I jumped on the back of a rental Honda at curbside and yelled at the driver to take off.

Bill chased me down to my aunt's house.

He sat outside and waited for me to come out. When I didn't, he sent a young boy in to get me. "Tell Mai if she doesn't come out to talk to me, I will come in there."

Reluctantly I went outside.

He was calmer, not so angry as before. Quietly he asked me, "Mai, do you have another boyfriend?" I didn't answer. I just nodded my head without looking at him.

"Then you have to make up your mind," he said. "It's either me or him, Mai, you can't have us both."

Without looking up, I said,

"Him."

Ten days later Bill came back to see me. He was more reasonable. He invited me out to have coffee, so I did. After all, I told myself, I owed him an apology. We sat down and ordered. Before I could speak, Bill said, "Mai, did you know that your man, Mr. Bernard Donohue, will leave Vietnam in a short time, that his tour of duty is almost over?" He was twisting his glass of iced coffee in his hands. I was close to tears, watching him.

"I know," I said. "He told me."

"He didn't promise to come back, did he?"

"Yes, Bill, he did."

"Do you believe him?"

"Yes," I said. I pushed my glass aside. "Bill, I am sorry things didn't work out between us. I didn't mean to—"

"Mai, no harm done," he said. "I owe you the apology—I behaved very badly the other day. It was my fault. I assumed you were my girlfriend. Then when I found out you were in love with someone else, I just went nuts."

There was pain in his face.

"Mai, please, tell me the truth. Did you ever love me?"

I was choking and couldn't find the right words. I didn't dare look at him. "I thought I did. I did care for you and I still care for you, but I'm not in love with you." I was crying and unable to stop.

He reached for my hand and held it tight.

"Mai, please don't cry. All I want is for you to be happy."

He brought me back to my house. Always a gentleman, he thanked me for going out with him. He asked if he might come in for just a few minutes. I said yes. He walked in, went over to the table, picked up my picture and took it out of the frame. Then he took his pen out and wrote on the back of my picture. He turned to me.

"Mai, I can't give you my address here because of my job, but here is my address in the States. If you ever need to reach me, for any reason, I will get to you. No matter where I am."

He put my picture down slowly.

"I hope your boyfriend is as true to you as you are to him."

I wanted to say something but my throat was tight. Bill's thoughtfulness, his kindness, made me feel ungrateful. I still cared for him as a friend. It was sad and emotional for me to say goodbye to him.

After Bill's visit I knew there was no one I wanted in my life but Brian.

Even though I knew Brian only had a short time left in Vietnam, I wanted to make every minute count. I used my connections to get police papers so we could go out in the evenings without being harassed, so we could have a few weeks of happiness together.

There were times we spent the whole evening in my room.

We used the excuse that the evening heat was too intense to go out. We played strip poker. We made love. We laughed. We lived in our own little world. There were only the two of us. When eleven o'clock curfew came, it was hard for us to part. Brian would return to his compound. I would be alone in my bed, holding his pillow, letting my senses relive our evening, waiting for our reunion the next day.

Then Brian went back to the United States.

He told me his father was really sick now. He was going back on emergency leave to see him. He promised he would return for me, that he had extended his tour of duty in Vietnam. As much as I wanted to believe him, his absence took its toll. I couldn't eat or sleep. Worse, it got to the point that I didn't bother to get out of bed or even take a shower.

My friends tried to cheer me up. They offered to take me to the zoo, to movies, out to clubs, but I would refuse. They were so worried that they asked my godmother to come and see me.

At first Vu Linh tried to talk to me but it didn't work. She got angry. She dragged me by the hand to the shower.

"This will wake you up and get you out of bed! You silly girl! No man on this earth is so important to kill yourself for!"

While she scolded me she poured buckets of cold water over my head. "Now clean yourself up, get dressed and come downstairs! I brought some of your favorite food. Get something in you and then we talk."

She shook her hand at me.

"Do you think Bernard would like to see you like this? If I were him, do you know what I would do? I would go find a woman who can take care of herself! Lovesick, hah! Lovesick is all in the head. Of all people, you should be strong, not weak!"

The pep talk and the hot broth revived my soul but I still missed Brian so much. My heart still ached. Vu Linh could see this. She said quietly, "Mai, you must keep yourself looking good. When Bernard comes back he must not see you like this. Who can love a half-crazy woman? You must look good so that when he first sees you, he remembers how pretty you look!"

From that day on, I got out of bed every day.

I started counting the days. For nine days I took my shower, got dressed, put on my makeup and went downstairs. I sat on the couch and waited. On the tenth morning, I was too tired, too depressed. I gave up.

I got off the couch and, holding onto the rail, slowly dragged my feet up the stairs. Someone was knocking at the door, but I had no energy to go back down.

"Tu, please open that door," I called. "If someone is looking for me tell them I am sick." When I was at the top of the stairs I heard her cry, "*Dai Uy, Dai Uy!*"

My feet light as feathers, I took two steps at a time down the stairs.

Brian was standing outside in the courtyard. When I saw him I screamed.

His blue eyes met mine, his incredible smile melted my heart. I leaped up into his arms, burying my face against him. He held me like a child. I let myself cry.

Gently he kissed me. He whispered softly. "Froggie, It's *okay*. I'm here. I missed you so much." I held onto his neck, afraid to let go. My tiny body fit in his strong arms. He carried me upstairs to my room where we stayed into the evening.

I remember how happy I was.

That night, sitting on the bed, I told Brian I wanted to have a child with him.

"A little *Dai Uy* just like you." I said. "So when you leave me, I will still have your child." Suddenly I felt sad. "When you go, promise you never forget me?"

My words made Brian very solemn.

"Froggie..." he said, and held me tight in his arms.

There was a mosquito buzzing inside the mosquito net. I pushed Brian back down and jumped up, trying to kill the little bugger with my bare hand. Brian laughed and pulled me down onto him. "Do you know why I call you Froggie?"

Playfully I pushed him away.

"Why? Because I look like a frog?"

There were frantic knocks on the door and a shaking voice, "*Co Mai*, you have to come downstairs. It is urgent!" It was the maid.

"Tu, what is it? Can you tell me?" I was still in Brian's arms.

"Hurry up, come down," she cried. "I am scared the other American is at the gate!"

My heart bumped. I didn't want Brian to think I had another boyfriend while he was gone. I jumped out of bed and gathered my clothes scattered on the floor.

"I'll be right down," I said to Tu.

I turned to Brian. "Please, don't come downstairs. It's nothing. I'll be back soon."

Quick as a flash I was out the door and down the stars. Tu's face was as white as a ghost. I opened the front door and went out to the courtyard. The moon was full, but I didn't see anyone.

"Psst, psst, I'm over here."

I looked over at the side alley. Bill was outside the fence under the shadow of the house. My heart dropped down into my belly.

"What are you doing here?" I hissed.

I walked down the long side of the house toward him. I could not see his face clearly but I could smell the alcohol on him even through the fence.

"Bill, you are drunk. I don't want to see you," I said quietly.

He ignored me. "I know your boyfriend is back today. I just wanted to see you one last time," he blurted.

All I could say was, "Why?"

"I just got married," he said.

I said, with a little envy for her married state, "Bill, who is the lucky woman?"

"No one you know. Her name is Mai, too."

He chuckled drunkenly. "So, now your boyfriend is back and I am married—how about you and me have an affair?"

I was shocked. "Bill, are you crazy? I didn't sleep with you when I dated you! What makes you think I want to have an affair with you now? You are drunk! Go back to Long Binh!"

Then his words hit me.

"Bill, how do you know my boyfriend is back?"

He chuckled again. "That's for me to know and you to find out. I am CIA. Do you know what that means? Go upstairs and ask your boyfriend. He will tell you."

I pleaded. "Bill, for God's sake, please leave. Go back to your new wife."

"Okey dokey," he slurred. "If you say so."

As he staggered out to the street, I stood there wondering. how he knew Brian was back and what made him come to see me? Was he really married and why did he need to tell me?

When I went back upstairs Brian had already dressed to go to his compound.

"Froggie, is everything okay?"

"Yes," I said, but I didn't go any further.

291

CHAPTER 27

Family Matters

A few months later, Brian returned to the United States once again. His father was dying.

I thought I had learned from my mistakes the first time but my fear that he wouldn't come back this time was even greater. I knew his extended tour was almost over. I didn't tell anyone, even my godmother. I just packed a small bag and left the city, trying to get back home. Brian had returned to see his family twice in the United States yet I hadn't seen my own family for a long time. My ex-husband was dead now and my son was somewhere in my old district. I wanted to see him.

So I bought a bus pass and headed out.

It took two days to get to Quy Nhon. The war was getting worse. Parts of Highway One north to Quang Ngai were blocked. The Viet Cong blew up bridges at night and the government and the Americans couldn't rebuild them fast enough. I stayed in Quy Nhon for several days waiting and then decided to return to Saigon. On the way back I stopped at Tuy Hoa to see my brother An. During my visit, I told him about Brian.

My brother was so angry at me for shaming our family.

"How dare you date a foreigner! You are betraying our family, our family name, our society! I thought you'd changed, but you haven't. You are still a spoiled child. You always want the biggest fruit on the tree. You will do anything to get it, even if you break your arm. Now you are a grown woman and you still do unspeakable things! Mother was right, you are more trouble than you are worth. I can't believe you do this to your family!"

I protested. "Brother, that is not true and you know it! I was never a spoiled child! I've taken care of everyone in our family! I am the one who always had to take crap from everybody!"

"Here you go again," he retorted. "You are living an immoral life. You are sleeping with a man not your husband!" I was so angry I yelled. "Brother, how many women have you slept with who are not your wife?" "That's different, I am a man," he said. "And I found you a good man so you could have a good life and what did you do? You betrayed me!"

"Oh, I see." I said. "Not because I date an American, but because I made you lose face with Phuc, is that it? Brother, that was not my fault. You did that one!"

"Sister, whenever did you think anything was *your* fault? Never. You lived only for what *you* wanted, never caring what effect it would have on our family! Like when you were little, and you climbed up to the tallest branch to pick the best fruit, no matter what. Then you fell out of the tree and broke your arm. That wasn't your fault either, right? It's never your fault!"

"Brother, what are you talking about?"

"The custard apple and the black chicken! Mother had to kill our best and most profitable chicken. That chicken would lay many eggs to feed our family! But no, you had to have that fruit. You broke your arm. Did you even think it how much it would cost us? No, you never think of that, and now you have a love affair with a foreigner. Do you care what your selfishness will cost our family this time? No, you don't!"

My brother was right. I had done many things unacceptable to my family and to my society. I remembered that incident clearly now. Being a girl, I was not allowed to climb trees, but I did. The custard apple tree wasn't the first time I did it. I had climbed betel trees to pick the leaves for my mother to chew with areca nut, but that was different. She told me to do it.

Tree climbing ...

I could suddenly see that custard apple tree again, that one big fruit dangling. Every day I had looked up at the big beautiful fruit dangling on the high branch. Our ladder wasn't tall enough and my brothers and sister were afraid of falling. They wanted that fruit but they didn't dare climb. My mother knew I wanted that fruit, too. She warned me not to climb that tree and pick that fruit.

"Cam, leave that fruit alone," she said. "Don't climb up that tree and rip your clothes. You will be punished if you do not obey me!"

The more she warned me the more I wanted that fruit.

One day when she was out, I climbed as high as I could and stretched out to grab the fruit. The branch broke and I landed on the ground, the fruit in my hand. I was excited to have the fruit but soon my fear was greater than my excitement. How would I explain the broken branch to my mother?

Luckily, she didn't look at the tree. But my nightmare had just begun. My right wrist was in such pain. It got bigger and bigger as the day went on. The pain was unbearable but my fear of my mother was greater.

I managed to do my chores with my left arm but pulling the water bucket out of the well with one arm was hard. My mother saw me using my feet and my teeth to draw up the rope, but not my right hand. She got suspicious.

She ordered me to roll up my shirtsleeves to show my arms but I couldn't, my wrist was so swollen. My mother got angry that I was defying her. She grabbed my shirt and stripped it down. I gave a howl and passed out.

She must have realized instantly that I had injured my hand because when I regained consciousness she was using scissors to cut off the sleeve. My wrist was dark purple and blown up like a sausage.

Surprisingly, she didn't hit me. She went out to the yard and trapped the closest chicken. It happened to be the black hen, the special kind. She didn't even bleed it. She just cut off the head, opened the body, and wrapped the body around my wrist, the feathers still sticking to the chicken. By that afternoon the swelling had gone down. When my wrist was nearly back to its size, my mother went to the neighbors and picked some kind of leaves. She ordered my sister to pound the leaves to a paste. She put the paste on my arm and wrist and then used banana leaves and bamboo strips to put my arm in a cast.

No, my family had never forgiven me for that.

Now my brother was using the accident to show me how insensitive I was to date an American man, that my foolishness affected other people in my family, not just me. I had to agree with my brother so I no longer argued with him.

I also didn't try to explain how I felt. I respected his opinions, but my heart belonged to Brian, the man I had fallen in love with. Even though I wasn't sure he would ever return for me, I'd rather have him in my life for a short time than not at all.

I was not angry with my brother. I wasn't sorry I had told him about Brian. What I was sorry about was my mistake in leaving the city. I was to regret every hour, every minute and second while I sat on that bus.

The trip back was dangerous.

The road to Saigon had major damage. The Viet Cong had attacked everywhere. Parts of the road were destroyed. Dead bodies lay alongside the highway. Villages and hamlets nearby were still burning, the smoke coming in the windows. Most of the time my stomach hurt and my throat was tight. I could see my fear and anxiety on the other passengers' faces. The bus drivers didn't want to take any risks. They only traveled in the late morning or early afternoon.

It took us three long days to get to Saigon, a trip that normally took a day.

I was so glad the bus reached the city in daylight. I took a taxi home. I wanted to rest but the emptiness surrounded me. I couldn't stand it. I took a quick shower and went out again. Aimlessly I roamed the streets of Saigon. There was nothing I wanted and nothing I needed. I was uncertain what my future would be if Brian didn't come back.

I watched couples walk hand in hand on the streets. I felt lonely and hollow. Suddenly, the idea struck me hard that Brian had already come back and didn't want to see me! I stopped at Brian's compound on Le Qui Don Street. I found his roommate, Tom. I asked him if he had heard from Brian.

"Mai, Bernie and I just share a room," he said. "Most of the time he's at work or out with you. Since he went back to the States, I don't know where he is. I am sorry but I don't have his address." I thanked him and went to see my godmother but I didn't feel like staying long. She offered me food, but I said no.

It was late at night when I got back to my house. A big party was going on.

Boys and girls were drinking and dancing to loud music. So much for our house rules, I thought. No sex, no drugs, no drinking. Obviously, Thuy didn't know I was back from the countryside. She'd had more than a few drinks herself. The maid came out of the kitchen as I walked in. She took one look at me and went back in the kitchen.

Thuy came up to me, laughing and swaying.

"Hi, Mai! We're having a party for Tan. He didn't pass his final exam. His father was angry with him. He won't pay for Tan's diploma. Tan can't be a lawyer. So he will join the South Vietnamese Army to be an officer. He will fight for our safety."

I was too tired. All I wanted was to go to my room but the boy Tan staggered over to chat with me. I was annoyed but I tried my best not to be rude. "Tan, I am sorry that you have to go out to the battlefield," I said. "I would like to stay and party with you, but I am so tired. I have traveled for three days. I need to sleep."

He put his hand out and blocked my way. He yelled out for someone to bring me a chair. He sat me down and handed me a tall glass of rum and coke. His speech was slurred. "Mai, forget about that American *Dai Uy*. He won't come back. I didn't tell you before but I always loved you. I will return after the war for you. I will be your *Dai Uy!* Please, just one drink with me. Who knows, maybe I will be dead and never return."

Normally I didn't let peer pressure get the best of me but somehow the drink looked so inviting. I could feel the noisy crowd, the cheer, the pressure around me. "Tan, one drink, that's all," I said. "Then I go to bed and wait for my love, not *you*." We all laughed.

"Drink, drink and be happy!" they cried. Everybody raised their glasses.

"Drink, drink!"

I lifted my glass, closed my eyes and let the sweet drink slide down my throat. That was all I remember. The next thing I knew I was in my bed, still wearing my purple outfit. I was blurry. I could not remember what had happened to me.

The maid was sleeping at the foot of my bed.

"Tu, Tu, wake up!" I said. "How—who brought me up here?"

Half asleep, she opened one eye.

"Miss Thuy and I."

I had passed out soon after that drink. Tu and Thuy had taken me up to my room and Tu had stayed there to guard me in case some of the guys got fresh.

I was still dizzy but hungry. I sent Tu out to get me a bowl of *phở* and a Vietnamese iced coffee. I ate my soup and drank my coffee. I took a long cold shower and returned to bed. I soon fell back to sleep.

I dreamed a big black bear was chasing me, over mountains, hills and sand dunes. No matter where I ran the big bear was after me. I tried my hardest to escape but my feet were stuck in quicksand. I waved my arms and called for help but the words wouldn't come out. I felt the bear claws pulling on my arms. I gathered all my strength and kicked my feet and screamed. The scream woke me up.

When I opened my eyes, my heart still pounding, my legs tangled in bedclothes.

Brian was sitting beside me on the bed, his hand on my shoulder.

"Froggie, it's me," he said softly.

"Your father?" I said.

He shook his head, unable to speak.

I buried my face in his chest and cried and cried.

Twice now, Brian had gone home to safety and twice he had returned to the war. For me. There were no words to express it. It didn't matter how long he would stay in Vietnam with me. One hour, one day, one week. My heart was filled with joy and love.

Brian was still in uniform but he had resigned his commission. After he was released from active duty he would stay in country as a Defense Department official. The Admiral, now in Washington, had asked him to stay and direct all the training programs.

It was time to introduce him to my godparents' family.

I wasn't happy about it. Deep down in my heart I was afraid I wasn't good enough for him. There were many more beautiful girls in Vietnam, especially my godfather's daughters. They were very beautiful and highly educated.

I told Brian my concerns. He assured me that I was his girl, no one else. It didn't help. My insecurity made me very nervous to take him there.

But it really was time.

I remember how carefully I dressed that day and also the impression Brian made on my godfather.

As for me, my mini-skirts and bikinis had disappeared. After I met Brian I gave them all away. Now I wore an *ao dai* everywhere, covered from neck to ankle. The day of the visit, I stood in front of my mirror for hours checking over every inch of my body, trying on every dress I owned. Finally I chose the pink *ao dai*, high heels, and my fashion statement dark sunglasses.

When we got there I was very tense.

Godmother had prepared the dinner and would serve it in Godfather's private study. There would be just the four of us, no First Wife and no children. I was so relieved but I shouldn't have been.

Godfather was so impressed with Brian that he wanted all his girls to meet him. After our meal, Godfather said in his grand voice, "Vu Linh's Daughter, take Bernard to see your sisters."

Nervous and worried, I had no choice but to obey.

Most of them were out. One of the younger ones, my friend, was there, since she knew me best and had come to my house many times with her boyfriend. To me she was more like a little sister. However, one of the most beautiful of the older sisters, Kim, happened to be in her room.

When I say beautiful, I mean *beautiful*. Her black shining hair hung down to her waist. Her eyes were stunning, deep and inviting. She was about five feet two. Her breasts were firm, succulent fruits. Her nipples stuck out underneath her loungewear. Her skin was soft and creamy, like polished egg shell. Her teeth were perfect and gleaming. Her nose was high and elegant. Her lips were wet and soft and pink. She was so beautiful and so charming, and she was also the queen of flirtation. She could speak at least three languages, especially French.

Men and boys hung around Kim like flies. Sometimes she dated three or four men at the same time. She hid them from each other in her sisters' rooms. She was the beautiful daughter of a rich man so she got away with it. If she'd been poor, people would have called her a different name, or maybe not. Whatever, she was the master of her game. To her, my boyfriend was nothing. It was a game she and her sisters played, the thrill to see how much power they had to make men wilt, especially each other's men.

I didn't warn Brian. I wanted to see his reaction to her. If I was going to lose him, it would be today.

Kim was lying on her bed in her elegant, short, baby blue peignoir.

"Oh, Sister Mai, this must be *Dai Uy!* It is *Bernard*, isn't it?" She pronounced his name the French way. She held her hand out to be taken by him.

"Welcome, welcome to our little family!" She smiled up at him. "I must apologize to you, *Bernard*, I didn't think you would be coming to my room. Otherwise I would have gotten up and dressed for you!"

Oh, sure, I thought. *You didn't have any warning. Hah!*

She motioned her hand to a chair as if she were Cleopatra.

"*Bernard*, please, bring that chair over and come sit here by me. Would you like something cold to drink? And you, Sister Mai?" She didn't wait for us to answer. She turned her body, enough to lift her gown so we could see the suggestion of her beautiful thighs. She opened her little refrigerator and took out the Vietnamese cola. "Bernard, would you like some?"

I tried not to be alarmed but I knew I was no match for her.

I glanced over to see how Brian was reacting.

He grinned at me and shrugged his shoulders.

"Oh, Sister Mai," Kim went on, "You never told us how handsome Bernard is!" Slowly she leaned forward toward his face.

"Bernard, you have the most beautiful blue eyes."

As she looked in his eyes she said quietly, "How was the lunch with my father, Bernard?" She smiled at me. "Sister Mai, Father must have been so pleased with Bernard." Looking at Brian again, "Father has been a powerful man in his life. He's a good judge of men. He likes you, doesn't he?"

Brian kept smiling.

After a bit more small talk we excused ourselves and returned to Godfather's room. Either it was the big lunch or the opium but he was deep in his dreams. Vu Linh wanted us to take a nap in her room but we declined. We said goodbye to her and caught a taxi.

In the taxi I asked Brian what he thought about our visit.

"It was interesting."

"Which part?" I teased, "With Kim or with my godfather?"

"Oh, both."

I couldn't keep the jealousy out of my voice. "What do you think about Kim? She's beautiful, isn't she?"

"Oh, she's beautiful, but—"

"What do you mean? Do you like her?"

"Oh, yes, I do!"

"For real?" I said.

"No, Froggie, I just wanted to tease you."

"You are fibbing," I said as I moved away from him.

"Froggie, she's just like other girls. You are the one I want." He pulled me over to him and gave me a kiss.

"You are my girl."

Brian needed a place to live. As a civilian, he couldn't stay in the BOQ (Bachelor Officer Quarters). He was looking at hotels, and asking his civilian ESL consultants where they lived.

I asked him to move in with me, but he refused.

"Why not?" I cried, sobbing. "You will no longer be a military man! And Thuy and I have been arguing a lot lately. I want to move out and get another place but the rent will be too expensive!"

He still shook his head.

I cried harder. "You don't love me enough to make a commitment! Okay, then, if you won't move in with me I will go back to work!"

So he gave in.

We rented a smaller villa on Tran Khanh Du in the Phu Nhuan section, not far from his headquarters. Brian could walk to work. He always dressed casually so no one would suspect who he was. Our neighborhood by the canal was filled with Viet Cong sympathizers but nobody bothered us.

Shortly after we moved in Brian asked me to marry him. "Froggie, I want to do it the right way. You have no family here, and your godfather loves you very much. I want to ask his permission to marry you."

I was so moved by that.

Since the first visit, we came to see my godparents more often. My godfather was always glad to see Brian. He respected Brian for his intelligence, his courage and honesty. He enjoyed talking with him about what went on in the political world. My godmother was always delighted to serve us her special dishes. This visit would be different, though. We were not coming as boyfriend and girlfriend but as a couple now choosing to spend their lives together. We were coming to ask their permission to get married!

Happiness, excitement—I was on Cloud Nine all the way to Truong Minh Giang Street. In the taxi I dreamed of a home, of children, of love and happiness. I had not realized love can do many things. It can turn your head and make you forget who you are.

Until my godfather reminded me.

We sat down in godfather's room. Carefully, Brian asked him for permission to marry me. To my surprise godfather rejected it, and was outright rude to me.

"Bernard, you don't know what you are doing!" he exclaimed. "You are a young American. You have been a Naval officer, a *Dai Uy*, and so young! The future is waiting for you. Someday you will be President of the United States. Why do you risk your life, your future, to marry this poor Vietnamese girl? She was an orphan when my wife took her in. She has very little education. You will not be president if you marry a Vietnamese girl. No, Bernard, you must go back to your own kind."

I sat on the floor helping Vu Linh prepare our meal. Now I was trying my best not to cry in front of Brian. Vu Linh looked at me curiously. She didn't understand what the men were talking about, but I did. godfather was talking about me as if I weren't there!

I couldn't hear what else godfather said. My tears were about to fall. My hands were trembling. I wanted to die rather than listen to him talk any more. I leaped up and ran to the bathroom. My breath was short. My stomach hurt. I began to vomit.

In a flash I realized I had missed my period.

Oh, my God, am I pregnant?

If I was I would not tell Brian. *Oh, God, help me.* No, I don't want him to marry me just because I am carrying his child! No, I won't tell him. But, should I?

Oh, God!

I had a panic attack. I looked around for a way to escape but there was only one way out, past Godfather's room. I collapsed on the floor. I cried and cried until I had no more tears. Finally, I got hold of myself.

Stop it! Go back in there. Pretend you didn't hear a thing.

I washed my face and combed my hair. I took a long breath to calm myself down and walked back down the hall and into Godfather's room.

Brian was looking down at the floor, his hands playing with his cigarette lighter. My godmother's face was red with anger. Godfather was explaining to her in Vietnamese what he had just told Brian. When he saw me he said, "My Goddaughter! The truth hurts but I had to tell him. If you love him you have to think of his future. Don't be selfish. Take your godmother for example. She gave up her life just for me!"

There were no words to express my feelings.

I didn't even try. I couldn't even pretend. My throat was too tight. I desperately needed fresh air. I was about to throw up again. I covered my mouth and ran for the door. "Wait!" Brian called. He bowed to them quickly and came after me.

The ride back was long and dark.

Brian was doing his best to cheer me up, but I didn't hear a word he said. No matter how much he tried to talk to me, all I could think about was what my godfather had said about me, about Brian. All I could think was that I was not good enough for him. That what my godfather had said was true.

Was I carrying Brian's child? Oh, God, what should I do? I could hear my brother's voice scolding me, "What you do affects other people, not just you!" I was so confused.

One minute I was happy because Brian was telling me he loved me and the next I was crushed at my selfishness. *How could I destroy his future?*

It was a terrible ride home. One minute I wanted him to hate me, to break up with me and return to the United States. Yet even as I said these words to him, I held onto him, sobbing, afraid to let go.

Brian was getting exasperated with me.

"Mai, stop it. I'm not going anywhere. I love my country and I've got a job to do here. I loved the Navy, too, but I love you more. Mai, we are going to be married. I want you to be the mother of my children. So calm down, it's all right."

He smiled at me.

"Forget about Godfather. What he said about me was very flattering. And I'm sorry he was so rude to you. But none of it matters. Those are just his opinions. I'm a man. I'm doing what I want, what I need to do."

He tried to tease me.

"I came back to Vietnam twice! Good grief, if that didn't prove I love you, there is nothing else I can do. I can't believe you doubt my love for you. Don't let other influences take over your heart."

He hugged me. "It's a beautiful night and you are my beautiful girl." I sighed and held him.

With or without Godfather's blessing, we would not be parted.

CHAPTER 28

Going to Bien Hoa

One month later we were married in a civil ceremony. I had hired a lawyer and asked Auntie Moi to be our witness. She knew what she was getting into, but she loved being a part of our life now. She was very fond of Brian. She was the only one in the family to stand by me. The civil ceremony was performed by a village chief in an empty room out in Bien Hoa. But it was legal.

On the ride back, Brian looked at me and smiled.

"Hello, Mrs. Donohue."

When we returned to our villa, Auntie Moi was so happy that she didn't want to leave. She just sat on the couch smiling. The maid served her tea and sweets. Auntie Moi just looked at Brian and looked at me, asking question after question, excited. Sometimes she repeated herself. She just sat there smiling, thinking up more questions, more reasons not to leave.

I tried not to be rude and I couldn't tell her to go home, but I wanted to be with Brian as husband and wife. After a while Brian got up and started walking through the rooms from one end of the villa to the other, from the kitchen courtyard to the living room, back and forth.

"Tell your aunt to go home."

"I can't."

After an hour of listening to her say, "Oh, Bernard such a good boy, Bernard such a good boy." Brian just nodded his head, over and over. "Thank you, thank you," he kept saying in Vietnamese.

Finally Auntie Moi laughed her way out to the gate. "Bernard is hungry. You should cook him something to eat. You are his wife now, you know."

"Yes, Auntie, I will."

I walked with her out to the road and flagged down a cyclo. I handed the driver the money and gave him directions back to her place. I waved as she drove away and then dashed back to the villa. Brian was waiting for me at the gate. I pulled him toward the house but he stopped.

"No, no," he smiled. "We have to do this the right way."

He picked me up and carried me over the threshold. Inside, he put me down on a chair and knelt down. With his hands on mine, he looked at me with his blue eyes and said, "Mrs. Donohue, will you marry me? Will you be the mother of my children? I want a dozen of them. They will all be beautiful like you."

He stood up and bowed.

"Now, may I have this dance?"

Just the two of us in our living room, slowly dancing to music. The music stopped and we sat together quietly. Brian lit a cigarette. I took a deep breath and looked up at him. It was now or never. Very quietly I said, "Yes, I will be the mother of your child."

Brian looked at me and put his cigarette down.

"What?" he said.

I could barely speak. I whispered, "We're.... I think.... We're going to have a baby." He was speechless. He just blinked his eyes. "Are you sure? I mean . . when?"

"I don't know. I think I am pregnant."

He looked at my belly, then up at me. Then he smiled from ear to ear. I was sobbing. "I am so sorry. I was afraid to tell you. You are a good man —I didn't want to make you have to marry me."

I couldn't stop crying.

He kissed me. "All the more reason for us to be married." He sat me on his lap and held me close, his face against mine.

"Froggie, don't cry. Our child will have a father. Our child will have my name."

I looked at him in wonder. I never thought having a baby could be that important to him. The next moments were a daze of happiness and love. I loved him so much.

The maid brought us dinner from the street vendors in the alley behind our house. By now Brian's cigarette was all ash in the tray. He had forgotten to smoke it. His eyes were on me all the time. We laughed and talked as he ate. I just picked at my food.

Over us the ceiling fans moved the air slowly.

The maid was peeking at us from the door to the kitchen courtyard. She was waiting for us to move to our bedroom so she could watch her Vietnamese soap operas on our TV.

Brian looked over his shoulder at the maid and laughed.

"Mrs. Donohue, let's go to bed."

Our bedroom was air-conditioned and our bed was neatly made. Two beautiful pillows embroidered with "Hanh Phuc," meaning happiness, lay against the headboard. Brian had not stopped smiling.

Just to see his face shining was so thrilling, there was something about him. It made it so romantic to be in love.

Truly, nothing he did was wrong in my eyes. I worshiped him.

We lay on our bed, his hand on my tummy. He talked about our future, what he wanted for us. In each other's arms we planned our future.

"Mai, do you want to be a Catholic?" Brian asked me.

"It's up to you," he went on. "Either way, I want to marry you in the Church. I want our vows sanctified. I want our baby to have a chance to be baptized."

"Oh, *yes*, I do!" I said to him. "I want to become a Catholic like my Godmother. She gives so much love to others from her heart and from her faith. I want to be like her."

I hesitated.

"I didn't tell her, or you, but I was secretly studying the Bible at the church by my old house. I wanted to surprise her. Then, when we moved here I went to a church nearby and a Vietnamese priest said he would teach me privately."

I didn't want to go on.

"He was nice at first but then he wanted to know more about our... relationship."

"Such as?" Brian asked.

"Oh, about how we made love, how I held you. At one point he wanted me to show him. He wanted me to demonstrate."

Brian sat up and looked at me. "You mean physically, not just explaining?"

I nodded. "I didn't like the way he looked at me then... so I left. And I stopped going to class."

Brian's face turned from red to white. He started to get up.

"Where is this creep?"

I put a hand on his arm.

"Honey, it's okay. Bad men don't make a bad faith. I still want to be a Catholic. Our landlady is also a Catholic. When I told her what had happened she said she could help me, that her uncle is a good priest."

Even without a phone, the news of our civil marriage had traveled fast. Godfather sent Vu Linh to see me.

She brought Brian his favorite steamed buns, *ban bao*, and a delicious Vietnamese sandwich for me. While we were eating she said to me, "Daughter, your Bo has heard that you were married in Bien Hoa. He sends you both his congratulations. He wants you both to come see him. Please come."

So Brian and I went over to Truong Minh Giang Street to see him. It was fine with me. There was nothing Godfather could say. We were legally married.

When we got there I was, once again, surprised.

I don't know what had changed his heart but Godfather was sincerely happy for us and was glad to be a part of our lives. First, he gave us his blessing. Then he offered to pay for our church wedding.

"Bernard," he said, "In American tradition the bride's family pays for the wedding. Mai doesn't have her parents so Vu Linh and I will pay for the church wedding and feast to celebrate and bless your union. We must do it right."

Brian thanked him respectfully but declined.

"No, Godfather, since I am marrying Mai here in Vietnam, it is proper to follow your tradition that the groom's family pays for the wedding. My family cannot be here but I am a grown man. Since I am the groom I will pay for the wedding."

Over whisky the two men politely argued over who would pay for my wedding. I was too happy to care who paid—as long as I had my beautiful four-tiered layer cake with flower sculpture icing from the French bakery!

Our wedding was unlike any wedding I had ever heard of.

In America, planning the wedding can take a year or more. I know one wedding that took more than a year and then the couple filed for divorce six months later! In Vietnam weddings take even longer. So many traditions to observe. Two years can pass from the engagement to the wedding day. Astrologers, readers of the Asian zodiac, all have to be consulted. The year, day, even the hour, for the wedding has to be determined.

Our wedding planning took us five weeks.

It took that long because two governments in a war zone were involved. Also, we wanted to be married in the Catholic faith. Brian was a Catholic. I was studying but had not yet been baptized. I had to complete my studies. And Brian had to prove to the American priest that he was a Catholic and had never been married. Brian had to wait for his baptism and confirmation papers, and a statement that he had never been married from his old pastor. On top of it all, Brian had to find a best man. Finally he found a friend, a Catholic classmate who was still in country.

It was right out of a crazy movie script.

No plans, no rehearsals, no printed invitations, and no one in charge. There were so many people involved I didn't know who was doing what. Nothing matched, anything might go wrong, but in the end everything fit together.

For instance, my godparents took it upon themselves to make the arrangements for our reception but I didn't know where, somewhere in Cho Lon, they said. Brian himself took care of the paperwork and the church. He also invited his Vietnamese and American staffs and his boss, Admiral Rauch, the chief of staff. Many of them I had never met.

My closest family in the city was Auntie Moi. She couldn't do much for me, but I had done a lot of business with her bosses, who didn't have a daughter and who always treated me like a niece. They went out and purchased my engagement and wedding rings—matched and flawless blue diamonds – as well as our gold wedding bands.

Auntie Moi invited all my relatives, but no one came except one old man. So Auntie Moi, her bosses and their children, would be my guests. It was Auntie Moi who ordered the beautiful French cake I wanted.

My landlady, a Catholic, arranged for my baptism in time for my wedding. She was the nicest, most wonderful landlady I ever had. Her first name was also Mai so we had decided I was Miss Mai and she was Mrs. Xuan Mai. She was in her thirties and beautiful. Her husband had worked for Ngo Dinh Diem and had been killed during the coup along with Diem and Nhu. She had no suitors but she had a close friend, a doctor, so she borrowed him to escort her and her children.

I didn't mind and I didn't see why not. It was the happiest day of my life. I wanted to share it with people who cared for me. I invited the First Wife and all her children who could make it. Many of my student friends would also come.

When the chaos got too much for me, Vu Linh would tell me not to worry, that my job was to be pretty, to have my dress made and to get to the church on time. I told her I wanted my wedding dress in the Vietnamese style. I also told her I wanted it to be white.

She didn't agree. Neither did Auntie Moi.

Vu Linh said, "No, you are not a virgin, you shouldn't wear white." My aunt said, "No, you cannot wear white. White is the color for a funeral, not for a wedding!"

When I told Brian he said it was all nonsense.

"Honey, you should wear whatever you like! This really is your first wedding, the one where you say *yes*. Besides, in America first-time brides always wear white and I guarantee you, many of them are not virgins! They also wear a veil on their heads and they carry flowers. So should you. Because it's beautiful, and your dress will be beautiful!"

That solved that. If Brian said so, it must be right.

He also said, "In America it is a tradition that the groom shouldn't see the wedding dress. So the couple usually don't see each other the night before the wedding."

So I asked Godmother if could leave my dress at her home.

She said yes, that I could also stay over.

I was happy and busy but deep in my heart I wished that my mother, my sister and my brother An were with me. I wished they could see how happy I was. I wanted so much for them to accept Brian as my husband, not just as some American I married.

Don't hold your breath, I told myself. *They'll never accept you or your husband.*

That afternoon I came home to find An standing in my living room.

He was nervous and tense. I was stunned. I had thought after my last visit with my brother that I would never see him again. Brian came into the room and I introduced them. Brian put out his hand. My brother bowed, not speaking, but he did shake hands.

I sat down in a chair. Brian and An sat on the couch.

My brother started speaking very fast, too fast for Brian to understand.

"Younger Sister, I heard the news of your wedding from Auntie Moi. So I have come to speak to you. I am sorry that I have said harsh things to you. I should not have said them. This American man must love you very much. He looks like a good man. You look happy. I know he

313

has come back to the war twice now, when he didn't have to, because of you. I wish you every happiness but I cannot attend your wedding."

He couldn't look at me.

"I hope you understand why." He went on. "It is not easy in our village. I have my wife to protect, my children. I must look after them. I don't want anything to happen to them. Please keep this visit just between us. I don't want anyone in the family to know I came to see you and this American. Not even Auntie Moi."

After he finished he was more relaxed. He turned to Brian. This time he stuck out both of his hands to shake Brian's hand, which is the respectful way in Vietnam. He and Brian were both smiling and nodding. "Good, good, very good," my brother said, smiling.

Brian took out his cigarettes and offered one to An. Brian lit their cigarettes with his Zippo lighter and they smoked. I was so happy to see my older brother and Brian in the same room.

Brian gave the cigarette lighter to my brother.

My brother accepted it, nodded his head, and soon after that he stood up and left. There were no kisses, no hugs.

A very Vietnamese goodbye.

I didn't cry when he left. I just watched him go.

I was still trying to understand what had made my brother come. Guilt or curiosity? Or maybe it was his love for his little sister. Maybe he just wanted to see for himself if I was truly happy.

It must have been hard for him to be that humble, I thought.

CHAPTER 29

Our Wedding

January 24, 1970, our wedding day.

I had slept over at my godmother's house.

Brian's classmate at the Naval Academy, Tom Barnett, another PBR division commander, had flown into Saigon and would be Brian's best man. I hadn't seen either of them since the night before when they left the villa and went downtown for a bachelor drink.

That morning as I left her house, my Godmother told me to get to the church on time.

I laughed. I had plenty of time. I told her I would return to dress.

On the way to my hairdressers I stopped by the bakery shop to make sure my cake was done. The cake was beautiful. Then I happily went to the hairdressers. Although I didn't go to hairdressers much since I stopped working, my hairdresser was good to me.

When I got there I discovered my hairdresser had quit.

The place was packed with fussing women. Everybody in the shop was busy. The only person free was a new guy. *Oh well*, I told myself, *what can go wrong?*

"I only want banana curls," I said.

"Yes," he said.

"Vietnamese style, of course," I said.

"Yes," he said.

Whatever I said, he said, "Yes." The truth was he didn't have a clue.

It took him more than an hour to do my hair. I was running out of time. When he finished and I saw what he had done, I burst into tears. I was angry, tired and upset. When I protested he insulted me.

I leaped from the chair, grabbed him by the neck, leg-dropped him to the floor, and started choking him. He had been sneering when I leaped for him. He definitely wasn't ready for that one. No one was. There was absolute silence in the shop. Everyone was in shock. I was astonished at what I had done.

The owner dropped what she was doing and came to the rescue. She took me to the back of the shop and calmed me down. Through my tears I told her it was my wedding day, and I wanted to be pretty, and look what he did to my hair! She went back out into the shop and fired him. Then she did my hair herself.

The crisis of my wedding day was not yet over.

Godmother was at her gate, my wedding dress in her arms.

"My daughter, you cannot get dressed here. The First Wife has said she has seven unmarried daughters. She said you cannot walk out of this house in your wedding dress. That if you did, you will take all the charm from her daughters. I am so sorry."

I was so distressed I couldn't speak. I couldn't even cry.

I gritted my teeth, grabbed my dress and my veil and ran out to the main street. I didn't wait for a taxi. I flagged down a motorized cyclo with an open carriage. I jumped in, not bargaining or even telling the man where I was going. We took off, the motor belching, the wind blowing, the hot sun beating on my skin.

"Faster, faster, please!" I howled at the driver.

He howled back, "Miss, where are we going?!"

"Phu Nhuan! I don't know – I'll show you!"

Distraught as I was, I had my wedding to go to. For all I knew Brian was already at the Queen of Peace church, waiting for me.

I told the driver to drop me off at the backdoor of our villa, at the entrance to our landlady's upstairs quarters. My fist banged on the door, my other hand twisting the door knob. The landlady, Mrs. Xuan Mai, had been upstairs getting ready to go to my wedding. She was half dressed when she opened the door.

"Heaven and earth, Mai!" she cried. "What has happened to you?"

I scooted under her arm to get inside.

"Please, I need a place to get dressed! Please, help me."

In the large front quarters of the villa below, I could hear Tom and Brian leaving. I wanted to call out to Brian, but I remembered he had said it was bad luck if he saw me before our wedding. Mrs. Xuan Mai hustled me up the stairs.

"How will you get to church?" she asked.

"I don't know!" I cried.

"All right, " she soothed, "Rinse off and get dressed. I will drive you."

I ran inside the bathroom and rinsed carefully, not wetting my hair. Standing in front of the wall mirror, I tried to put on my makeup. The heat was unbearable. My sweat was dripping from my chin onto my chest. Then Mrs. Xuan Mai came in and turned the ceiling fan on high. But she turned it on backwards. Suddenly the blades were sucking up all the air. My hair flew upwards.

Mrs. Xuan Mai gave a shriek and started to laugh, her hand pointing at me.

"Shut it off! Shut it off!" I screamed.

She shut it off but she couldn't stop laughing, her mascara smeared, her false eyelashes half hanging over her eyes. There was nothing I could do but laugh with her. Somehow we managed to get ourselves dressed and dainty looking.

By now I knew I was very late.

Meanwhile, Vu Linh and my godfather had been worried since I had left. They had come looking for me. They found me with Mrs. Xuan Mai. After discussions it was agreed that Mrs. Xuan Mai would go in her own car.

Godfather said, "I will take our daughter to the church."

He looked at me. "I will take you to the altar."

Hustling and bustling, we all piled into the cars. I sat in the back of Vu Linh's old car beside my eleven-year-old flower girl. My stomach was tight and my heart was pounding. There were traffic jams on every street, every corner.

Vu Linh drove. Godfather sat in the passenger seat giving orders.

"My love, go this way," he said. "Sweetie, turn to the left." Then, "Oh, never mind, go straight." My godmother just smiled and drove. She knew the way. Then Vu Linh called over her shoulder to the flower girl, one of the little daughters.

"Nu, did you remember to bring Sister Mai her flowers?"

"Yes, Auntie, I did."

I looked around. No flowers.

"In the trunk," Nu whispered to me.

I stroked her black shining hair. "Thank you so much, Nu! I am so glad you are my flower girl. You look so pretty in your dress!"

When we arrived at the church, we were an hour late.

Nu hopped out to get the flowers from the trunk. I got out of the car, walked into the courtyard, and stood there, looking up at the church. Outside of old movie scenes, I had no idea what to do next.

Nu brought me a long bunch of white gladiolas wrapped in frilled white paper. I took the flowers gratefully and held them to myself. As I held them she stood there, staring at my dress. "You are so beautiful," she said. Then she turned and walked into the church.

"Okay, Mai," I whispered, "It's now or never."

With my Godparents on either side, I entered the church.

The doors were wide open. Breezes and singing birds were flowing though the lattice windows of the church. In front of the altar stood the tall American priest in bright gold robes. Brian and Tom stood next to him in tailored dark suits and boutonnieres.

Along the aisle, the guests were rising, their heads turned toward me. A large group of men in white Navy uniforms proudly stood up, a woman officer in light blue with them. Music was playing. The small songbirds flew back and forth across the ceiling.

Halfway down the aisle my legs started to buckle.

"*Vu Linh, Bo*, I cannot walk," I whispered.

Their hands went under my elbows.

"Daughter," said Vu Linh. "You will make it. Bernard is waiting."

Then Godfather was handing me over to Brian.

I nearly collapsed.

Brian smiled at me. He didn't ask where I had been or how come I was so late. He just held onto my hand. Throughout the ceremony all Brian did was look at me. We sat or stood as directed. We gave our vows and our rings. Finally, the priest signed the book on the altar rail.

Then Tom signed and then my godfather. The priest pronounced us, in the eyes of the Church, as husband and wife. It was over.

As Brian kissed me, the church filled with applause and cheering.

I don't remember walking down the aisle. I was in a dream.

Outside the church there were many congratulations. I don't know who arranged for the photographer but he was there. He took all our pictures, both at the wedding and the reception. After our pictures with individuals there was a group photograph on the steps of the church. Then everybody drifted toward their cars.

Brian and I still stood there in the courtyard smiling, too happy to wonder how we were going to get to our own reception. No matter. The chief of staff, Admiral Rauch, had loaned us his driver and his black car for the evening. The Admiral himself took a taxi to the restaurant, followed by his security jeep.

The reception was in Cho Lon in the salon of the Pavillon de Jade.

At the restaurant, after we held the receiving line, Brian and I entered the salon. In the center of each table, on a gleaming platter, was placed a whole roast suckling pig, red apple in its mouth. Other courses would include shark-fin in asparagus soup, crab, abalone and mushrooms in sauce; almond jelly; Chinese vegetables steamed or stewed; rice and noodles, both steamed and fried; and of course, magnums of champagne chilling in silver buckets. All this was to be followed by exotic desserts, fruits, rich coffees and liqueurs.

I didn't think the Americans were too thrilled to see a whole pig on their table. They were probably wondering what to do with it. When waiters in white gloves appeared at each table to carve and serve, I could hear grunts of satisfaction. I was told the meat in its juices was succulent beyond compare.

I don't remember eating. Or drinking.

Soon Brian and I were moving from table to table with flutes of champagne in hand to toast our guests, standing behind their tables for group photographs. When we toasted, I would touch my lips to the flute, not daring to drink.

As the afternoon drifted into golden evening, people began visiting and talking. The room was filled with laughter and the happy noise of people trying to talk in four different languages, Vietnamese, English, French, and Chinese, some even using hands and body language to make themselves understood.

We had no band, no music of any kind, just a lonely microphone. So the Navy officers decided, with much laughter and merriment, to provide the entertainment and sing for us. We had our own Navy glee club!

The First Wife had come to the reception. I had never seen her so happy. Not only happy for me, she was so proud to hold court at her table, surrounded by many of her beautiful daughters. As for her daughters, the young Navy officers couldn't take their eyes off them.

Everything was joyous. Food, drink and laughter. The cutting of our majestic cake. More speeches and laughter. We partied into the night.

The most beautiful moment of all happened after the party.

Brian and I were walking alone up the dark alley that led out to the street. Brian was holding me close to his side. Body to body we walked through the darkness. Vietnamese do not show affection in public but, with no one looking, Brian bent down to steal a kiss.

"Mrs. Donohue, you are beautiful. I love you."

I poked him with my elbow and giggled. He laughed.

We reached the bright street. It was a short narrow street. Our black car was parked at the other end, the driver sitting on the hood, smoking.

So many bright lights were shining on us now. So many people were out on the street or crowding the sidewalks, old men standing in doorways of small shops, men and women of all ages talking, children in rags playing. It was a tough neighborhood, a poor one. These people lived very hard lives and had no love for strangers, or Americans.

When we stepped out from the alley, people spotted us and pointed. Soon they had all turned to stare at us.

Down the street I saw our driver leap to his feet, alert for any danger. But we felt no fear at all. We were so young, so happy. We just walked slowly through the crowd, smiling. We were shining, glowing.

And then it happened.

Everyone stepped back, cleared the way for us. The men were looking at Brian, at me, nodding thoughtfully, respectfully. The women's eyes were glistening, smiling at our happiness. Some people started clapping, murmuring, some of them shouting.

"Co dau, chu reu, dep qua, dep qua! Hanh phuc tram nam!"

"Bride and Groom! You are too beautiful, too beautiful! Be happy for a hundred years!"

I had always loved fairy tales, and that night we wrote one.

We waved and smiled, waved and smiled.

Young children were following us now, dancing and yelling. At the car the driver opened the door and we got into the back seat. As we pulled away we looked back at the crowd and waved again. They were still clapping and smiling as we disappeared into the beautiful night.

CHAPTER 30

I Was Told

Brian was my hero, my protector. I thought he was my God. He had pulled me from the mudslide and brought me to safety. He showered me with tender love. He shared my dreams and my hope. I gave him my heart and my soul.

Yet, the week after our heavenly honeymoon, I began to have terrible dreams. Dreams of my ancestors' spirits screaming at me for marrying outside of my people, outside my race. Dreams of the terrifying face of the fortuneteller raging at me that I would die before I was thirty. I hid my dreams. I went secretly to the Buddhist temple, not in faith, but in fear, bearing gifts like the rich. Inside my head a little voice reminded me of the death I owed the teller. Before I met Brian I had nothing to live for. Now I had everything to live for. Why was I so scared?

Not knowing quite why, Brian tried many ways to comfort me. But the more he tried the more guilty I felt. Guilty of being in love. Guilty of a comfortable life when my family was so poor. Guilty to have such happiness that I did not deserve. One night the dreams were so horrible I woke up in a cold sweat, shaking and sobbing. Brian was holding me in his arms, comforting me. Finally I told him my dreams. This couldn't go on. The baby in my womb needed peace.

Brian held me gently.

"Mai, I love you. You are not a bad luck girl reborn. You are a free spirit, a new spirit! Your life belongs only to you, free to share with those you love. No demons can harm you. You are my beloved wife! Believe me, no fortune tellers would dare to harm you, and they cannot harm your spirit. They have no power over you! They are all fakes. Do you think they would live on the street like they do if they had real power? They are a hoax! Believe me, no one in this world has the power to make you die before you reach thirty! If you don't believe me, then who do you believe? God?"

It took me days to realize what Brian had said. God had sent his angels who kept me alive—my sister, my godmother, and now Brian to guide me through to my new life. I did not know why, but I believed God had a good reason to keep me alive.

I WAS TOLD

I was told.
You are a poor Vietnamese girl.
A bad luck girl reborn.
You have no right to cry, to ask us why.
This is our way.
You must pay, and pay.
Tradition.
I was told.
But I refused my mother, my neighbors.

CROSSING THE BAMBOO BRIDGE

I chose my path.
I chose the life I lead.
Now I tell.
The ghost of all childhood fear
Is gone from my river
The ghost of all fortune teller curses
Gone from my soul.
My son, I promise I will return for you.
My husband, the child in my womb, and I.
Together
We cross the bamboo bridge.

Epilogue

After giving birth to our oldest daughter Maura in Vietnam, Brian and I moved to the United States. Over the next six years we had five more children.

In 1982, eleven years after we left Vietnam, I found and reunited with my son Han. He lived with us for a time in the States, then joined the U.S. Navy where he served for 14 years. He is now married and lives in Arizona.

In 1993, I returned to Vietnam and met my family from the North and South. When I returned home I raised funds to help deaf orphans attend school and to build a bridge in my hamlet.

After many years of struggle, we sent our children to college. I wanted to fulfill a college dream too. After a dozen years of study I received my GED, Associate's Degree, and, finally, a Bachelor's of the Arts degree. I worked with Special Education students for 15 years in the local school system. I recently retired.

In 2012 with the help of my colleagues I cooked 350 meals to raise $22,000 to support a high school in Staten Island, New York after it was devastated by Hurricane Sandy.

My friends tell me I have lived the American Dream, from a Vietnam country girl to American soccer mom.

(Photo credit: Tom Barnett)

The Day after the Wedding in Saigon

Acknowledgments

With my deepest gratitude I wish to thank the men and women who served in Vietnam to fight for my freedom. My thanks also to my departed ancestors, my mother, sister and brother, uncles and aunts, whose spirits are always with me; my nieces and nephews who love me for who I am; and my sole surviving sibling, my Viet Cong brother, Mang, who kept the bond between us in spite of our differences. I thank the spirits of my father-and-mother in-law who gave me a wonderful husband, and his sisters and brother Mary, Kathy, Sheila, and Paul, who accepted a stranger into their home and helped me enter the American way of life.

Thank you to the Reilly family, the Braman family, and Steve and Sheila Burke for your friendship that helped me grow. Thanks especially to my first American friends, Donna and Kent Clarkson, for welcoming me with open arms, kindness, love and support.

Thank you to my children Anh, Maura, Maeve, Bernard, Patrick, Aileen and Eirene. You are the reason this book is being published. You have supported me in every project of mine. You taught me many things about America, especially how to be a mother. Thanks also to their spouses Michelle, Perry, Dave, Hilary, Amber, Rob and Brad. You all brought your own rich artistry to our family. Together you gave me the most wonderful of gifts, the light of my life, my grandchildren Steve, Alexander, Sasa, Jet, Dempsey, Mirabel, Bowyn, Selkie, Harkin, Leo, Simon, Arwen, Tofino, and future blessings, too. Thank you for all the love, hugs and kisses.

Thanks to Tom Barnett, Brian's Naval Academy classmate, who came into Saigon from his own combat command to be his best man. Thanks to my Godmother Vu Ba who always gave me hope, my

Godfather Bo who walked me down the aisle at my wedding, and to my God-sister Bernadette 'Mama Thai' for believing in me.

Thanks to all my professors who shaped my education, especially Margaret Connell, my ESL teacher who forced me to write my first paper, a personal journal. Thanks to Marion Colella and Leisa Young, my mentors through years of college. Thanks to Kathy Henry's writing group too. Thanks to Don Saracen for bringing me to Toastmasters, and especially to Scott and Marie Saracen for filming the PBS video about me, "Mai: A Lesson In Courage, Passion & Hope." Thanks to Marty and Porter Halyburton for sharing Porter's POW stories, and to Professor Emeritus Gerry Tyler, URI, who invited me to speak in her Vietnam History classes.

Thanks to my long-time neighbors and friends Julia Califano, Diane Stanley, Lois Cone, Maureen Lombardi and Marianne Russell. You all contributed to my independence. Thanks to the Barrington community, our home for over forty years. Thank you, Josh Bickford, editor of the Barrington Times, for writing news stories about my life. Thanks to my colleagues at Barrington High School. Your trust and respect kept me committed to our work. A special thank you to all my students for their endless letters that made me want to share my stories.

Thanks to Leigh Medeiros who helped me organize this book, and who brought me back to earth whenever I was out of focus. Thanks to Dawn and Steven Porter. I am extremely lucky to have you as my publishers. Also, I thank everyone who pre-ordered this book. Your contributions helped to finance its publication.

Most of all I would like to thank my first editor, my husband Brian. He is my rock and my love. He shared all my sorrow and tears so I could write this book. He listened to me from the first day we met. He loved me without knowing anything about my family. His help is present in every sentence in this book. His belief in my efforts is what kept me writing.

About the Author

Mai Donohue is a writer, beloved home cook, and retired educator of special needs students. After leaving Vietnam in 1970 she and her husband Brian settled in Barrington, Rhode Island. They have seven children and thirteen grandchildren. Mai holds a B.A. from the University of Rhode Island, an accomplishment that was the culmination of more than twelve years of study. Mai is known in her community for supporting various charitable causes with her delicious Vietnamese cooking. A PBS short documentary about Mai's life was nominated for a New England Emmy award in 2006. More information about her can be found at www.MaiGoodness.com.

Made in the USA
Middletown, DE
12 August 2016